IN DEFENSE OF PUBLIC ORDER

The Emerging Field of Sanction Law

IN DEFENSE OF

The Emerging Field of Sanction Law

NEW YORK 1961

IN LITTERIS LIBERTAS

PUBLIC ORDER

Richard Arens &
Harold D. Lasswell

COLUMBIA UNIVERSITY PRESS

Library of Congress Catalog Card Number: 61-7946
Manufactured in the United States of America

ACKNOWLEDGMENTS

THE AUTHORS acknowledge with gratitude permission to quote from *Children and Families in the Courts of New York City,* by Walter Gellhorn *et al.,* published by Dodd, Mead & Co., New York; *The Crime of Imprisonment,* by George Bernard Shaw, published by Philosophical Library, Inc., New York; *Criminal Justice and Social Reconstruction,* by Hermann Mannheim, published by Routledge & Kegan Paul Ltd., London; *Holy Deadlock,* by Sir Alan Herbert, published by Doubleday & Co., Inc., New York and Methuen & Co., Ltd., London; *Law and the Modern Mind,* by Judge Jerome Frank, published by Coward-McCann, Inc., New York; *New Horizons in Criminology,* by Harry Elmer Barnes and Negley K. Teeters, published by Prentice-Hall, Inc., New York; *Our Criminal Courts,* by Raymond Moley, published by G. P. Putnam's Sons, New York; *Principles of Criminology,* by Edwin H. Sutherland, published by J. B. Lippincott Co., Philadelphia; *The Road to Justice,* by Lord Alfred Denning, published by Stevens & Sons Ltd., London; *Sexual Behavior in the Human Male,* by Alfred C. Kinsey *et al.,* Indiana University Institute for Sex Research, published by W. B. Saunders Co., Philadelphia; *The Urge to Punish,* by Henry Weihofen, published by Farrar, Straus & Cudahy, Inc., New York; *Wigmore on Evidence,* published by West Publishing Co., St. Paul, Minn.; *You Can't Get There From Here,* by Ogden Nash, published by Little, Brown & Co., Boston; and from the *Midwest Journal of Political Science* and the *Yale Law Journal.*

CONTENTS

FOREWORD

THE GREAT PROBLEMS of our legal system cannot be understood in isolation from the more general problems of modern society. So many of our legal problems are, in fact, nothing more than symbolic expressions of these other underlying issues. But the intellectual workers in this country seem to be evolving into a community of experts with limited vision. As a result, the primary subject on which they concentrate in limited ways—namely, the individual, his purposes and potentials—is lost in a maze of technicalities which are comprehensible only to the experts. The authors of this book are aware of the need to comprehend the whole man and the essentials of the social order in which he functions.

This assessment is overdue. The authors, however, have done more than merely suggest the assessment which is so sorely needed. They have shown that many of our sanctioning policies are indeed "confused, inconsistent, and fraught with dangerous consequences for the basic values and institutions of the United States."

Beyond that, they have explored the use of intellectual tools and modes of practical action to bring sanctioning in line with the ideal of a democratic social order; a democratic social order which by definition places "a prime value on the individual—any individual, be he citizen or alien, useful or harmful, sane or mad."

This book deserves the careful and earnest attention of all those concerned with our sanctioning system.

DAVID L. BAZELON

Circuit Judge
United States Court of Appeals
Washington 1, D.C.

PART I. *The Challenge of Present Failures*

INTRODUCTION

THE STUDIES that appear here are designed to clarify a field of legal study and professional practice that has begun to emerge only in recent times, and then gradually. Every legal system employs sanctioning measures to protect the integrity of the system of public order whose fundamental values and institutions are to be maintained and fulfilled. Nevertheless, the choice of sanction is frequently carried out in improvised, confused, and even contradictory fashion. The "penalty" provisions of a statute are often thrown into the draft at the last minute or left to the discretion of a hurried draftsman who must operate with little practical or theoretical guidance. Within the frame provided by statute, administrators and commissions fill in sanctioning as well as substantive detail, subject to the relatively haphazard vicissitudes of judicial review. The courts themselves reveal diverse conceptions of the proper standards to apply in the imposition of negative, or the granting of positive, sanctions. The vast machinery of imprisonment, parole, and clemency alters the lives of hundreds of thousands of human beings every year and affects the fate of basic social loyalties, faiths, and beliefs.

An examination of the curricula of the law schools in this country and abroad will confirm the fact that no courses are offered in "sanction law." There are standard topics such as contract, tort, criminal law, property, procedure, constitutional and administrative law; and in recent years the number of less established specialties included is a tribute to the determination of modern law faculties to keep in step with the fast-moving pace of contemporary developments.

The omission of a course in sanction law, once it has been called to the attention of layman or specialist, looks "exceeding strange." After all, the legal order is a vast system whose sanctioning operations are of enormous importance. So far as most people are concerned the very idea of law conveys the notion of enforcement.

There is, however, a subject usually taught outside United States schools of law that is at least partly occupied with the study of sanctions. This is criminology. We shall suggest that the conception of sanction law is far wider in scope than treatment of offenders against the prohibitions laid down by the community against common crimes. In fact there are grounds for complaining that the prominence of sanctioning activities in the criminal field has distracted attention from the sanctioning system as a whole. A principal point to be made in the present book is that there are great advantages for science and public policy in viewing sanction law as a whole in any given system of public order.

When the community is called upon to "umpire" a dispute having to do with an alleged breach of contract the party who the Court decides has committed the breach is liable to sanction. In conventional legal language, however, the deprivations to which defendants are exposed are not labeled "sanctions." Lawyers in our system are trained to talk of "damages" or "specific performance." Our point is simply that when one looks into the factual situation, one finds it entirely apt to speak of sanctions in such cases.

The most obvious similarities between sanctions that result from controversies over contract and from criminal action are two: deprivations are involved in both; and both are imposed by decision makers representing the entire community. Differences relate to the antecedents of the deprivation. In the case of allegedly criminal acts the community is officially involved from the beginning, since public officials invoke the authoritative prescriptions of the community when they assert that an offense has been committed. The typical sequence of events in a contract case is that a private party initiates the action and draws in the decision makers of the body politic to "umpire" the controversy. Private settlement may occur at any time up to the moment the spokesmen of the community render a decision. If liability is formally established, the target of deprivation is proceeded against with the full weight of community authority.

We also call attention to the fact that sanctions of varying severity may be imposed upon any person adjudged to have committed a "wrong" in a tort action. Traditionally a tort is called a private wrong as a means of distinguishing it from a "crime," or public wrong. For the moment we shall not comment further upon this distinction, since the immediate point is that the "tort-feasor," like the "criminal," is subject to deprivations imposed by authority of the entire community. In the case of a breached contract, the factual deprivations are given special labels in legalistic vocabularies.

Further deprivations in fact, though not "sanctions" in name, occur when the community, acting through its officials, successfully establishes the allegation that "regulatory" norms have been broken. Although legalistic speech does not necessarily call these breaches "criminal," the defendant may experience a loss, like license revocation, imposed in the name of the community.

The questions that are perhaps already suggested, we now pose expressly: Why bother to extend the meaning of the term sanction to include so much? What do we expect to see accomplished?

The first proposition that we put forward in reply is this: the failure to consider the sanctioning process as a whole has resulted, to a significant degree, in some of the most damaging faults of our legal order.

One of the main tasks of the present undertaking is to summarize evidence that bears on this assertion. We show that many sanctioning arrangements now current in the United States are on their face inconsistent with the articulated goals of the American system of public order, and that in actual operation the goals of our system suffer chronic and substantial defeat.

As American society operates today, much responsibility for taking a comprehensive look at large institutional processes rests with universities and professional associations. So far as sanctioning law is concerned, the failure of the law schools to examine the subject in a unified perspective is indicated by the absence of appropriate courses. The law schools do not focus the minds of future members of the bar upon the sanctioning *system* and it is not astonishing that the associations display little sensitivity to the problems that relate to its operation. To a limited extent the gap has been filled by departments of sociology. Departments of political science, despite their formal concern with public law, have not stepped into the breach. Although several other departments touch upon pertinent questions they have not perceived the larger framework. Economists assess trade regulation, and philosophers have relevant things to say about normative questions. But neither economists nor philosophers deal with sanctions as a whole.

The second proposition that we affirm is this: *When sanctions are examined as a whole the result is to strengthen the factors that tend to bring sanction law into more consistent and effective harmony with the goals of the American system of public order.*[1]

We predict that when members of the law faculties of the United States busy themselves with the theory and practice of sanction law they will be impelled to bring into the open a flood of discrepancies between aspiration and performance. In order to base judgment upon knowledge it will be necessary to employ all the instruments at the disposal of modern research, especially the methods of interviewing and participant observation. As research results accumulate, teaching materials will make it possible to bring more comprehensive and better selected items to the notice of students. Law school curricula will be remodeled in order to provide opportunity for examining the whole sanctioning system with fundamental criteria of appraisal in mind. A new field of specialization will appear, composed of all who devote themselves to research, teaching, consultation, and administration of sanction law. As a cumulative result it is in no sense daring to predict that the failures of our legal system insofar as they are connected with sanctioning operations will be significantly reduced.

Perhaps it will be possible to forestall and prevent misinterpretation if we take occasion at this early stage to utter a few disclaimers. We desire to emphasize that sanction law is not properly conceived as a minor subdivision or an extension of criminology and criminal law. It is a frame of reference that includes some criminology, all criminal law, and substantial parts of all the legal specialties having to do with sanctioning prescriptions of any kind. Criminologists have made valuable contributions to our knowledge of how "the common crimes" are affected—or unaffected—by sanctioning prescriptions and applications. Criminologists have not been helpful, however, in meeting the problems relating to the social regulation of business, or of political parties, pressure groups, and other private associations; and such questions are especially pressing in large-scale modern societies. As we conceive of the scope of sanction law, it takes in much of the conventional content of criminology though it is not limited to the study of deprivations imposed upon criminal offenders.

The proposed generalization of this field is not intended to provide an exercise in the art of "truth by definition," in the sense of jurisprudential systems undisciplined by empirical data. It will, of course, be indispensable to the cultivation of sanction law to clarify the meaning of key postulates such as recognizing "the dignity of man" as the overriding goal of public order in this commonwealth. We cannot abolish differences of opinion about the scope of specific definitions, or the most practicable lines of inquiry. Legal scholars and practitioners can look forward with confidence to the continuation of controversy, a stimulant to which they are so frequently and so happily addicted. But injections of data obtained through research and consultation can prevent controversy from having the sterile results to which it has so often led.

A third caveat: we expressly disclaim the view that sanctioning problems are "strictly legal questions" and that the joint experience and special methods developed by scholars of history, psychology, and the social sciences ought to be neglected. By this late date in the twentieth century it is to be hoped that jurists, legal scholars, and practising attorneys are cognizant of the advantages of the incessant interplay between legalistic language and the language of those who describe the past and predict the future. Actually, the distinctions to be made are more numerous. In the interest of clarity of thought—and ultimately of communication—we are not insensitive to the importance of recognizing the distinct though interrelated roles of the languages of "jurisprudence" and of "conventional legalism," and of "science" and "policy." Jurisprudence refers to language *about* law. Conventional legalism refers to the whole body of authoritative prescription whose terms are used by parties to advance and justify "claims" addressed to community decision makers, who in turn legitimize what they do in the same terms. "Scientific" statements are wholly descriptive; they describe the place of law in the social process. The primary language of "policy" is the vocabulary of preference or determination; it may, of course, refer to the legal process.

Jurisprudence is the distinctive intellectual instrument at the disposal of scholars or practitioners of law by which they can detach themselves from any *one* system of public order for the purposes of examining *any* system comparatively, or of gaining the perspective required to navigate effectively within a particular system. It is unhappily true that jurisprudence has acquired a bad reputation in America for empty and pretentious verbalization. However vehemently jurisprudential thinking may be deplored, it cannot be avoided. At its crudest level such thinking is utterly unsystematic and is applied to immediate and limited problems, as a lawyer who calculates which judge will probably be most receptive to a particular argument on behalf of a particular client. At its highest level it involves formidable intellectual structures designed to summarize and guide the scholarly investigation of law in the social process.[2]

The recent growth of workable systems of jurisprudence has contributed greatly to research and policy in many fields of law. Our orientation is that of value-institution study, with whose development one of us has been actively identified.[3] We find in this concept a frame of reference sufficiently comprehensive in scope and refined in detail to guide the evolution of sanction law as we understand the field.

At this point we shall say nothing about value-institution analysis except to recall the fact that it conceives of law as authoritative decision, hence as a fundamental feature of the decision process within the social process of every body politic. The scholar or practitioner who has a problem related to legal process has five basic methods of approach at his disposal: he can clarify goals, ascertain trends, analyze factors that condition (explain) trends, project the probable course of future development, invent and assess policy alternatives for the purpose of maximizing his clarified goals. The goals of the individual, if they are to be realized, must be widely and effectively shared.

In thinking about the decision-making and -executing process it is convenient to identify seven stages and in this way to arrive at rather precise comparisons of corresponding decision phases.[4] The *intelligence function* is the obtaining and processing of information and of estimates of the future. The *recommending function* is the promotion of results. The *prescribing function* lays down authoritative general rules. The *invoking function* makes provisional characterizations of concrete circumstances by interpreting prescriptions. The *applying function* makes final application of prescriptions. The *appraisal function* assesses the conformity between decision activities and the goals sighted. The *terminating function* puts an end to prescriptions or arrangements growing out of prescriptions.

Prescriptions can be roughly classified as primary and sanctioning propositions, the former articulating a norm of conduct preferred by the body politic, the latter specifying the actions to be taken especially when breaches of the norm occur.

In modern states the making of written prescriptions is a conspicuous activity carried on by constitutional conventions, legislatures, and top executive organs. It would, however, be a mistake to assume that the words found in statute books or in written constitutions are entitled to be classified as "laws" in the fullest functional sense of the word. We define a law as more than words, as authoritative prescription *and* high levels of conformity. Hence, not until the necessary research has been done to disclose the degree of conformity and the extent and result of enforcement activities when deviations appear are we justified in speaking of a rule as a law. This calls for an examination of behavior levels in the body politic, and notably of policemen, judges, and kindred enforcers.[5]

If all printed statutes are not laws it is also correct to say that all laws are not printed statutes. The norms of society are continually made and unmade in the interaction of everyday living. It is to these norms that we must look if we are to make an exhaustive inventory of the laws of any organized society. Since we have the perspective of entire communities in view it is clear that economy of effort calls for selection, and that we choose for legal study those prescriptions that are expected to be enforced with a high degree of severity against deviates and that involve specialized representatives of the community in the process of sanctioning.[6]

Some years ago the late Professor Dession and Professor Lasswell became interested in the implications of the study of sanctions for jurisprudential science and policy and for professional practice. In fact the choice of the term "sanction law" as a suitable designation for the field was an outgrowth of their collaboration in a seminar at the Yale Law School. The present investigations were originally planned by Professors Dession and Lasswell as part of a series intended to outline the conception of public order and giving prominence to sanctioning processes.[7] From the beginning, Richard Arens, now a practicing member of the bar of the District of Columbia, has been closely associated with the approach, first as student, then as assistant, and eventually as independent scholar. It has therefore been decided to proceed as much as possible with the original program.

It should be understood from the outset that the present book has a highly limited set of aims. One objective is to give currency to the conception of sanction law. Another is to present a sufficiently detailed characterization of the American sanctioning system to justify the claim that the sanction-law field is important enough to be developed. A further aim is to provide a brief outline of how we believe the scope of sanction law can now be most usefully conceived. Hence the present enterprise does not itself coincide with the scope of the proposed specialty. It is in the nature of a prolegomenon, a proposal, a justification; we are certainly not producing a textbook, casebook, or definitive treatise on the subject. Our hope, of course, is that we can contribute to a chain of development that produces all these results, which in turn will affect the American legal system.

The obligation of the authors to various individuals will be apparent—and, we trust, properly acknowledged—at appropriate places. Professor Richard C. Donnelly of the Yale Law School has been particularly generous in connection with the current enterprise. He has graciously allowed us to incorporate the substance and often the wording of an article published in the *Yale Law Journal* and written in collaboration with one of us. In addition he has read much of the manuscript at its various stages and has been helpful in every possible way. The *Yale Law Journal* has kindly agreed to our use of the article.

We desire further to acknowledge the assistance and cooperation of distinguished Professor Emeritus Arthur Lenhoff of the University of Buffalo Law School, Dr. Harold Graser of the University of Buffalo Medical School, and Professor Jerome Skolnick of the Yale Law School. We are also grateful to the editors of the American Sociological Review and of the Midwest Journal of Political Science for permission to draw freely upon published material.

Professor Myres S. McDougal of the Yale Law School could not fail to be implicated in this undertaking because of his close—even guilty—association with the authors. He has been as usual articulate, opinionated, and brilliant in his comments, and shares our hope that this relatively modest part of the total task will inspire—or provoke—the work that needs to be done. He is, of course, to be absolved from the limitations of the present sketch.

I. THE FUNCTION OF SANCTIONS IN OUR SYSTEM OF PUBLIC ORDER

WE BEGIN by highlighting the need for a comprehensive conception of sanction law in the study of the American legal system. We do this by offering an overview of the limitations characteristic of the present state of affairs. We shall show that sanctioning policies are confused, inconsistent, and fraught with dangerous consequences for the basic values and institutions of the United States. Our point is that by enlisting more talent and energy for research, analysis, and modification of the current situation we may reasonably expect to bring American institutions into closer harmony with the fundamental goals of the nation.

It is not to be assumed that because confusions, contradictions, and destructive consequences inhere in the functioning of the American system that imperfections are more flagrant here than elsewhere. Discrepancies of this kind come to light in varying degrees when any legal system is looked into. As Americans we are directly concerned with what happens at home. It is therefore appropriate to focus upon the sanctioning process in the United States before including comparative studies made elsewhere.

Essential to the present analysis is the idea of a legal system as a means of defending and fulfilling a system of public order. The public order of a body politic is composed of the goal values and basic institutions of the community as a whole. The goal values are the events whose occurrence is the overriding aim of public policy. Any community can be viewed as a social process in which everyone is seeking, consciously or unconsciously, to maximize his value position. In American society this includes the demand to defend and fulfill the requirements of a collective way of life in which values are widely rather than narrowly held. It is evident from the formal requirements of constitutional charters and from effective acts of government that the emphasis in the United States is upon broad rather than narrow participation in social values. The value patterns of any body politic can be described for purposes of comparison with the aid of a short list of categories (like power, wealth, rectitude, skill, enlightenment, well-being, affection).

Besides the prevailing pattern of general or limited participation a system of public order includes the specific practices by which values are shaped and shared. We use the term "institution" to designate the practices that are relatively special to a value. The institutions of federalism and the separation of powers, for instance, are part of the institutions relatively specialized for the decision process, which is the shaping and sharing of the power value. Commercial and industrial undertakings are among the institutions of wealth. Established patterns of social acceptance or discrimination are special to the respect value (including of course the negative as well as the positive side of the value). Churches are among the agencies significantly concerned with formulating and applying criteria of right and wrong (rectitude). The skill value is exemplified in art, craft, and occupational technologies. Enlightenment is afforded (or withheld) by the mass media of communication. Hospitals and recreational facilities are particularly related to physical and mental well-being. Affection, of course, is expressed in the circles of family and friends, and in loyalty to the nation and other large social units.

Among the institutional practices by which a system of public order is maintained or fulfilled we are singling out the sanctioning process for attention. Sanctions are deprivations or indulgences of individual and group values for the purpose of supporting the primary norms of a public order system. The deprivations; i.e., negative sanctions, spring readily to mind. The list of fines, imprisonments, and similar penalties that figure in our system is very long. Often we lose sight of the part played when the positive is accented and bounties or honors are used to reward conduct conforming to community prescription. We may also speak of "sanction equivalents," which operate in place of unequivocal indulgence or deprivation (such as warning or instruction). It is evident that sanctions are used in a much wider range of situations than those conventionally called "criminal." We shall consider the special problem of a "criminal" sanction when we look into the place of the "criminal" category within the context of public order activities.

The following inventory of positive and negative sanctions according to the value involved is intended to provide examples explicit enough to make clear the meaning of each category. The enumeration is in no sense exhaustive, and is subject to certain limitations which will be indicated as they become important.

POWER

Positive sanctioning—expressed in the conferral and recognition of rights of participation in the decision-making process—is exemplified by the naturalization of an alien, or by the qualification of a citizen as a grand or petit juror upon a showing of "good moral character." [1]

Negative sanctioning—expressed in the withdrawal of such rights—is often provided for. Expatriation may result from unauthorized service in the armed forces of a foreign state.[2] Officeholders may be removed by impeachment; [3] and the reduction of legislative representation, for example, may be enforced against a state for denying the right to vote to qualified citizens within its jurisdiction.[4]

WEALTH

The conspicuous role of wealth among the rewards and inducements available to government for sanctioning purposes is apparent throughout history. One recalls the creation of a new landed gentry and the dispossession of the old in the reorganization that followed the Norman Conquest. In more modern days assets other than land have played their part. Veterans' benefits are paid in money, often for specific purposes, and the underwriting of approved business activities is an inducement offered by the government. The grant-in-aid device is a favorite means of encouraging local initiatives.

"[F]ederal stimulus to the passage of state unemployment compensation laws" during the Depression took the form of positive sanctioning exemplified by "grants [to the states] from federal funds." [5]

Legislatures frequently provide financial rewards for the informer which are taken from the amount assessed against the delinquent for the reported violation. *Qui tam* suits by the informer are well-known, if not edifying, spectacles. In brief, "statutes providing for actions by a common informer, who himself had no interest whatever in the controversy other than that given by statute, have been in existence for hundreds of years in England, and in this country ever since the foundation of our Government." [6]

Negative sanctions in this field are illustrated by the well-known civil penalties of the Sherman Antitrust Act. The multiplication of licensing requirements in response to the pressure of special interests [7] has made license revocation a more serious sanctioning tool than it once was. The penalty of property forfeiture has been prescribed in a variety of circumstances, when such property is used in violation of the law—*e.g.*, the illicit use of an automobile for the transportation of bootleg liquor (even without the owner's knowledge); [8] the operation of an illicit still; [9] interstate transportation of property in violation of the Sherman Antitrust Act.[10] The most obvious wealth deprivation, of course, is the fine.

AFFECTION

Permission to marry or to enjoy other rights relating to family and social life are granted to those who conform to requirements laid down in legal codes. A by no means insignificant reward for maintaining a marriage relation is the substantial and often munificent tax relief to family units—a relief which may progress geometrically with the size of the family—under the federal and state income tax laws.

Freedom of association, whatever its purpose, so long as it is not unlawful, is constitutionally guaranteed and hence receives judicial protection. Thus the right of keeping the company of one's choice, presumably therefore congenial, is subject only to the requirement that the company, however suspect, is kept for a lawful purpose.[11]

On the negative side we observe that indulgences may give way to varying degrees of deprivation. Loss of conjugal rights, of custody of children, and of financial assets are among the negative sanctions imposed for breach of a marriage relationship and violation of parental duty. Moreover, these sanctions may occur in connection with the less final separation, a divorce *a mensa et thoro,* as well as with the absolute termination of marital status, a divorce *a vinculo matrimonii.*[12]

However legal at its inception, a grouping of individuals once oriented to an unlawful end or to the pursuit of a lawful end by unlawful means, is transformed in the eyes of the law into a conspiracy to be shunned by all. Confederation is now evidence of crime, and continued adherence increases the stringency of the penalties that the participant may suffer on the basis of direct and vicarious liability, especially since conspiracy and conspiracy-type laws are becoming more numerous.[13]

SKILL

Positive sanctions typically include the protection and encouragement of socially useful skills. Socially desirable forms of creative work are rewarded by affording patent and copyright protection to the enjoyment of income and control related to the products of discovery, invention, and artistic imagination. Exceptional national needs have led to such emergency programs of indulgence as the naturalization and governmental employment of ex-enemy specialists in guided-missile research.

We may summarize national policy by saying that "authors, composers, inventors, and others are protected by patent and copyright laws from people who would misappropriate their works or contrivances." [14] Patent and copyright laws, passed pursuant to the authority given Congress by the Constitution, "to promote the progress of science and useful arts by securing for limited times to authors and inventors the exclusive right to their respective writings and discoveries," [15] operate to "make the infringer liable to injunction and for damages resulting from [his] infringement." [16]

Under contemporary conditions more frequent positive sanctions are provided by administrative acts that confer the "privilege" of exercising a skill within the growing number of fields which are subject to licensing restrictions. Although "[u]ntil the end of the nineteenth century few occupations other than those of the lawyer and the physician—were subject to state licensing," the twentieth century witnessed

> a veritable deluge of licensing laws. By 1952 more than 80 separate occupations, exclusive of "owner-businesses" like restaurants and taxicab companies, had been licensed by state law, and in addition to the state laws there are municipal ordinances in abundance, not to mention the federal statutes that require the licensing of such diverse occupations as radio operators and stockyard commission agents.[17]

The other side of the coin in licensing administration, namely, license denial or license revocation for failing to meet a legislative or administrative norm, emphasizes the deprivational use of sanctioning in this area. Potential severities are not to be underestimated, since, in Mr. Justice Douglas's aptly expressed dissent, "it does many men little good to stay alive and free and propertied if they cannot work." [18]

ENLIGHTENMENT

A frequent reward of conformity with community norms is the obtaining of access to, or aid in the dissemination of, enlightenment. An increasing number of scientists throughout the nation receive "restricted data" or "classified information" in the field of their research when granted "security clearance" by administrative authorities.[19] For some years the Postmaster General has been authorized to give "second-class" mailing privileges to publications which are recognized as devoted to "the dissemination of information of a public character or . . . to literature, the sciences, arts or some special industry." [20]

The Internal Revenue Code provides substantial tax relief to institutions qualifying as "educational" in character; and part of the activity of these establishments is the cultivation of enlightenment as well as skill.

The denial of enlightenment benefits is a well-entrenched penalty for nonconformity. Forfeiture of access to "restricted data" or "classified information" follows the revocation of "security clearance." [21] The Postmaster General is authorized to exclude from the mails materials characterized, *inter alia,* by "obscenity," [22] "fraud," [23] "sedition," [24] incitement to arson, murder, or assassination,[25] as well as materials providing information on birth control.[26] It is obvious that the department may take into account more than the manifest content of the communication, and may examine affiliations or official conclusions about the communicators in question.

State and municipal agencies effectively exert powers of censorship over motion pictures which are deemed morally offensive under varying standards.[27]

WELL-BEING

The modern community provides many facilities designed to safeguard and improve the health, comfort, and safety of its members. In addition to the minimum available to everyone, other value indulgences are given to those who have made special contributions to the realization of community values. Hospitals, convalescent homes, and old-age care are provided for those who have served the nation in war or in highly regarded peacetime capacities.

It is hardly necessary to underline the reliance upon deprivations of well-being in connection with sanctioning policy, since capital punishment, compulsory labor, whipping,[28] and mutilation are among the best-known penalties which have been historically or are currently applied to offenders.

RESPECT

On the positive side we have not reestablished a peerage, or its equivalent, since the Revolution. But there is ample evidence that we are making more frequent use of citations, awards, and honorific occasions to reward with suitable symbols of deference those who have served satisfactorily in civil no less than military branches. But these affirmative instances are rather weaker than the impact of negative measures.

The ex-convict, as we shall have further occasion to observe, is under a myriad of disqualifications, including those involving respect status, as exemplified by the New York law excluding the "habitual criminal" from the pale of official protection against unreasonable searches and seizures. A product of more recent years is the attaint of the so-called loyalty and security risk, not infrequently on the sole basis of suspected associates as a result of the contemporary "revival" "of a principle [of guilt] discarded in Judah three thousand years ago." [29] "It is true," as the late Professor Max Radin perceptively commented,

> that those condemned "by association" are not put to death, but merely publicly defamed and black-listed as potential traitors. That

[however] is no mild punishment and the irresponsible publicists who inflict it, might with profit have their attention called to Deuteronomy, the Second Book of Kings and the book of prophet Ezekiel.[30]

RECTITUDE

Positive sanctioning is exemplified by the law of Justification and Excuse within the field of crimes. Acts which are otherwise punishable are exempted from negative sanctioning upon a showing that their net effect contributes to the maintenance of existing modes of public order. Thus the defense of the self, of others, and of property under appropriate circumstances is encouraged by general exemption from criminal liability. Similarly, "acts done by qualified officers in performance of their duties, within the limits of reasonable necessity or official privilege, are . . . legally justifiable." [31] The same is true of disciplinary action *in loco parentis*.

In connection with the bestowal of "honors" upon individuals for public service, stress is often laid upon the moral integrity of the recipient. Strictly speaking the characterizing of anyone as "good" or "God-fearing" is an invocation or application of "rectitude" norms. It may or may not be closely associated with respect.

The rectitude value figures heavily on the deprivational side of sanctioning policies. Informal expressions of a condemnatory character often result in mobilizing the legislature and other organs of government to establish new sanctioning prescriptions or to terminate old ones, and enforcement officials are spurred to invoke or apply established codes. The formal terminology of "guilty" or "not guilty" in connection with criminal trials testifies to the moralistic connotation that suffices to carry out the sanctioning process at many points.

It is perhaps superfluous to remark that the specification of any particular pattern of sanction as deprivational or indulgent in terms of a given value category is highly provisional. The significance of a given practice in a concrete case or in a representative series of cases during a given period can only be discovered when appropriate methods are used to disclose the actual state of affairs. Since we describe a sanction in functional terms as "severe" it must be shown that a tentatively classified activity is expected to be, and is, more than mild in its social context.

Another remark is perhaps pertinent here. Although a given practice is indulgent or deprivational in terms of one value, it is not to be assumed that no other values are affected. On the contrary, our expectation is that in every specific case *all* values will be affected to some extent. Experience indicates that it is typical to find that one or a few values are relatively more involved than others. Our classification suggests only that the practices referred to are relatively important in the situations referred to.

It will also be observed that chains of value changes are found in sanctioning activities. By definition all lawful official acts are viewed as exercises of power in the jurisdiction where they occur. Hence all sanctions are positive or negative exercises of power regarding some targets. But values which are not necessarily tied up with power are also involved to a degree that gives them prominence in the sanctioning sequence. This is true of wealth, respect, and the other values which figure in our analysis. Sometimes the value is immediately affected by the use of power; often it occurs later in the sequence that separates the official act from the impact upon the value position of the target. Officials affect wealth immediately when they levy a fine; and they affect respect immediately when they confer an honor. Some affection sanctions are less direct, as when an official act stands in the way of marriage or clears the path. We classify sanctions according to the value impact which the official act exerts upon the target.

Despite the decisive role of sanctions in perpetuating or undermining a system of public order it cannot be successfully maintained that they have been adequately explored at the level of theory or action. We have no doubt that the main responsibility for raising the issue of adequacy rests with legal scholars and with the bar. It is generally understood that the study and practice of law is more than a craft or a livelihood; it is a profession. This implies concern for the aggregate effect of the legal system as a whole.

Accepting this view of legal scholarship and professional obligation we propose to call attention to the sanctioning process as it now operates. The first step was indicated above: to establish the proposition that confusions and contradictions abound and that their effects upon the American system of public order are genuinely grave. The second step is to propose a number of intellectual tools and modes of practical action.

Strictly speaking, we are in no position at this time to make a definitive report upon how the sanctioning system works. Information is scattered, incomplete, and of varying authenticity. Before needed information becomes available it will be necessary to obtain wider recognition of the importance of the problem. We are relying upon present research and opinion, unsatisfactory as these sources are, in the hope of arousing enough scholarly and professional interest to correct the situation.

Fortunately our principal proposition is likely to win the consent of a substantial number of those who have good reason to know the detailed working of the American system. However, we do not want to rest the case entirely upon such impressions, valuable as they are. The plan is to go beyond an inventory of opinion and to call attention to available indications of the true state of affairs.

We have said that systems of public order include preferred patterns for the arrangement of social values and institutions. Our inventory of sanctioning will deal with each of the principal values. Sometimes it will be apparent by studying the formal language (the *prescriptions*) of constitutional documents, statutes, and regulations that the sanctioning function is out of order. Similar situations will be dissimilarly treated; by contrast, no allowance will be made for states of affairs that diverge sharply from one another. Sanctions may be entirely omitted; or, if provided, they may be left in an ambiguous state.

To some degree it is possible to push beyond the presumptions based upon the language of formal prescription to the actual *applications* made in the sanctioning process. This is a matter of what officials do, or fail to do, within the framework of authority. Ideally we would provide an account of the invocation of formal prescriptions. To what extent are they invoked by the appropriate individuals or organs when they are supposed to be? Further, we would go beyond invocation to what we consider to be "application" in terms of the seven-phase analysis of decision process mentioned in the Introduction. Once invoked, are the prescriptions fully applied? With what effect? It must be borne in mind that deficiencies in formal requirements are often remedied by the nullification of obnoxious rules, or by the tacit adoption of more satisfactory prescriptions by administrative officials. Hence the inferences drawn from studying formal language may be substantially modified when we examine the available sources of information about consequent events. No one will be surprised to learn that admirable prescriptions found in statutes and affirmed as authoritative by the courts may find no echo in actual operations.

We shall draw back from the current situation long enough to glance at the historical *trend* in sanctioning measures in theory and fact. The object of this exercise is to put the positive and negative features of today in the longer—and often more reassuring—perspective of time. The current deprivations inflicted upon our preferred system of public order are, however, not infrequently the result of quite recent developments in the sanctioning process.

We plan to deal successively with the eight value-institution categories that we use in analyzing systems of public order and the social process as a whole. If placing "a prime value on the individual—any individual, be he citizen or alien, useful or harmful, sane or mad" is accepted as the overriding objective of our legal system, this inquiry will raise disturbing doubts about the degree to which sanction law now defends or advances our system of public order.

2. SANCTIONING MEASURES AND THE SHARING OF RESPECT

ONE OF the principal instruments available to community decision makers is the withdrawal of respect from those who violate the primary norms of the legal system. It is well known that one sign of tension in any society is an increase in the number of people who feel no shame when they flout lawfully prescribed rules and remain indifferent to the breaches committed by others, or go so far as to admire and praise the lawbreaker. If deprivations of respect are to operate formally and informally as sanctions of the public order system it is evident that sanctioning measures must harmonize with the sentiments of the community and that they must be exercised on behalf of norms supported by the community. Manifestly this is no simple matter in a complex modern nation where a multitude of special environments create a multitude of specialized experiences and perspectives. Where such ideals as absence of discrimination are at stake the indications are that the many component elements of American life differ more or less radically from one another in their acceptance of the norm or in their interpretation of the specific conditions in which the norm is to be given strict application.

Whatever deviations we find in the sanctioning practices of the nation may be the result of the definitions that we ourselves give to the conceptions involved. Without overloading this discussion with problems of definition we shall seek in every context to make obvious the sense in which we understand the key terms employed; and, in the main, our usage will be kept as close as possible to a well-recognized stream of tradition. As we shall see, there are facts of sufficient gravity to justify attention even if norms are narrowly rather than broadly construed.

Perhaps the quickest way to indicate what we refer to by respect is to say "absence of discrimination"; or, affirmatively, acceptance on the basis of individual qualities as a human being. The giving and withholding of respect goes on continually in human affairs. It is accorded or withheld in the forms of etiquette; and it is codified in the treatment of A by B as a member of the same social class or of a higher or lower one.

We review the language of statutes and the rules employed by judges, and we uncover some instances in which explicit discriminations are required in the process of sanctioning. The most far-reaching discriminations are those to be inferred from the existence of many inconsistent prescriptions among the various jurisdictions in the United States. In a mobile industrial society sharp contrasts in legal rules are discriminatory in practice, unless, of course, it can be demonstrated by inquiry that the rules make no difference.

The analysis of formal language can establish a strong presumption that rules of formal equality are actually discriminatory. By studying the regulations relating to summary or nonsummary procedure we can lay the foundation for the view that summary procedures are unnecessarily prevalent. By examining rules it can be shown that many wrongs connected with sanctioning activity are left without an appropriate remedy. For example, we shall see that police invasions of privacy are accorded wide latitude. We shall find that the language referring to specific discriminations is often vague to a degree that invites evasion.

Our review of available information about how rules work in practice draws attention especially to the influence of class position and personality factors upon discrimination.

Finally, study of the trend suggests that there has been a long-term rise in effective demand for widespread sharing of respect, despite certain notorious countermovements.

PRESCRIPTIONS

Explicit Denials of Equality

The tradition of equality of access to respect on the basis of individual merit is so deeply implanted in American life that explicit denials of equality are seldom found in statutory or court language. Our survey, which is restricted to the prescriptions made by public authorities, has, however, uncovered a flagrant example in connection with the sanctioning process. We refer to the position of the ex-convict, who is regularly deprived of the right to vote and the right to pursue gainful occupations, ranging from the practice of medicine to taxi driving. He is alleged to be devoid of good character.[1] Many jurisdictions require the ex-convict to give notice of his outcast status, upon pain of further penalties, by registering with local authorities.[2] In the isolated challenges that have been made in the courts these legislative disqualifications and penalizations have usually been sustained as constitutional.[3] Some statutes in fact seem to read particularly "heinous" ex-prisoners out of the human race by attempting to put them beyond the pale of any protection against certain forms of arbitrary official action. The protection of the Fourth Amendment, authoritatively viewed as essential to "ordered liberty," [4] is withdrawn by the State of New York from the person adjudged a "habitual criminal" whose "person and . . . premises" are explicitly declared "liable *at all times* to search and examination by any magistrate, sheriff, constable or other officer, *with or without warrant.*" [5]

Here, then, is the handicap that confronts the ex-prisoner. He finds himself, not a "new man" as one might expect since he has done penance for his crime, but an ex-convict with all that this implies.[6]
The dignity of the human being is a very late discovery in history, especially the dignity of those who have been unsuccessful—the criminals and other asocials.[7]

Inconsistent Doctrines of Criminal Responsibility

When we look into the principal doctrines defining criminal responsibility in American jurisdictions we are at once struck by the inconsistencies that prevail. Thus the District of Columbia has joined the State of New Hampshire [8] in rejecting the M'Naghten Rules, which embody the "right-wrong" test of criminal responsibility, as contrary to the "legal and moral traditions of the western world." In so doing, the United States Court of Appeals for the District of Columbia Circuit has declared that "our traditions . . . require that where . . . acts . . . [which violate the law] stem from and are the product of a mental disease or defect . . . moral blame shall not attach, and . . . there will not be criminal responsibility." [9]

Beyond this the United States Court of Appeals for the District of Columbia Circuit has gone on to declare that "it is both wrong and foolish to punish . . . where punishment cannot correct" and that there were obvious and numerous instances in which for that reason "the community's security . . . [would] be better protected by hospitalization . . . than by imprisonment." [10]

Numerous other cases in other jurisdictions have considered but rejected the Durham Rule, as thus enunciated in the District of Columbia,[11] viewing it essentially as "a radical departure from the rules theretofore adhered to in all English-speaking jurisdictions with the exception of New Hampshire." [12] The law of criminal responsibility in the rest of the country can be summarized as follows:

> A person is not criminally responsible for an offense if at the time it is committed he is so mentally unsound as to lack 1. Knowledge that the act is wrong, or 2. (In fourteen or more states) will power enough to resist the impulse to commit it.[13]

It follows that the same "act," concurring with the same "state of mind," may lead to hanging, gassing, or electrocution in one jurisdiction and commitment, perhaps for psychoanalysis, in another.

Any survey of the penalties now provided also shows tremendous variation in severity from one jurisdiction to another. A few drastic examples must suffice. Attempted as well as actual rape may validly be punished by death in Virginia.[14] The same penalty, one may note in passing, may be meted out for rape in the nation's capital.[15] No penalty of comparable severity is permitted to be imposed for the offense of actual or attempted rape in New York, to mention no other jurisdiction.[16]

Robbery, without the use of a dangerous weapon, may incur a maximum term of ten years' imprisonment in Wisconsin.[17] In Alabama the same crime may carry the penalty of death.[18] In this context the report contained in a recent news dispatch to the effect that "[a] 55-year-old Perry County Negro . . . [was] held at Atmore Prison [in Alabama] under death sentence [imposed pursuant to state law] for robbing a white housewife of $1.95 at Marion, Ala. . . ." [19] needs no comment.

Variations in the severity of penalties for sex offenses are particularly extreme, ranging, as in the case of sodomy, from a sentence of one year to a sentence of thirty years (and beyond), *i.e.*, to an indeterminate sentence of from five years to life, depending solely on the geographical location.[20]

Depending only on the *locus in quo* the law thus lays "an unequal hand on those who have committed intrinsically the same quality of offense. . . ." [21]

When certain formal prescriptions are examined critically the inference is inescapable that equality is nominal and discrimination is genuine. Some of the more archaic doctrines of criminal law, if applied in practice, cannot fail to work in favor of the well-to-do, and thence to constitute a deprivation of respect (among other values) for the less well situated members of the community.

This is exemplified by common-law and statutory gradations of the gravity of larceny upon no other basis than the existing market price.[22] Professor Hermann Mannheim's trenchant analysis is revealing:

> From the very beginning the *value* of the object, and consequently the distinction between grand and petty larceny, has played a pre-

dominant part in criminal legislation, not only in the sense that, in order to be the object of theft, a thing must have some value, however small, but also that penalties have to be imposed in accordance with the value of the object. . . . [This] is characteristic of the loving care which criminal law, throughout its history, has bestowed upon the interests of the big property owner who alone can, as a rule, become the victim of grand larceny. . . . There is more in it than just another example of the general principle of criminal law that the damage done should be taken into account when meting out the penalty. If to kill a man was more expensive to the offender than to knock out a front tooth, this was justifiable as everyone had a life as well as (presumably) a front tooth, and everyone therefore enjoyed increased protection for the more important parts of his body. If, however, the thief was more severely punished if he stole a hundred sheep than if he took one or two, this in most cases, favoured only the owner of a hundred. Sometimes, it is true, grand larceny may betray stronger criminal tendencies in the thief which justify a sterner sentence; often, however, this does not hold good and the thief may even be unaware of the high value of the stolen article.[23]

Another example is provided by the widespread use of the alternative criminal sentence of fine *or* imprisonment.[24] For reasons which are too obvious to require elaboration, this sanctioning mechanism cannot fail to work in favor of the well-to-do and against the economically underprivileged. The record shows only one judge who has thus far raised the issue of its constitutionality.[25]

The point is further exemplified by the provision that requires maximum severity in the treatment of a homicide committed in the perpetration of a felony when property rights are violated.[26] The classic common-law illustration depicts the application of the celebrated Felony-Murder Rule to these facts:

A. shooteth at the poultry of B., and by accident killeth a man; if his intention was to steal the poultry, which must be collected from circumstances, it will be murder by reason of that felonious intent; but if it was done wantonly and without that intention it will be barely manslaughter.[27]

Mr. Justice Holmes's observation is apposite:

The fact that the shooting is felonious does not make it any more likely to kill people. If the object of the rule is to prevent such accidents, it should make accidental killing with firearms murder, not accidental killing in the effort to steal; while if the object is to prevent stealing, it would be better to hang one thief in every thousand by lot.[28]

In view of its patent unsuitability for the prevention of homicide, it is difficult to believe that "the object of the rule" is anything but the concern of men of property for property.

Another case in point is the contrasting criminal penalization generally provided for "assault" and "robbery." In New York, for example, an assault upon a human being either with "a loaded fire arm" or by the use of "poison . . . so as to endanger life," and in either case *"with an intent to kill,"* [29] is punishable by *a term [of imprisonment] not exceeding ten years."* [30] In contrast, a robbery, defined as the "taking" of *"personal property* from the person or in the presence of another, against his will, by means of force, or violence, or fear of injury, immediate or future, to his person or property," [31] is punishable, on a showing of any of several circumstances of aggravation (including the use of an accomplice or an automobile) [32] by measures of greater severity—*i.e.*, by a term of imprisonment of *"not less than ten years and . . . [not more] than thirty years."* [33] Once more, the paramount consideration appears to be the concern of men of property for property. Evidently the assumption is that if one has property one is a more serious loss to society than if one is merely a human being.

Consider, too, the following contrast in criminal sanctions in New York. "[A] term not exceeding *ten years"* [34] is provided for *"a person who,* with an intent to kill a human being . . . *assaults* another with a loaded fire arm, or any other deadly weapon," [35] while a term "for not more *than twenty-five years"* [36] is provided for a *"person who* unlawfully and maliciously . . . *destroys or damages any building"* [37] under circumstances productive of danger to human life. The moral of the law, as indicated by the comment of a contemporary journal of public opinion on the recent case of the "mad bomber," who was theoretically triable under both sections of the statute, is that a man "who plants bombs because he resents society's indifference to the individual should obviously concentrate on maiming his fellow citizens; he is foolhardy if he turns his rage on the real estate." [38]

Moreover, thus far at least, none of these forms of discriminatory legislation has met with serious challenge on constitutional grounds.

Summary Proceedings in an Unnecessarily Large Number of Cases

When we turn our attention to the authorization of summary action by public officials the conclusion is that existing requirements do not give enough protection against discriminatory practice. Summary proceedings are accepted in an unnecessarily large number of cases to the prejudice of individual rights.

While it is difficult to quarrel with the summary power of quarantine exercised by appropriate public health officers, it is equally difficult not to quarrel when this power is not subject to effective judicial control. In *State ex rel. McBride* v. *Superior Court,*[39] a petitioner, confined for hospital treatment under a city ordinance authorizing the summary quarantining of persons found to be suffering from "syphilis, gonorrhea, or any other contagious or infectious disease . . . or [from] any disease . . . dangerous to the public health" by the municipal Commissioner of Health,[40] sued for his release on habeas corpus. In so doing he alleged

> being held on a pretended claim vexatiously instigated by some police officer that he . . . [was] afflicted with some dangerous, contagious and infectious disease; that such charge . . . [was] unfounded and in fact untrue; . . . that, as he . . . [believed], the alleged cause of his detention . . . [was] but a subterfuge in furtherance of a conspiracy on the part of the police department, aided and acquiesced in by the health department, to unjustly deprive him of his liberty; that he . . . [had] been detained in unsanitary, filthy and poorly ventilated quarters, crowded with inmates . . . suffering from various ailments, . . . forced to use the same soap and a common drinking cup; . . . fed on unwholesome food and forced to submit to arbitrary medical treatment in furtherance of the design to detain him, without the privilege of having or consulting a physician of his own selection.[41]

We shall never know the truth about this allegation because a hearing on habeas corpus was denied upon the ground that there was no "legal reason for denying the power to quarantine *summarily,* or to restrain for treatment a citizen . . . because the authority may be abused or the law maladministered in a given case," [42] and that "to assume to review a finding of a properly constituted officer vested with authority to determine a fact in a critical situation involving detriment to the life and health of a community . . . [was] tantamount to a declaration that the police power of the city . . . [was] moribund and useless." [43]

While proceedings for the commitment of the mentally ill appear to be uniformly subject to judicial review, existing law in this field is, characteristically, summary,[44] and contemporary judicial conceptions of fair play are notoriously short of "due process" in other fields.[45] Illustrative of the situation even in "enlightened" jurisdictions, New York has authorized the detention of a person who is alleged to be mentally ill up to a period of ten days in a mental hospital upon certification by two physicians, without any manner of hearing in "emergencies." [46] The State has authorized indefinite detention after a "hearing" that is hardly recognizable as such. Thus, New York statutory law permits judicial examination of the alleged mentally ill person "in or out of court" and allows notice of the proceedings to be dispensed with, at the discretion of the court, to the one immediately and directly affected,[47] even in the more formal proceedings of "admission on court certification." While legislative history of these extraordinary measures shows that they were justified on therapeutic and humanitarian grounds (to save needless distress to all concerned), it cannot be denied that they are peculiarly vulnerable to arbitrary and irrational abuse. Despite the severity of the deprivation at stake for the one detained, the New York State law does not provide for the assistance of counsel or for effective steps to obtain independent psychiatric testimony. We may speculate that such aid may perhaps be obtained by the wealthy or other elite elements; it remains largely beyond the reach of the poor.

While the substitution of a "clinical" for an "accusatorial" investigation in Juvenile Court proceedings is generally held to be an advance toward corrective treatment, no legal scholar can fail to think of the dangers of unfairness that will arise when judgment is based on evidence that is not received in the presence of the alleged offender and is not open to appropriate cross-examination and reply.[48] Whatever the original legislative purpose to be served, it is appropriate to question the actual outcome of procedure which may not always be administered by competent or unbiased officials. We are accustomed to think in terms of a justice which "hears before it condemns." Condemnation, however, can be readily discovered in the "emollient terms" of a finding of "juvenile delinquency," as distinct from "crime." In the words of Mr. Justice Musmanno, dissenting, in *Holmes's Appeal:*

> A most disturbing fallacy abides in the notion that a Juvenile Court record does its owner no harm. The grim truth is that a Juvenile Court record is a lengthening chain that its riveted possessor will drag after him through childhood, youthhood, adulthood, and middle age. . . . What is punishment? It is the infliction of pain, sorrow, and grief. To take a child from the comfort of his home, the joy of his companions and the freedom of field, river and wood, and confine him to a building with whitewashed walls, regimented routine and institutional hours is punishment in the strictest sense of the word. To say . . . that this institutionalized incarceration is "for the care and treatment" of the juvenile does not make it any less abhorrent to the boy of spirit, health and energy.[49]

In sum, as expressed by Judge Crane, dissenting, in *People* v. *Lewis,*

> We must minimize the chance of abuse and place limitations even upon those who have the best of purposes and the most benevolent dispositions. To send a young man to prison for a crime is a serious matter for him and his family. To take a young lad, filled with the wild dreams of childhood, from his parents and his home and incarcerate him in a public institution until he is twenty-one years of age, is equally as serious, and the consequences are not lessened by the emollient term, "juvenile delinquency." [50]

The problem of summary action can be rationally raised in seeking to appraise one of our ancient institutions, the Grand Jury, whose "invoking" function is critically important in our system. Judicial control over the inquisitorial powers of the Grand Jury has traditionally included the dismissal of indictments deemed to be devoid of all evidentiary support or to rest upon no competent evidence.[51] Although this has been prevailing practice in numerous jurisdictions,[52] the Supreme Court has, in the recent case of *Costello* v. *United States,*[53] furnished *carte blanche* to federal Grand Jury investigators to found their indictments on gossip, hearsay, and suspicion. With strange unanimity the Court appears to have repudiated the traditional requirement at the level of federal practice of insisting that an indictment be based on competent evidence. In voting an indictment in a federal court the Grand Jury thus obtains greatly enhanced summary powers. In collecting evidence the Grand Jury is henceforth no longer subject to any perceptible control on behalf of a free citizenry that limits its discretion or that of the prosecuting officer. Perhaps such power could be justified if an indictment had no significant deprivational effects. In the apt words of the late Judge Jerome Frank, this is

> an astonishingly callous argument which ignores the obvious. For a wrongful indictment is no laughing matter; often it works a grievous, irreparable injury to the person indicted. The stigma cannot be easily erased. In the public mind, the blot on a man's escutcheon, resulting from such a public accusation of wrongdoing, is seldom wiped out by a subsequent judgment of not guilty. Frequently, the public remembers the accusation, and still suspects guilt, even after an acquittal.[54]

The drastic debilitation of the role of the Grand Jury as a watchdog against improvident prosecutions—highlighted by the Costello Case—has reinforced previous misgivings about its continuing social utility.[55]

Unusual and questionable scope has been given to summary procedures in another important area, the exclusion of aliens. The Supreme Court has held that administrative officers are not answerable even to the courts as to the evidence underlying an act of exclusion.[56] An American citizen may thus be denied knowledge of the specific grounds for excluding his alien wife from this country. An "abrupt and brutal exclusion of the wife of an American citizen without a hearing" [57] becomes possible. In the apt words of Mr. Justice Jackson, dissenting, in *Knauff* v. *Shaughnessy:*

> [An] American citizen is told he cannot bring his wife to the United States, but he will not be told why. He must abandon his bride to live in his own country or forsake his country to live with his bride.
>
> So he . . . [goes] to court and . . . [seeks] a writ of habeas corpus, which we never tire of citing to Europe as the unanswerable evidence that our free country permits no arbitrary official detention. And the Government tells the Court that not even a court can find out why the girl is excluded. But it says we must find that Congress authorized this treatment of war brides and, even if we cannot get any reasons for it, we must say it is legal; security requires it.

Security is like liberty in that many are the crimes committed in its name.[58]

We observe in passing that a measure of callousness in dealing with aliens appears to be a modern characteristic of American policy. Even after an alien is admitted to these shores he is hampered at every turn by formal and informal barriers. Access to many values and institutional situations is restricted to citizens; and eligibility is circumscribed in many ways.[59] Those who supervise the alien, whether an applicant for citizenship or not, are granted wide latitude for summary action.[60] The courts appear reluctant to seize opportunities to assess the fairness of the procedures employed.

In recent times one of the most notorious offenders against respect for human dignity by the use of summary action has been our legislative bodies. Congressional "'loyalty committees' have become a sort of irregular and irresponsible security police force, operating on a mounting scale which is rapidly approaching an overt and acknowledged inquisition." [61] In this process, they have exerted their "power of office and the pressure of publicity to inflict severe punishment, outside the due and regular processes of criminal law," and have hence "increasingly [resembled] the special people's courts, established by the Nazis to execute the 'healthy feeling of the people,' and in Communist countries to enforce Party standards of individual behavior and attitude." [62] It is gratifying, in this context, to note that the Supreme Court has reversed a conviction for Contempt of Congress encompassed in the refusal of the defendant "to testify [before the House Un-American Activities Committee] about persons who may in the past have been Communist Party members or otherwise engaged in Communist Party activity but who to [the petitioner's] best knowledge and belief . . . [had] long since removed themselves from the Communist movement" [63] —on the ground that the information sought to be elicited appeared to have no valid legislative purpose and that there was "no general [congressional] authority to expose the private affairs of individuals without justification in terms of the functions of the Congress" [64] or, in sum, "no congressional power to expose for the sake of exposure." [65] It is questionable, however, if anything but the more bizarre type of punishment by "exposure" has been checked by available judicial precedent. In the words of Mr. Chief Justice Warren himself, "the mere summoning of a witness and compelling him to testify against his will, about his beliefs, expressions or associations is a measure of governmental interference. And when those forced revelations concern matters that are unorthodox, unpopular, or even hateful to the general public, the reaction in the life of the witness may be disastrous." [66] The secure abatement of such practices, however, has not yet come in sight.[67]

Thus far, in sum, punishment by "exposure" can be inflicted, in most cases, without significant judicial restraint.

Widespread denial of passports to Americans, subjected in consequence to a summary form of "house arrest," has become yet another phase of a mounting infringement upon the traditional freedom of the individual. Less than thirty years ago, it can be recalled, a responsible observer of the American scene "viewed our ten dollar passport fee as a wrongful interference with the right to travel. Today, the objection seems bizarre in view of the widespread ban upon travel by Americans whose views on domestic and foreign policy do not accord with those of the State Department." [68] "Passports, [in brief,] are denied today for one reason alone: to impose a sanction upon political non-conformity." [69] Progress has been made in the judicial exaction of a "hearing" as a condition of passport denial though the nature of the "hearing" and the "evidence" upon which a passport may be denied has remained unclear.[70] Whether or not the recent invalidation of some of these practices by the Supreme Court on narrow statutory grounds [71] has in fact written finis to this form of sanctioning is very much to be doubted. It is probable, therefore, that the summary power of this form of "house arrest" continues to haunt the lives of political nonconformists.

The climax of summary action in recent years, however, has been reached in connection with the federal loyalty-security program.[72] "It is an ironic and not altogether happy reflection," it has been observed, "that although Congress has written into the law the elementary requirements of fair procedure for the government to follow in administrative hearings involving property rights, the same safeguards have been . . . denied [in loyalty-security matters] to its own employees." [73] In essence, "without trial by jury, without evidence, and without even being allowed to confront . . . [his] accusers or to know their identity, a citizen of the United States . . . [may be] found disloyal to the government of the United States," [74] notwithstanding the tradition "that no man shall be condemned to consequences resulting from alleged misconduct unheard and without having the opportunity of making his defense." [75] In this context the proceedings allow the combination of prosecuting and judicial functions, notwithstanding the tradition that "it is the right of every citizen to be tried by judges as free, impartial and independent as the lot of humanity will admit." [76]

"The heart of the matter," it may well be said in comment, "is that democracy implies respect for the elementary rights of men, however suspect or unworthy; a democratic government must therefore practice fairness; and fairness can rarely be obtained by secret, one-sided determination of facts decisive of rights. . . . Secrecy is not congenial to truth-seeking and self-righteousness gives too slender an assurance of rightness." [77]

In brief, the federal loyalty-security program has imposed the gravest possible deprivations upon reputations (to say nothing of economic, political, and other assets) without adhering to the safeguards customarily invoked in such relatively more trivial proceedings as those involving revocation of a driver's license.

It may be suggested that the answer to the current loyalty-security dilemma does not necessarily lie entirely in the direction of procedural improvement, exemplified by confrontation and cross-examination of witnesses, demanded by many a well-meaning advocate of reform. Traditional judicial techniques, however trustworthy in the traditional courtroom setting, are singularly unsuited to the exploration of the subjective state of mind, connoted by loyalty or disloyalty, the sole issue in a loyalty contest. Even if this were not the case, the adoption of some of the more elaborate safeguards of judicial trial would still not render the loyalty-security program unobjectionable. Armed with spurious respectability, the transformed administrative tribunal would brand the citizen found guilty of a "disloyalty" encompassed not in acts but thoughts with the same "badge of infamy" as before. In sum, the citizen would still face punishment for a crime of the mind by administrative adjudication. However "fair and enlightened" the underlying procedure, the assessment of "guilt" and the consequent stigmatization of the individual for "dangerous thoughts" would still seem intolerable under democratic justice.

The justification for summary action appears to have been in effect a presumption of "guilt," notwithstanding the tradition "that . . . [the] presumption [of innocence is essential to] every code . . . which has reason, and religion, and humanity, for a foundation." [78] Without the apparent benefit of poetic license, Ogden Nash has caught the quintessence of such official attitudes in these lines:

> Our fathers claimed, by obvious madness moved,
> Man's innocence until his guilt be proved.
> They would have known, had they not been confused,
> He's innocent until he is accused.[79]

Inadequate Remedies for Acknowledged Wrongs

When we analyze the formal requirements of a legal system one pertinent question is the inclusiveness of the remedies that have been provided. In connection with the application of sanctions, for example, can we say that the American system is complete? Our review suggests that several important gaps have been left unfilled.

The doctrine of sovereign immunity in its presently overextended form appears to foreclose remedial action beyond reason and conscience. In 1744, Lord Mansfield declared that

> to lay down in an English court of Justice such a monstrous proposition, as that a governor acting by virtue of letters patent under the great seal, is accountable only to God and his own conscience; that he is absolutely despotic and can spoil, plunder, and affect his Majesty's subjects, both in their liberty and property, *with immunity,* is a doctrine that cannot be maintained.[80]

In 1949, a Frenchman, asserting that he had been willfully and maliciously interned on the pretext that he was a German enemy alien during the Second World War by action of officials of the Department of Justice and that by such action he had been deprived "of his liberty contrary to law," was held to have failed to have stated a claim upon which relief could be granted in an American court.[81] The contemporary rationale for the "proposition" viewed as "monstrous" by Lord Mansfield was that it is "in the end better to leave unredressed the wrongs done by dishonest officers than to subject those who try to do their duty to the constant dread of retaliation." [82]

Adequate opportunity is not given at present, we suspect, for the judicial examination of adjudicated cases in the light of newly discovered evidence. Regardless of the merits of the situation a motion for a new trial (in civil and criminal matters alike) is strictly limited to the time prescribed by statute or by a judicial rule of procedure.[83] This restriction works the most obvious and far-reaching discrimination in the criminal case where new evidence is discovered only after the expiration of the time available for such a motion. The extraordinary remedies of the writs of error *coram nobis* and of habeas corpus are largely ineffective in common law or statutory form for the pure case in which newly discovered facts establish innocence, though involving no suppression of evidence, fraud, or judicial error. In such cases, existing law leaves the victim subject to the hazards of executive clemency.[84]

A further important point remains in this connection. On those rare occasions when the fact of a wrongful conviction has been authoritatively acknowledged, what remedy is open to the individual? Although he has been singled out for unjustified deprivation by the long arm of fate in the guise of courts, few arrangements have been made to create a right to compensation, capable of judicial enforcement. In the handful of jurisdictions where the remedy exists [85] only token measures are provided.[86] In most of our jurisdictions, not even the financial loss directly attributable to the cost of a trial that ends in a wrongful conviction is compensable under existing law. Although legislatures may decide to vote a compensatory award as a matter of grace, it has not been the general practice for them to assume any part of the "financial burden" of a miscarriage of justice. And we may note that wrongful convictions occur more often than prosecutors care to admit.[87]

We must not lose sight of the somewhat ironical fact that when measured in terms of financial loss there appear to be as many, if not more, "hapless victims" of "just acquittals" as there are of "wrongful" convictions. Our sanctioning arrangements typically make no more provision for compensating from the public treasury the victim of a false charge, found groundless after judicial trial, than for compensating the victim of a judicial conviction found groundless after executive scrutiny. In either case the end of the trial may leave the victim partly or completely impoverished. However, the victim of the "just acquittal," unlike the victim of the "wrongful conviction," will have no substantial hope of compensation by grace of the legislature even when he has spent months in custody preliminary to acquittal or has expended his life's savings for his defense.

The contrast furnished by Soviet law is not rendered less embarrassing by the fact that on this, as on many other scores, Soviet doctrine can safely be assumed to present a paper guaranty belied by the realities of everyday practice. Yet Soviet law purports to secure to the accused, once acquitted of crime, recovery of his back wages for the period of his incarceration *pendente lite.*[88] Without such or similar remedies for the loss inevitably thrust upon the accused despite acquittal, our system, characterized as it is by the broad discretionary role of the prosecution,[89] operates without significant restraint in the initiation of the criminal proceeding, and therefore tolerates the infliction of an often irremediable hardship upon the sanctioning target, regardless of the outcome of the litigation. We note, parenthetically, that the Grand Jury, essential only to the indictment stage in the case of the indictable offenses (as distinct from most misdemeanors), has not been conspicuous in dampening the zeal of the prosecution, especially in the case of unpopular characters. Transformation of the Grand Jury into the rubber stamp of the prosecution, one may remember in this connection, is, if not invited, at least facilitated by the unanimous ruling of the Supreme Court in *Costello* v. *United States,*[90] which we have previously discussed.

It is generally known that prosecutors who are unable to obtain a penalty in the regular way may succumb to the temptation of securing informal but nonetheless equally effective results by harrassing prosecutions which eventually leave the victim formally vindicated though penniless. Under such circumstances innocent defendants yield to the temptation of pleading guilty, or decide to retain less expensive and competent legal assistance in the hope of salvaging at least part of their financial assets for their families. These dangers appear particularly acute in cases that involve unpopular political figures [91] as well as the members of middle- and lower-income groups. Our conclusion is that our sanctioning process needs to be brought into line with the ancient maxim, "*ubi jus, ibi remedium.*"

Neglected Rights of Prisoners

Another gap of some magnitude in our system of remedies is that concerning the rights of prisoners. Existing statutes are singularly dumb on the subject, leaving duly convicted individuals liable to the uncertainties of custodial discretion on behalf of prison "discipline." [92] Concealed behind prison walls, convicted men and women would seem peculiarly vulnerable to the arbitrary infliction of punishment above and beyond that specifically prescribed by the sentencing court. In many instances the added penalties may arise from nothing more legitimate than the whim of the custodial personnel.[93]

Invasions of Individual Privacy

In American tradition a significant theme has been the attempt to protect zones of individual privacy from encroachment, especially on the part of public officials. Mr. Justice Frankfurter has stated that theme in saying that "the security of . . . [our] privacy against arbitrary intrusion by the police" is "basic to a free society." [94] It is unnecessary to remind any lawyer or student of law-enforcement problems that police officials are under perpetual temptation to penetrate the curtains that stand in the way of apprehending offenders and obtaining sufficient evidence to convict. To the incentive associated with ordinary law enforcement must be added the motives that are inseparable from the changed structure of world politics. The chronic crisis in world affairs has filled the nation with apprehensions relating to national security that are without recent precedent short of active war. Moreover, the technological revolution has put new instruments of surveillance in the hands of public officials and of prying private parties. In such a setting the proper limitations upon police activity remain in rapid flux; and there are ample grounds for concern about the state of respect for individual privacy. A variety of electronic devices of surveillance, including though not limited to wire tapping,[95] have been accepted by the Supreme Court as outside the ambit of constitutional prohibition against state or federal action. The contemporary situation has fulfilled a prediction by Mr. Justice Brandeis, in dissent, in *Olmstead* v. *United States*,[96] that "by means far more effective than stretching upon the rack . . . [the government would] obtain disclosure in court of what . . . [was] whispered in the closet. . . . [and that the] progress of science in furnishing the government with means of espionage . . . [would not] stop with wiretapping." [97]

More conventional and ancient forms of intrusion by the police into the citizen's privacy have indeed been brought within the express protection of the Constitution at state and federal levels. "The knock at the door," declared Mr. Justice Frankfurter for the Supreme Court, "whether by day or by night, as a prelude to a search, . . . solely on the authority of the police, did not need the commentary of recent history to be condemned as inconsistent with the conception of human rights enshrined in the history and the basic constitutional documents of English-speaking peoples." [98] While, however, "the security of one's privacy against arbitrary intrusion by the police . . . [is held] implicit in the concept of ordered liberty" [99] we must give full weight to the fact that no uniform rule now defines the standards by which this security is to be judged or the appropriate remedies to be invoked against its violation.

The Supreme Court has required the federal courts to exclude evidence of whatever character, including the most pertinent, whenever the evidence is the direct or indirect result of unreasonable search and seizure by federal officers.[100] At the same time the Court has left the "ways of enforcing . . . [the] basic right" [101] of the party in the context of state proceedings to action by the state.[102] About half of the state jurisdictions accept with varying degrees of qualification the product of unreasonable searches and seizures in evidence, and provide for trespass suits, criminal prosecutions, and administrative action against offending officials.[103] The employment of efficient remedies, other than the exclusionary rule, was correctly foreseen by Mr. Justice Murphy as most improbable (dissenting in *Wolf* v. *Colorado*).[104] In his own words:

Self-scrutiny is a lofty ideal, but its exaltation reaches new heights if we expect a District Attorney to prosecute himself or his associates for well-meaning violations of the search and seizure clause during a raid the District Attorney or his associates have ordered. . . . A trespass action for damages is a venerable means of securing reparation for unauthorized invasion of the home. . . . But what an illusory remedy this is, if by 'remedy' we mean a positive deterrent to police and prosecutors tempted to violate the Fourth Amendment. The appealing ring softens when we recall that in a trespass action the measure of damages is simply the extent of the injury to physical property. If the officer searches with care, he can avoid all but nominal damages—a penny, or a dollar. . . . The conclusion is inescapable that but one remedy exists to deter violations of the search and seizure clause. That is the rule which excludes illegally obtained evidence. Only by exclusion can we impress upon the zealous prosecutor that violation of the Constitution will do him no good. And only when that point is driven home can the prosecutor be expected to emphasize the importance of observing constitutional demands in his instructions to the police.[105]

A search of the law reports of all states reveals but a handful of actions in behalf of "the security of one's privacy"—since the Wolf case—although no responsible observer has claimed any significant decline in lawlessness in law enforcement during that period of time.

Speaking through Mr. Justice Traynor, six years after the Wolf case, the Supreme Court of California "concluded . . . that evidence obtained in violation of the constitutional guarantees" was henceforward to be "inadmissible" in California courts and explained that it had

been compelled to reach that conclusion because other remedies . . . [had] completely failed to secure compliance with the constitutional provisions on the part of police officers with the attendant result that the courts under the old rule [admitting the product of unreasonable searches and seizures in evidence had] been constantly required to participate in, and in effect condone, the lawless activities of law enforcement officers.[106]

It was plain, declared Mr. Justice Traynor, for the Court, that "experience . . . [had] demonstrated . . . that neither administrative, criminal nor civil remedies . . . [were] effective in suppressing lawless searches and seizures." [107]

In sum, the contention "that exclusion is the only practical way of enforcing the constitutional privilege" [108] appears to be vindicated.

Inadequate Protection against Violence toward Minorities

No doubt broad prohibitions of discrimination have a fundamental role in our legal system. But experience suggests that general standards need to be supplemented by specific standards, and by sanctions whose incidence is clear.

When we examine American legislation and legislative proposals we note the absence of prohibitions aimed directly at such an ancient abuse as lynching. An anti-lynching bill, designed to supplement federal sanctions by making local officials criminally responsible for neglect or refusal to make reasonable efforts to protect lynching victims, and establishing the civil liability of every subdivision of a state in which a lynching takes place,[109] has always been buried in committee.[110]

APPLICATIONS

Up to this point we have relied mainly on the phraseology that appears in statutes and in the opinions of courts. Hence the picture of the significance of the sanctioning process for respect relations in America is highly inferential, even though on many specific points there is no reasonable basis for predicting that further study will add or subtract. We now turn directly to sanctions in operation. Regardless of the formal requirements of statute and doctrine, are deprivations of respect regularly imposed upon discernible categories of individuals? Are these deprivations discriminatory; do they depend upon characteristics of the target that are logically extraneous to the result? For instance, do the elite—those whose class position is high in terms of wealth, power, and other values—have an advantage over the mid-elite or the rank and file who constitute lower strata?

Class Position Affects Outcome

Observers of the actual operation of the sanctioning process are quite generally impressed with the impact of class position on outcomes. Class position is defined according to the degree of control that one has over values. As plaintiff or defendant the values at one's disposal are available to serve as base values for the accomplishment of specific purposes (the scope values). The late Judge Jerome Frank summarized the importance of money in criminal or civil litigation in these forthright words:

With the ablest lawyer in the world, a man may lose a suit he ought to win, if he has not the funds to pay for an investigation, before trial, of evidence necessary to sustain his case. . . . Without the evidence which such an investigation would reveal, a man is often bound to be defeated. His winning or losing may, therefore, depend on his pocketbook. He is out of luck if his pocketbook is not well lined with money. For neither his lawyer nor any legal aid institution will supply the needed sums. For want of money, expendable for such purposes, many a suit has been lost, many a meritorious claim or defense has never even been asserted.[111]

We take as an example in the "civil" field, litigation over water rights. The standards that have been set prescribing the rules for the allocation of water are, on their face, relatively unobjectionable. When we examine the attempts made by public or private parties to invoke the sanctioning process in order to conform conduct to prescription, many discrepancies appear. The presently existing remedies are actually invoked in a comparatively small number of controversies. A gross disparity exists between the number of individuals who need water, and who are seriously affected by injurious water uses, and the number who actually present their claims before the bars of the state trial and appellate courts. Under such circumstances adjudication proceeds by fits and starts. The pace is set in the main by the claimants who are capable of defraying the requisite cost of litigation. Many of the claims are unrepresentative of the problems confronting wider strata of the populace. In this field as in so many areas a host of formally recognized "rights" continues its amorphous existence *in nubibus,* not for lack of meritorious claimants but for lack of a happy pairing of merit and money. The growth of an adequate pattern of precedent is inhibited by the cost factor.

We note in conclusion in such a context that the "law's delay" is the special nemesis of the man of modest income and capital.[112]

When we probe into the realities of "criminal" justice it is apparent that results are distorted in substantially the same direction in response to essentially the same cluster of dominating factors.

Consider in the first place the invoking function, "the making of a provisional characterization of an act as constituting a violation of (or a conformance to) community prescription." It is well known to lawyers that in federal and state systems of criminal prosecution the prosecutor has, with few exceptions, ultimate discretion as to the initiation of proceedings, *i.e.*, the exercise of the invoking function.

We have previously mentioned the possibility of purely harassing prosecutions in spite of the traditional role of watchdog that has presumably characterized the Grand Jury (but which was seriously undercut by the Costello case).

A recent trend is for the prosecution to abandon criminal action in favor of mental commitment proceedings when confronted by troublesome characters who at any given time are chargeable only with violations that carry light maximum sentences.[113] A case in point is the District of Columbia's notorious "Bad Man of Swamppoodle" who, when arrested for nothing more serious than public drunkenness, was the target of mental commitment proceedings. At a stroke of the pen the "bad man" was transformed into the "sick man," [114] and instead of receiving the statutory maximum of ninety days for public drunkenness became the target of what for practical purposes could have become a term of life imprisonment in a mental hospital. Evidently there are grave dangers developing that "medicine" can be used as punishment without strict observance of due-process requirements.[115] The danger is indicated by such common statutory authority as that which permits summary, though temporary, mental commitment of an individual answering a "criminal" charge, when the prosecuting officer initiates the motion. No other evidence is required than courtroom observation.[116]

We now take note of the possibility of culpable inaction by the prosecution, a contingency for which effective sanctions are not provided in the present state of the law. For "how to compel the prosecutor to initiate prosecution where the circumstances of the case demand it," it has been aptly observed, "is a legislative problem which has found no solution to date." [117]

Furthermore, most prosecutors have, subject to a few restrictions, effective discretionary power to dismiss criminal proceedings after they have begun, though usually before trial.[118] Besides, the prosecutor has discretionary power to "compromise cases" upon "plea-bargaining," the "great majority of convictions in both federal and state courts . . . [being] based on pleas of guilty, most of which result from compromises involving waiver of felony or some other reduction in the charge or a recommendation for suspension of sentence." [119]

No informed lawyer doubts that "*bargaining* in regard to the plea is common. The district attorney asks the accused if he will plead guilty to a lesser offense in order to insure a lighter sentence. In the slang of the courtroom, the prisoner 'dickers for a light rap' in return for his plea. Roscoe Pound discusses this much condemned power of the prosecutor to compromise his cases: 'Ninety percent of these convictions are upon pleas of guilty, made on bargain days in the assured expectation of nominal punishment as the cheapest way out.' " [120]

More striking perhaps, since less discussed, is the continued invocation by the prosecution of sanctions which are unlikely to meet the test of constitutionality, yet remain outside the effective scope of federal review. When we ask why, the answer is that policemen and prosecutors find these instruments convenient, and the typical target of the sanction is either poor or unpopular. "Dragnet" statutes, which are notoriously out of harmony with the principle of legality and in accord with the totalitarian doctrine of analogy, continue upon our statute books.[121] There has been no sustained incentive to lay down the constitutional gauntlet, presumably because these measures are used by the prosecution against "vagrant," "heretic," and friendless "troublemakers."

The atmosphere created by these conditions can by no stretch of the tolerant imagination be made consonant with the democratic ideal. The prosecutor's power, whatever it may once have been, is dangerously without restraint. A startled Supreme Court recently was confronted by the admission of the State of Texas that its prosecuting counsel had knowingly offered in evidence the perjured testimony of his principal witness in a capital case. The court was reviewing the case on habeas corpus. An enraged husband, suspecting infidelity, had shot his wife whom he had discovered in a parked car with the State's witness. The witness told the prosecuting counsel before trial that he had engaged in numerous acts of sexual intercourse with the defendant's wife. The prosecutor, however, directed him "not [to] volunteer any information about such intercourse"; hence the witness had pictured his own behavior with the deceased as unimpeachable and thus had testified about an unprovoked shooting in cold blood. The conviction of murder in the first degree which had been obtained below was of course held by the Supreme Court to violate the due-process clause of the Fourteenth Amendment.[122] The most significant feature of the situation is that it took action by the highest tribunal in the land to secure a new trial on the basis of facts which were not in dispute.

A study of the flow of daily criminal court business is enough to support the popular maxim that "money talks." We Americans not only pride ourselves upon our idealism but upon our realism; and recognizing the role of wealth, power, and related values in the administration of criminal justice is in no sense outside that strand of the national tradition that includes self-criticism alongside the "screaming ego." We are impressed by the tone of moral indignation with which these matters are usually considered. In fact there is rather more rhetoric in this field than serious-minded, comprehensive, and competent reporting. The normative approach is aptly exemplified in the unequivocal language of Mr. Justice Black, speaking for the Supreme Court. "There can be no equal justice where the kind of trial a man gets depends on the amount of money he has." [123] Yet "the kind of trial a man gets" does in fact appear to bear a close relationship to "the amount of money he has" in the practical administration of criminal justice.

Consider the most extreme case first, the indigent prisoner. The assistance of counsel for the defense of an indigent is not a matter of constitutional right in all circumstances in state courts.[124] Moreover, the "right to counsel," even when recognized, has not been deemed to impose a constitutional duty, at least upon a state court, to appoint private psychiatrists for pretrial examination to aid the defendant in presenting a defense of insanity, even in a capital case.[125] Need one add that the "best" of rules for the determination of criminal responsibility is a sham without *adequate* psychiatric facilities for the defense in a system of adversarial justice?

The results are deplorable. The following summary succinctly presents available data on the current situation:

> Approximately 60 per cent of defendants in criminal cases are unable to employ counsel. In 1947 an estimated 97,000 persons who could not afford a lawyer faced prosecution on serious criminal charges of a type classified in many states as felonies. Not more than 22,000 were assisted by public or voluntary defender organizations. Approximately 36,000 received the . . . services of assigned private counsel, and at least 38,000 went without any form of Legal Aid whatever.[126]

When counsel is made available by virtue of "constitutional" requirement (or legislative, judicial, or civic charity), it is rarely if ever as effective as the services obtained by the criminal defendant who is better off financially. Counsel is not generally assigned to the defense of indigent prisoners until the arraignment, directly preceding trial. The overwhelming majority of indigent prisoners, unlike the paying "criminal" clientele, "waives" the "preliminary hearing," and hence forfeits the opportunities of pretrial discovery and the perpetuation of evidence inherent in that right. The enormity of the disadvantage incurred is realized by any experienced criminal trial lawyer. In this connection a suggestion that deserves serious consideration is that legislatures prescribe a hard and fast rule of mandatory preliminary hearings at least for all felonies. We might do worse, in fact, than to follow the English example of substituting the preliminary hearing for the grand jury investigation.[127] This step toward fairness and economy would, however, have to be preceded by constitutional amendment in view of the Fifth Amendment guaranty of grand jury indictment in the federal prosecution of "infamous crimes."

It is well known to the bar that counsel for indigent defendants are mostly appointed pursuant to some mechanical or haphazard scheme by the courts, and frequently exhibit the most amazing ignorance of elementary criminal practice. Compensation is not usually paid; hence an assigned attorney often lacks incentive to put up the spirited defense which is essential under the adversarial system. Time and again counsel devotes himself, regardless of the merits of the case, to persuading the client to enter a plea of "guilty" or to waive an appeal.[128]

These strictures apply even to the most advanced administration of existing criminal procedure under the Federal Rules. These Rules do not entitle indigent prisoners to have counsel assigned to represent them in preliminary proceedings, "assigned counsel [appearing only at a later stage and significantly] . . . without compensation. . . ." [129]

One of the most obvious and frequent proposals for improving the situation is to establish a Public Defender's office at public expense. It cannot be demonstrated as yet that these offices have been sufficiently numerous or well supported to make a substantial dent in existing practice.[130] Remedial action by the states has failed to improve the situation significantly.

The Supreme Court has held that indigent defendants are entitled as a matter of due process and equal protection to free stenographic transcripts for appellate purposes, assuming that the right of appeal had been provided under state law.[131] If "destitute defendants must be afforded as adequate an appellate review as defendants who have money enough to buy transcripts" [132] and if this principle is extended to include all other means of effective legal assistance, an improvement may at last be in sight. At this stage, however, the possibility is highly speculative.[133]

In the meantime, moreover, Pelion is piled upon Ossa by requiring the "exhaustion of state remedies" to include a petition for certiorari to the Supreme Court, as the foundation for a federal review of a state criminal conviction by habeas corpus.[134] "This rule," to say the least, "has been puzzling" to many responsible observers.[135]

Under the circumstances now prevailing, the trial court of first resort is generally the tribunal of last resort as well. It is estimated that "probably 95% of all cases end in the trial courts." [136]

Insofar as nonpaying litigants are concerned this implies minimum opportunity for appeal. It is not surprising if the bench, occupying a rather privileged position in fact if not in form, displays unwarranted caprice and erratic judgment.[137]

Variation of Judicial Response to Similar Situations

When we make a more intensive examination of the factors that result in discriminatory treatment of litigants, especially in criminal cases, we obtain some enlightenment from psychoanalysis and other methods of probing the personality system as a whole.[138] However, personal differences are often not rooted in the structure of the total personality; they may reflect the continuing impact of exposure to special patterns of culture, class, interest, or even crisis level. All these complexities are involved, although somewhat blurred by the results obtained when the conduct of judges is subjected to satistical comparisons. For instance:

A survey was made of the disposition of thousands of minor criminal cases by the several judges of the City Magistrate's Court in New York City during the years 1914 to 1916 with the express purpose of finding to what extent the "personal equation" entered into the administration of justice. It was disclosed that "the magistrates did differ to an amazing degree in their treatment of similar classes of cases." Thus of 546 persons charged with intoxication brought before one judge, he discharged only one and found the others about 97% guilty, whereas of the 673 arraigned before another judge, he found 531 or 79% not guilty. In disorderly conduct cases, one judge discharged only 18% and another discharged 54%. In other words, one coming before Magistrate Simons had only 2 chances in 10 of getting off. If he had come before Judge Walsh he would have had more than 5 chances in 10 of getting off. In vagrancy cases the percentage of discharges varied from 4.5% to 79%.[139]

Disparities of this particular kind seem particularly marked in the handling of sex offenses. As seen in the Kinsey studies:

The influence of the mores is strikingly shown by the study of the decisions which are reached by judges with different social backgrounds. There is still a portion of the legal profession that has not gone to college and, particularly where judges are elected by popular vote, there are some instances of judges who have originated in lower social levels and acquired their legal training by office apprenticeship or night school courses. The significance of the background becomes most apparent when two judges, one of upper level and one of lower level, sit in alternation on the same bench. The record of the upper level judge may involve convictions and maximum sentences in a high proportion of the sex cases, particularly those that involve non-marital intercourse or prostitution. The judge with the lower level background may convict in only a small fraction of the cases.[140]

Research on structural factors in personality points to one major finding of far from negligible importance for the sanctioning process. Relatively rigid and peremptory modes of thought are distinguishing traits of "authoritarian personalities." Translated in terms of the judicial process the implication is that predispositions in favor of asserting the power of the State against individuals, especially when "moral" issues are at stake, incline some judges to guide proceedings toward a verdict of "guilty." [141] We do not know the ratio of authoritarian to nonauthoritarian personalities on the bench, compared with the general public or with selected groups. But we are beginning to see that modern methods of personality study are providing ways and means of appraising with more precision than ever before the role of so-called "imponderable" factors in the decision process as a whole and in sanctioning measures in particular.

The defendant is subject to the "luck of the draw" in escaping or getting a judge who is disposed for or against "guilt." Closely connected with the same set of factors are the determiners of severe or mild sentences. Statistical comparisons of sentencing behavior are rather startling even to the blasé members of the least illustrious bar associations. Consider the court record of one county in New Jersey in which were tabulated all sentences handed down by six judges over a period of nine years for certain crimes. In all there were 7,442 cases. The results demonstrate "that these 6 judges . . . [had] sentencing tendencies which . . . [differed] markedly. Jail sentences . . . [were] given in 57.7% of the cases when Judge 4 . . . [sat] and 33.6% of the cases when Judge 2 . . . [sat]. Again, Judge 6 . . . [gave] 15.7% of his sentences in the form of suspended sentences, while Judge 2 . . . [gave] more than twice as many, namely 33.8%." [142]

In an experiment conducted in Erie County, New York, in 1955 under the auspices of the University of Buffalo Law School, a hypothetical fact situation involving a guilty plea to a larceny charge affording discretionary latitude of up to ten years of imprisonment in sentencing was submitted to six judges of general jurisdiction. The responses varied from a suspended sentence with an indication of probable discharge from probation after one year to a sentence of not less than five nor more than ten years in a state prison.

A *Questionnaire* sent by the *Yale Law Journal* to every federal district judge reports a recent study that reveals that 66 percent of the 140 judges replying consider the defendant's plea a relevant factor in local sentencing procedure. 87 percent of the judges who acknowledged that the plea was germane indicated that a defendant pleading guilty to a crime was given a more lenient punishment than a defendant who pleaded not guilty. The estimates of the extent to which the fine or prison term was diminished by a defendant pleading guilty varied from 10 to 95 percent of the punishment which would ordinarily be given after trial and conviction.[143]

In comparison, the wholly nondiscriminatory methods of Judge Bridlegoose, "who decided causes and controversies in law by the chance and fortune of the dice" [144] are models of judicial virtue, for Judge Bridlegoose, it will be recalled, used to "give out sentence in *his* favour unto whom hath befallen the best chance by dice." [145]

In passing it may be remarked that as studies multiply our factual knowledge, certain recommendations spring quickly to mind. It is proposed, for example, to provide for appellate review of sentences as well as convictions.[146] Insofar as the existing system tends to "deny adequate review to the poor" it is the poor who are most likely to be victimized by quirks in the function of the sanctioning process. They are most vulnerable to the loss of "life, liberty or property because of unjust convictions which appellate courts would set aside." [147]

Discriminatory Use of Capital Punishment

Of all sanction policies, the most irretrievable when applied is capital punishment; and it is precisely this penalty whose incidence is peculiarly discriminatory. In the words of a recent study:

> Where it is applied, it is applied in a shockingly haphazard and discriminatory way. Of the few who are actually executed, almost all are poor, almost all are men, and a disproportionately high number are Negroes. Defendants of wealth or education practically never go to the gallows or the electric chair. Neither do women. Warden Lawes of Sing Sing escorted 150 persons to their death. Of them, 150 were poor; 149 were men. During the twenty years from 1930 to 1950, there were 3,029 executions in the United States. Of these, 21 were women. And of these few, the majority were Negro women. In the southern states where capital punishment is retained for rape, it is used almost exclusively against Negroes.[148]

TABLE 1: PRISONERS EXECUTED UNDER CIVIL AUTHORITY IN THE UNITED STATES, BY RACE AND OFFENSE: 1930 TO 1959

(The figures in parentheses show the number of females included. Excludes Alaska and Hawaii except for two federal executions in Alaska, one in 1948 and one in 1950.)

Year	All offenses				Murder				Rape				Other offences*		
	Total	*White*	*Negro*	*Other*	*Total*	*White*	*Negro*	*Other*	*Total*	*White*	*Negro*	*Other*	*Total*	*White*	*Negro*
All years	3,666	1,653	1,972	41	(29) 3,179	(18) 1,578	(11) 1,562	39	426	42	382	2	(2) 61	(2) 33	28
Percent	*100.0*	—	—	—	*86.7*	—	—	—	*11.6*	—	—	—	*1.7*	—	—
Percent	*100.0*	*45.1*	*53.8*	*1.1*	*100.0*	*49.7*	*49.1*	*1.2*	*100.0*	*9.9*	*89.6*	*0.5*	*100.0*	*54.1*	*45.9*
1959	49	16	33	—	41	15	26	—	8	1	7	—	—	—	—
1958	48	20	27	1	40	20	19	1	7	—	7	—	1	—	1
1957	65	34	31	—	(1) 54	(1) 32	22	—	10	2	8	—	1	—	1
1956	65	21	43	1	52	20	31	1	12	—	12	—	1	1	—
1955	76	44	32	—	(1) 65	(1) 41	24	—	7	1	6	—	4	2	2
1954	81	38	42	1	(2) 71	(1) 37	(1) 33	1	9	1	8	—	1	—	1
1953	62	30	31	1	(1) 51	(1) 25	25	1	7	1	6	—	(2) 4	(2) 4	—
1952	83	36	47	—	71	35	36	—	12	1	11	—	—	—	—
1951	105	57	47	1	(1) 87	(1) 55	31	1	17	2	15	—	1	—	1
1950	82	40	42	—	68	36	32	—	13	4	9	—	1	—	1
1949	119	50	67	2	107	49	56	2	10	—	10	—	2	1	1
1948	119	35	82	2	95	32	61	2	22	1	21	—	2	2	—

Year	All offenses				Murder				Rape				Other offences*		
	Total	White	Negro	Other	Total	White	Negro	Other	Total	White	Negro	Other	Total	White	Negro
1947	153	42	111	—	(2) 129	(1) 40	(1) 89	—	23	2	21	—	1	—	1
1946	131	46	84	1	(1) 107	45	(1) 61	1	22	—	22	—	2	1	1
1945	117	41	75	1	(1) 90	37	(1) 52	1	26	4	22	—	1	—	1
1944	120	47	70	3	(3) 96	45	(3) 48	3	24	2	22	—	—	—	—
1943	131	54	74	3	(3) 118	(1) 54	(2) 63	1	13	—	11	2	—	—	—
1942	147	67	80	—	(1) 116	(1) 57	59	—	24	4	20	—	7	6	1
1941	123	59	63	1	(1) 102	(1) 55	46	1	20	4	16	—	1	—	1
1940	124	49	75	—	105	44	61	—	15	2	13	—	4	3	1
1939	159	80	77	2	144	79	63	2	12	—	12	—	3	1	2
1938	190	96	92	2	(2) 155	(2) 90	63	2	25	1	24	—	10	5	5
1937	147	69	74	4	(1) 133	67	(1) 62	4	13	2	11	—	1	—	1
1936	195	92	101	2	(1) 181	(1) 86	93	2	10	2	8	—	4	4	—
1935	199	119	77	3	(4) 184	(3) 115	(1) 66	3	13	2	11	—	2	2	—
1934	168	65	102	1	(1) 154	(1) 64	89	1	14	1	13	—	—	—	—
1933	160	77	81	2	151	75	74	2	7	1	6	—	2	1	1
1932	140	62	75	3	128	62	63	3	10	—	10	—	2	—	2
1931	153	77	72	4	(1) 137	(1) 76	57	4	15	1	14	—	1	—	1
1930	155	90	65	—	(1) 147	(1) 90	57	—	6	—	6	—	2	—	2

* 22 armed robbery, 16 kidnaping, 11 burglary, 8 espionage (6 in 1942 and 2 in 1953), 4 aggravated assault.

Source: Federal Bureau of Prisons, Washington, D.C., *National Prisoner Statistics*, No. 23 (February, 1960).

The preceding Table 1 is official and shows a shocking preponderance of Negroes over whites among persons executed in the United States between 1930 and 1959.[149]

Erratic Granting or Withholding of Bail

A much less dramatic and final sanctioning measure is the granting or withholding of bail. Yet bail is one of the most instructive instances when we are examining the relationship between the sanctioning ideal of equality and the coarse facts of elite advantage. Where the accused is financially able to put up bail, he may avoid spending a single day of imprisonment. The accused who is less well off may spend months or even years in prison regardless of his ultimate acquittal.

The situation is aggravated by the fact that under the pressure of chronically congested dockets most of our state courts repeatedly tolerate a lapse of many months between indictment and trial. These are the operational facts as distinct from the doctrinal prescription of a "speedy trial." One result is to deny appellate vindication, as a practical matter, to a large number of indigent prisoners. If the conviction carries a sentence of two or three years or less, the delays have often accumulated to the point that an appeal, besides depleting whatever funds are available, offers little alleviation even if successful. In contrast, the accused who is able to put up bail has the financial strength to make an appeal effective reality. Moreover:

> A poor and friendless person cannot get bail at all, while a well financed but infinitely more dangerous professional criminal has ample resources and means to buy his release. Moreover, in most instances a court attempts to arrange its calendar so that the cases of those detained in jail will be tried first. This practice, which court parlance calls "emptying the jail," means that those at large on bail are not called for trial until last. Since all delay is an advantage to the defendant, the state thus penalizes those who are so unfortunate as to be unable to get bail, and gives undeserved advantage to the adequately financed professional criminal.[150]

The Plight of the Middle-Income Defendant

It should not be supposed that the heel of discrimination is ground only in the eye of the indigent. In a sense the publicity given to the "down and outers" and the "dead beats" has contributed to the creation of a public stereotype that has perhaps done more harm than good to the cause of just administration of the criminal code. Very often the heaviest sufferers are the middle-income defendants who abhor any dependence upon others and who scrape the barrel and exhaust credit in the hope of meeting the extraordinary burdens that result from their entanglement in litigation, however undeserved. In this connection we recall the change in public understanding of the problem of medical care since the time it was understood, not in terms of charity for the indigent, but of reasonable prices for the nation as a whole and especially for the middle-income classes. A similar revelation and reevaluation has not yet occurred in the area of legal policy.[151] No doubt the difference lies in the suspicion of guilt that contaminates everything connected with the sanctioning process, no matter how innocent. Physical disease has succeeded in breaking with the historic tie of retribution. Mental illness, too, is coming out from under the ancient stigma. The "criminal," however, lags behind the "mentally ill" as a scapegoat of ancient images.

The situation that now obtains in the field of sanction law (including administration) is such that men of humane sentiment are driven to flashing phrases of indignation. With American forthrightness Professor Fred Rodell summed up the situation more than twenty years ago as follows:

> . . . The law's famous tautological boast about "equal justice for all" . . . is a lie. The law not only can be bought—although usually not in so direct a fashion as it was bought from ex-Judge Manton—but most of the time it *has* to be bought. And since it has to be bought, its results tend to favor those who can afford to buy it.[152]

TRENDS

When we step back from the present scene—which admittedly can be depicted in but fragmentary fashion—we encounter the usual dearth of definitive research on many points. Nonetheless, enough has been done by scholars in the relevant fields of institutional history to enable us to draw some conclusions with confidence.

The Progressive Liquidation of Legalized Discrimination

When all reservations have been made for countertendencies, the fact remains that for several generations the civilization centered in Western Europe has not only extended across the globe but has undergone an internal reconstruction of far-reaching importance. The direction of reconstruction has been signaled by the rise of democratic ideology and by the remodeling of social institutions in harmony with ideals of human dignity. Changes of these kinds are exhibited with great clarity in sanction law where, for example, all manner of discriminations have been abolished or attenuated. As late as the eighteenth century the social status of the accused under common law still afforded formal grounds for determining the form and substance of the proceeding. Nobles and commoners were judged by different standards. Caste and class could determine the character of the crime and the punishment. "Petty treason," for example, could be committed only by an inferior who murdered a superior, not vice versa. It was a far more serious offense for a wife to do away with her husband than for a husband to dispose of his wife, or for a servant to kill his master than for the master to end his servant's life. The dominant social pattern, exemplified by England's Statute of Labourers, was "that the unmoneyed and unlanded classes . . . [should] be compelled to work, and that they . . . [should] not have any voice whatever in determining their own remuneration." [153] The law which with majestic impartiality forbade rich and poor alike to sleep in doorways prescribed the same punishment for a minor theft, impelled by economic need, as for a premeditated murder: "In all, the penalty [was] hanging; in larcenies and petty thefts as well as in . . . murder." [154] The progress in this field is too well known for documentation.

The Modification of Arbitrary Judicial Processes

Not too many centuries ago the administration of justice was not held to be inconsistent with arbitrary and irrational judicial processes. "Down to the end of the sixteenth century, the accused could not call witnesses . . . [and] was not permitted the aid of counsel." [155] Today the right to call witnesses is unquestioned and the right to be assisted by counsel "at every step of the proceedings" is secured for numerous cases, at least on the doctrinal level.[156]

It is not entirely inaccurate to say that the quest for an "equal justice under law" has succeeded on the doctrinal level in reducing the last citadels of privilege. One of the most spectacular departures from tradition has been to abolish the immunity of heads of state under international criminal law. The contemporary law of nations, which is part of our law of the land, affirms that

> the principle of international law which, under certain circumstances, protects the representatives of a State, cannot be applied to acts which are condemned as criminal by international law. The authors of these acts cannot shelter themselves behind their official position in order to be freed from punishment in appropriate proceedings.[157]

In some areas, at least, doctrinal advances have been translated into effective outcomes that are in full accord with the newer ideals. For instance, cruel and degrading penalties significantly declined in favor of a more humane approach to the offender. Punishment "by boiling to death" [158] has gone out of fashion. Significantly, however, corporal punishment may still be inflicted for crime in at least one of our jurisdictions by court order,[159] although the death penalty itself has become relatively rare. This is a remarkable advance indeed when we recall the fact that in early nineteenth-century England most felonies were still viewed as capital—"at the end of the eighteenth century the death penalty was imposed both for the most serious crimes and for a great many trifling offenses, particularly against property." [160]

When we deal with refractory zones of social change—such as Negro-white relations—the modern trend toward nondiscrimination has made unmistakable headway in connection with the sanctioning process.[161] That the task of democratic reconstruction is not at an end is so obvious that it is easy to overlook the major drift of events.

In some important matters the trend is retrogressive. Above all we must single out the complex loyalty-security arrangement, for here is the battleground on which the cause of freedom in the modern state can bleed to death.

The map that we have traced of the effect of sanctioning measures upon the state of respect-sharing in America is far from complete. It is enough to show that in historic prospective extraordinary advances have taken place throughout modern times. Yet when we give the prevailing state of affairs a hard and honest look we cannot escape the impression that great discrepancies have been permitted to survive, or even to revive, between aspiration and fact. We shall defer drawing certain inferences from this survey of respect relations until we have given some attention to the other value-institution processes of American life.

3. SANCTIONING MEASURES AND THE SHARING OF ENLIGHTENMENT

THE SANCTIONING measures of society reflect the current state of enlightenment in society, and in turn influence the nature and distribution of information with a bearing on public policy. It is commonplace to recognize that the overriding objectives of any system of public order are unlikely to be realized if the influential members of the body politic are in the dark about how these goals can be reached, and about the present state of affairs. Policy objectives are continually re-specified as information becomes available about the past and as projections are made of the course of future developments. As we shall see, our survey of the impact of sanctioning measures leads to at least one firm conclusion: the existing system contributes greatly and continuously to the confusion of the nation about the goals or the consequences of sanctioning activity. We shall find that the eye of the public is blinded by the language historically used in formulating the prescriptions of sanction law. When we look carefully at current outcomes we discover many facts to corroborate the view that our established ways of doing things confuse the community. From a glance at historic trends we shall find the situation much like that which we described in the study of respect relations, save that advances to date in the direction of the overriding goals of a free society are less impressive.

PRESCRIPTIONS

If the community is to share an enlightened perspective on matters of sanction policy it is imperative for the overriding goals to be generally understood. When a sanctioning device is chosen, what values are supposed to be maximized? We have already said that sanction law is amenable to rational development if its function in safeguarding and fulfilling the values and the fundamental institutions of the prevailing system of public order are made clear. When we turn to the current prescriptions having to do with sanctions, do we find language that clarifies the goals to be sought by sanctioning activities? Is the language of statute, regulation, and traditional doctrine so lucid and comprehensive that it provides a valuable guide to police, judges, juries, correctional officials, offenders, and the community at large?

The answer is "no." We search in vain for a body of authoritative language in constitutions or statutes that bridges the gap between broad declarations of purpose and the hundreds—indeed thousands—of detailed provisions of the penal code. The absence of language of "intermediate generality" means that sanctioning arrangements are not explicitly integrated with the fundamental goal values of the body politic.

Are we arguing that behavior is moulded by the words that occur in official prescriptions? It is not necessary for us to go so far. The point is much more modest. We need assume only that official language *may* have some influence on judges and other participants in the decision process. The possibility of utilizing this influence, however slight, on behalf of the implementation of basic community policy is thrown away at present.

Actually, there is abundant evidence that prescriptions count.

They are part of the environment to which members of the court, for instance, are exposed in the consideration of a controversy. And they are imprinted in varying degree upon the predispositions with which the current controversy is approached.

There is evidence that general, not merely specific, propositions influence conduct. This is true even where we recognize, as we must, that consensus may change about the concrete meanings to be regarded as consistent with general propositions. During a given period of time—discovered by appropriate methods of investigation—general propositions do in fact constrict the frame of mind in which concrete situations are considered. The key terms in which highly abstract statements are formulated act as screens that filter information to judge and jury, and to all concerned. In varying degree cardinal terms and propositions are variously construed by men and women of diverging background and present purpose. However, the interlacing strands of belief, faith, and loyalty that cluster around the key symbols of the body politic provide the invisible bonds without which the polity, and especially a democratic polity, falls apart. Besides acting as a recurring impetus toward unity, the central symbols and propositions are means of channelling community policy in common directions. The sanction law field is one of the areas in which the advantages of unity and guidance have thus far been largely forfeited.

Absence of an Enlightening Penal Code

If we look only at the prescriptions of punishment the impression is chaotic. It is small wonder that they contribute no enlightening framework to the members of the body politic. The comment of a well-known expert is no less true now than when it was made more than a quarter of a century ago. "Specific forms of punishment . . . [are] . . . extremely diverse. They exhibit a jumble of purposes: vengeance, deterrence, expiation and finally reformation." [1]

Erratic Nature of Present Sanctions

An examination of the terms of art and the propositions employed in statutory codes and in the language of the courts reveals a rather startling situation. The presence or absence of procedural safeguards depends very largely upon whether the word "civil" or "criminal" is used to designate the *character* of the situation in which individual rights are to be determined. As a general principle we are well aware of the supposed ground upon which the distinction rests. "Criminal" actions are regarded as of exceptional gravity for the value position of the individuals concerned. That is to say, the targets of "criminal" prosecution are assumed to be liable to deprivations of such severity that community policy justifies the taking of precautions to make sure that deprivations are not suffered as a result of error or malice. The historic image has been that of the little man confronted by the organized might of society. In a legal system that aspires to maintain and protect the dignity of man it is held to be especially urgent to hold the official juggernaut in check. "Civil" matters, on the other hand, are relatively free of these precautionary arrangements. Apparently the assumption is that the targets of civil action are less vulnerable to deprivation as a consequence of the proceedings. Perhaps, too, there is some shadow of assumption that parties become involved in civil actions on a more "voluntary" basis. Presumably private parties, for instance, or even officials and private individuals, have bargained back and forth before committing themselves to the judgment of a judicial tribunal.

It is impossible to read the text of statutes or opinions and keep much confidence in the clarifying function of the terms "civil" or "criminal." The conclusion is inescapable that the terms spread intellectual confusion throughout the courts, the administrative system, the legislatures, and the community at large. As presently employed the distinction appears to be one of the silent enemies of enlightenment about the working of the sanctioning process.

Are the sanctions specified for "civil" liabilities uniformly less severe than the official deprivations visited upon a "criminal" offender? Some of the more extreme contradictions are obvious, shocking, and even ridiculous. On a "criminal" charge the protections of "due process" come into play, including the well-known requirements of specific and timely notice of the accusation and full opportunity to present a defense [2] before a tribunal "as . . . impartial . . . as the lot of humanity will admit." [3] If the defendant is charged, *e.g.*, with petty larceny, for which as likely as not he is liable to no more than a few months imprisonment or judicial probation, all these precautions are in force. The same man when confronted by the possibility of commitment to a mental institution may be speeded on his way without benefit of a hearing that comes up to the requirements of due process in criminal cases; or for that matter there may be no hearing. Instead of a definite sentence he may be sent away for indefinite periods of custodial care and branded with what is still generally regarded as the stigma of "insanity." All this may happen with few significant safeguards against prolonged custody without in fact receiving therapy. Or he may be subjected to unnecessarily radical or medically contraindicated treatment. All this comes about upon the assumption that "civil" deprivations are less serious than "criminal" ones. To continue with the same case: legislatures have been blind and hence indifferent to prescribing more "due process" protection in "civil" proceedings where grave psychiatric interventions are at stake. The "voice of caution" would advise a "prior restraint" against the transformation of a man at the discretion of a psychiatrist into a human vegetable, whether the job is done by prefrontal lobotomy, by the repeated administration of electric shock, by the more recently fashionable impact of tranquilizing chemicals, or by continued confinement without treatment. If we permit ourselves a glance at the outcome of present prescriptions it appears that the "voice of caution" is made mute by the familiar sound of the symbol "civil."[4] Unmistakably the two labels "criminal" and "civil" are blinding the minds of all concerned to the consideration of the severity of the deprivations at stake and barring the path to a proper clarification of sanction policy. Fossilized terms of art, long since divorced from the frame of whatever theoretical structure they once expressed, are distorting modern society in its approach to sanction law.

Perhaps another striking case will emphasize the point. Two terms of art closely connected with sanctions are "punitive" and "nonpunitive." If this distinction means anything it presumably has some relationship to the severity of the deprivations to which an individual is exposed. At least this would appear to be the justification for hedging "punitive" measures by the pervasive requirements of "criminal" due process. Charge a man with vagrancy and a penalty is imposed only when proof is "beyond all reasonable doubt." If, on the other hand, imprisonment is imposed, let us say, as "part of the means necessary to give effect to the provisions for the exclusion or expulsion of aliens . . ." [5] full due process disappears. Thus, if you charge a man with being an undesirable alien, he may be deported by a proceeding that moves in accord with a far looser standard. This is presumably allowed because deportation is not "punitive," though it must be conceded that it "is a penalty and at times a most serious one" and that "it visits a great hardship on the individual. . . ." [6] Nonetheless, it is not "technically a criminal proceeding." [7]

The Erratic Nature of Sanctions Imposed by Different Sources

Our analysis of official language clearly suggests that traditional terms of art relating to the *source* of a sanction confound the confusion created by terms that refer to the *character* of a situation.

Contrast, for instance, the status of deprivations of comparative severity when they are the work of a "court" and of a "legislature." [8] The imposition of a fine by the judiciary is deemed to require a ponderous machinery of procedural protection. If a legislative body imposes obloquy and economic ruin through "exposure" by an investigating committee nothing is done about it, as yet at least.[9] It must not be supposed that our legal system is so bed-ridden with formality that whatever is labeled a legislative body is thereby given *carte blanche* to perform any decision making or applying function that its members feel moved to undertake. A number of distinctions lurk in the doctrine of separated powers that provide pegs for recognizing the difference between a function that is chiefly prescriptive, and such a function as invoking or applying generalized standards to concrete circumstances. The applying function of the Congress has been restricted by such bounds as have been set by the judicial interpretation of the constitutional prohibition against "bills of attainder" and "bills of pains and penalties." Thus a rider attached to a Congressional appropriations act barring the payment to designated persons of any salary or compensation "out of any monies then or thereafter appropriated" has been held to be an invalid exercise of legislative power, since "punishment" is inflicted by "permanent proscription" of the parties from any opportunity to serve the government.[10] Legislative action "[stigmatizing] . . . reputation and seriously . . . [impairing respondents'] chance to earn a living," declared the Supreme Court, was punishment, which Congress was without constitutional power to impose.[11] While "the Supreme Court . . . did not [in that case] stop with holding that *Congress* could not dismiss employees for disloyalty," [12] "executive," as distinct from "legislative" dismissals of government employees for disloyalty, despite minimal procedural protections, have been sustained by the lower federal courts and an equally divided Supreme Court.[13]

Another pair of traditional terms that confuse the incidence and severity of sanctioning activity is "official" and "private." The Fourteenth Amendment, for example, is repeatedly reaffirmed as erecting "no shield against merely private conduct, however discriminatory or wrongful." [14] Where official action, exemplified by legislative enactment, will be struck down as violative of fundamental law, private action, essentially productive of the same result, is frequently said to be beyond the scope of judicial correction. Arbitrary deprivation *by the state* "of a right which is basic to the perpetuation of the race—the right to have offspring" [15] is readily struck down by the courts.[16] The same deprivation, effected by leasehold agreement, providing for the exclusion of dogs, cats, and children in the midst of a housing shortage, may be accepted as just and proper.[17] The invalidation of racial restrictive covenants between private parties was long delayed in the name of the immunity of *private* action. It is worth noticing that the Supreme Court, when it finally did invalidate such practices, based itself on the "discovery" of "official" discriminatory action. "We hold," declared Mr. Chief Justice Vinson for the Court, "that in granting judicial enforcement of the restrictive agreements in these cases, the *States* have denied petitioners the equal protection of the law and that, *therefore,* the action of the state courts cannot stand." [18]

The absence of "any consistently adhered-to objective and operationally formulated set of criteria for distinguishing between 'criminal' and 'civil' sanctions, or between 'sanctions' and 'non-sanctions' . . . [unavoidably] . . . leaves an avenue for evasion of the safeguards of the accused prescribed in any constitution and any code of criminal procedure." [19] The perpetuation of distinctions that have lost their point is a curtain against the prompt discovery by all concerned of the nature of existing deprivations. Thus it is that words may eat up men.

The Confusing Consequences of Denying "Judge-made Law"

The existing confusion is compounded by the persistent denial by the judges that there is such a thing as "judge-made" law. The matter has been lucidly put in these words:

> The doctrine of no judge-made law is not, generally speaking, a "lie"—for a lie is an affirmation of a fact contrary to the truth, made with knowledge of its falsity and with the intention of deceiving others. Nor is it a "fiction"—a false affirmation made with knowledge of its falsity but with no intention of deceiving others.
>
> It is rather a myth—a false affirmation made without complete knowledge of its falsity. We are confronting a kind of deception which involves self-deception. . . . When judges and lawyers announce that judges can never validly make law, they are not engaged in fooling the public; they have successfully fooled themselves.
>
> With their thinking processes hampered by this myth, the judges have been forced to contrive circumlocutions in order to conceal from themselves and the laity the fact that the judiciary frequently changes the old legal rules. Those evasive phrases are then dealt with as if they were honest phrases, with consequent confusion and a befuddlement of thought. Legal fictions are mistaken for objective legal truths and clear legal thinking becomes an unnecessarily arduous task.[20]

To sum up: we have been saying that the enlightenment value is sacrificed by the failure of the authoritative language of the law to clarify the connection between sanctions and the goal values of the body politic. Emphasis has been put upon the failure to build a bridge between propositions that articulate the basic objectives of the prevailing system of public order and the devices used in coping with offenders; and upon the failure to modify technical vocabularies by eliminating distinctions that propagate spurious assumptions about the sanctioning process.

When goals are left in a state of obscurity or confusion it can be predicted that consequences will be reported in a confusing and obscurantist fashion. Before we can confirm this expectation it will be necessary to look more concretely at the working of the present system.

APPLICATIONS

What expectations and demands now prevail among us about the relationship between community values and current sanctioning methods? To what extent can the state of clarity or confusion be attributed to the authoritative language of the law?

Very little can be said about American conceptions of goals, and especially about sanctions, on the basis of existing research. Everyone concedes that in a broad sense Americans favor a free rather than a caste-bound system. The specifics employed in the interpretation are closely related to the institutional practices to which present-day Americans are accustomed. With the aid of historical scholarship we can trace the rise and fall of some key symbols and of specific interpretations. But the instruments appropriate to the task of creating an exhaustive picture of past and contemporary perspectives have not been applied.

The indications are that "criminologists" are strongly disposed to see in the instruments of sanction law a repertory of "correctional" rather than "punitive" measures. "Deterrence," "reparation," and "reformation" are among the criteria that give definiteness to a "correctional" approach. When, however, we inquire into the outlook that characterizes other elements of the population, the "punitive" or "expiatory" criteria gain weight. It is well known to scholars that the latter was the dominant demand throughout Western civilization, at least, until rather recently. From our general knowledge of social dynamics it is not surprising to learn that older attitudes persist on a vast scale.

If we ask whether the language of the law has moulded the American outlook on sanctioning issues, the short answer is that we cannot answer the question conclusively. Students of social history have been busy in recent decades attempting to overcome exaggerated ideas about what can be accomplished by "passing a law." They are therefore inclined to tell us quite categorically that code books do not make "men" (that is, make society). Rather, the lesser is made by the larger. Code books reflect the whole context; they do not design it.

At the same time it is recognized that the chain of influence does not run exclusively in one direction. Verbal formulae do not exist in helpless isolation; they are part of a functioning context of belief, faith, and loyalty. Such subcontexts—which combine perspectives and operational activities—are the true factors that mould society. They interact with other functioning contexts of the same kind. When we recast the problem in this way we have a promising topic of study. At the time when a statute was passed, for example, what social elements were actively aligned for and against it? To what extent did these factors operate as predispositions capable of influencing conduct toward conformity or nonconformity? At any given cross section in the history of a legal system or of a particular formal prescription what was the strength of predispositional factors?

It has been necessary to refer, however briefly, to these rather fundamental considerations in order to clarify our position. We concur in the view that the gap between authoritative statements of goal and of sanctioning arrangements did originally reflect the social context in which official language was enunciated. Furthermore, the failure to bridge the gap has been and is sustained by important factors. We go far enough to suggest that research may eventually show that the omission is to be explained, not on the ground that people were confused, but that they were united and took punishment for granted. Fortunately, perhaps the omission of sanction formulations that would have been used at an earlier day has made it easier than it would otherwise have been for the enlightened few to influence the actual administration of justice in recent years. This is, of course, hypothetical: and there are counterindications too important to be left out of a complete account of the matter. The omission may have been a deliberate act of legislators in the hope of making it easier for older ideas of a punitive character to be circumvented. But it is not self-evident, by any means, that failure to connect our concern for individuality with sanctioning policies of a correctional type has left us better off. Indeed, we put forward the hypothesis that for want of an explicit bridge our sanctioning practices are inadequately recognized though in frequent and removable contradiction to our fundamental aims.

Official Reports Do Not Relate Operations to Social Goals

It is possible to state one highly probable and relatively narrow hypothesis, at least, concerning the influence of confusion in authoritative language upon the state of enlightenment: *the reports made by prosecutors, courts, and other sanctioning officials tend to perpetuate confusion, since they fall readily into the framework provided by statutes and regulations.* Since these prescriptions do not clearly state the results to be achieved by sanctioning measures, the most enlightening information is usually omitted from public systems of reporting.

The usual report issued by a public prosecutor tells us about "arrests" and "convictions." What of it? True, these details do tell us something about the busy work of the police, the prosecutor's office, and the courts. But what are the destructive social outcomes that are, presumably, abated or promoted by these activities? It is quite probable that in a given body politic comparative investigations are capable of making it possible to describe the amount of "speeding," or the amount of money diverted to the pockets of "trustees." To say the least, however, it is rare to have the objectives of policy couched in such explicit terms, and the result of sanctioning activities reported in a critical spirit.

The most obvious source of confusion comes from the practice of using terms of legal art as though they had explicit factual meaning. When we were comparing "civil" with "criminal" categories in existing codes it will be recalled that it was possible to impugn the dependability of the distinction as a measure of severity of damage done to all concerned, or of the severity of the deprivations to which the offender is exposed. Yet the reporting practices at every level fall into the trap—and a very understandable fall it is—of reporting "anticriminal" sanctions as though they gave the community more protection, case by case, than "civil" judgments.

Given our current modes of reporting, the public's attention is rarely focused upon situations in which "the law" has become obsolete (or obsolescent), or where new circumstances have arisen for which remedies are not at hand. Obsolete and obsolescent prescriptions in the statute books provide opportunities for mischief on partisan grounds or as a result of vindictiveness and ignorance. A sampling of obsolete or obsolescent provisions in the Penal Law of New York includes prohibitions directed against dueling,[21] hazing,[22] oyster planting by a non-resident,[23] and Sabbath breaking.[24] The federal criminal code still inveighs against misprision of felony,[25] piracy and privateering,[26] and private correspondence with foreign governments.[27] A cloud of instances can be found in every jurisdiction.

The complex division of labor in modern industrial society affords many new opportunities for destructive human relations. Nevertheless, current intelligence and appraisal operations do not characteristically guide public attention to novel forms of social damage, and display the limitations of traditional codes. We refer, for instance, to the field of "white collar crime." [28] For "though a man can get himself hanged for a momentary lapse of self-control under intolerable provocation by a nagging woman, or into prison for putting the precepts of Christ above the orders of a Competent Military Authority, he can be a quite infernal scoundrel without breaking any penal law." [29]

It is when one looks into the detailed operation of the sanctioning process that the scholar becomes most acutely aware of the degree in which the enlightenment value is jeopardized. Despite the fragmentary character of existing research many straws show which way the winds are blowing. We have challenged some of the traditional terms of art in this field by confronting formal prescriptions with one another, and suggesting that ancient distinctions are without a consistent and relevant difference. This type of criticism becomes more extensive and detailed when we concentrate upon the interpretation given to the terms in which offenses are classified by decision makers engaged in the application function.

Addressing the New York Academy of Medicine on "What Medicine Can Do For Law," Judge Cardozo analyzed the New York statutory distinctions between murder in the first and second degree, the first degree dependent upon a showing of "premeditation" and "deliberation," the second degree upon that of a "design":

The present distinction is so obscure that no jury hearing it for the first time can fairly be expected to assimilate it or understand it. I am not sure that I understand it myself after trying to apply it for many years and after diligent study of what has been written in the books. Upon the basis of this fine distinction with its obscure and mystifying psychology, scores of men have gone to their death.[30]

"The bite of the law," observed Mr. Justice Frankfurter, "is in its enforcement. This is especially true when careful or indifferent judicial administration has consequences so profound as does the application of legislation dividing murder into first and second degrees—consequences that literally make the difference between life and death." [31]

Failure of Disclosure of Evidence before Trial

For many years scholars who have compared our legal institutions with practices prevailing elsewhere have been shocked by the nondisclosure of evidence before trial. They have urgently recommended the principle of *pretrial discovery*. But the granting to each adversary of the right to require his opponent to disclose before trial the evidence which he expects to offer [32] has been painfully slow. "It is . . . [the] feature of games and sports that has influenced powerfully the policy of the common law in the present aspect. '*Nemo tenetur armare adversarium suum contra se.*' To require the disclosure to an adversary of the evidence that is to be produced would be repugnant to all sportsmanlike instincts. Rather permit you to preserve the secret of your tactics, to lock up your documents in the vault, to send your witness to board in some obscure village, and then, reserving your evidential resources until the final moment, to marshal them at the trial before your surprised and dismayed antagonist, and thus overwhelm him. Such was the spirit of the common law, and such in part it still is." [33]

While "discovery" of adversary parties and third persons and the inspection of documents *before trial* has been widely secured in "civil cases," [34] no comparable latitude has been afforded in "criminal" proceedings.[35] Whenever possible, the prosecutor jealously keeps his evidence from the criminal defendant until trial. The surviving "feature of games and sports" in this field is clearly inimical to an enlightened pursuit of the facts and imposes a particular handicap upon the indigent accused. Our practice contrasts sharply with the Civil Law countries. It is shocking for American lawyers to discover that in nonpolitical cases the criminal defendant enjoys incomparably wider facilities for pretrial discovery in Moscow than his counterpart in New York.[36] Our system tends to establish a monopoly of critical information in the hands of the prosecution in advance of trial.

Failure of Disclosure of Evidence at Any Stage

In recent times perhaps the most conspicuous failures of our system, when evaluated in terms of enlightenment, are to be found in the federal loyalty-security program. Judgment as to the existence of a loyalty or security risk may, under the program, be founded on "evidence" which is not open to scrutiny, not only by the accused but by the administrative judges who "try" him. Inquiry into the reliability of the alleged evidence may be foreclosed by the rule that allows the disclosure of information only to the extent to which "security considerations permit."[37] If the content of a report that is relied upon as evidence in the case is made available to the administrative tribunal it may not be made available to the accused. The source of the information (at least insofar as it involves the identity of a "confidential informant") may be screened from both.[38] In this context, the decision makers in a loyalty-security proceeding may have "no independent means of knowing whether . . . [the] source is a paragon of veracity, a knave, or the village idiot."[39] One of the nation's eminent scientists, for example, was the victim of just these quirks when he was removed from government service. Significantly he received vindication from the Supreme Court on narrow and scholastically technical procedural grounds, and not on grounds of due process. In the words of Mr. Justice Douglas, concurring, the evidence in his administrative loyalty security "hearing" was supplied:

> by faceless informers, some of whom were not known even to the Board that condemned him. Some of these informers were not even under oath. None of them had to submit to cross-examination. None had to face Dr. Peters. So far as . . . [the Supreme Court] or the Board . . . [knew] they . . . [may have been] psychopaths or venal people. . . . They may [have borne] old grudges. Under cross-exami-

nation their stories might . . . [have disappeared] like bubbles. Their whispered confidences might . . . [have turned] out to be yarns conceived by twisted minds or by people who, though sincere . . . [had] poor faculties of observation and memory.[40]

Indeed, our tradition has been that "the plea that evidence of guilt must be secret is abhorrent . . . because it provides a cloak for the malevolent, the misinformed, the meddlesome, and the corrupt to play the role of informer undetected and uncorrected.[41]

The procedure adopted by the federal loyalty-security program finds no parallel even in the annals of the Holy Inquisition, for the latter, although marked by "the crowning infamy in its treatment of testimony," namely, the "withholding from the accused [of] all knowledge of the names of the witnesses against him," [42] at least insisted that the reliability of all witnesses should be personally and carefully tested by its judges.[43] It does not even compare favorably with the secular inquisitorial criminal procedure of the French *ancien régime,* inherited from medieval times and redefined as late as 1670 under the *Ordonnance Criminelle.*[44] There a secret preliminary examination was made by the *lieutenant criminel.* A dossier embodying the result was handed to the judges and constituted all the evidence which they received outside of the *viva voce* examination of the accused which they might choose to undertake in person.[45] The end product was cloaked in obscurity. Its inherent antagonism to enlightenment, in a manner analogous to that of the loyalty-security program, has been poignantly described by a distinguished contemporary student of comparative legal procedure:

The results of the preliminary investigation were never carefully evaluated. There was no life in the trial procedure. The judges saw no witnesses. They heard no evidence. They examined only the written depositions resulting from the prior stages, and these documents provided only an imperfect idea of what the witnesses had testified or what had been done. The judges, therefore, received evidence at second hand and in a distilled form at that. Since they could not go back of the documents, they had no means of evaluating the evidence even had the rules of proof allowed it. . . . They added and subtracted evidence instead of weighing it.[46]

Yet even under this discredited system of a dead past, the accused would occasionally obtain a measure of disclosure in excess of that available in the contemporary loyalty-security proceedings of the federal government. The suspect was, more frequently than not, confronted by adverse witnesses during the preliminary examination.[47]

As a rule the criticisms which have been leveled against the loyalty-security proceedings of the Government have complained of their unfairness to the accused employee. In the present perspective it is evident that another and no less damaging stricture can be made upon them. These proceedings violate the requirements of enlightened judgment. They do not enable the decision makers who act in the name of the government to act as rationally as necessary to serve the national interest in obtaining the services of able and devoted Americans in positions of responsibility. We know that rational judgments depend upon more than good intentions. The most conscientious judge cannot act in an enlightened fashion unless he has all relevant factual information brought to his focus of attention, where it is subject to competent and full assessment. The procedures of the loyalty-security code, so often stigmatized as unfair, can therefore with equal justice be identified as irrational.

We have been summarizing two of the principal barriers to enlightened judgment in our sanctioning system: the ambiguity of the language of legal prescription when it comes to the attention of the decision maker; the omission of disclosure, and especially pretrial disclosure, of the facts to be evaluated. Even without ambiguity the hazards of judgment in the sanctioning field are high. One aim of the *rules of evidence* is to cut down risks by prescribing an orderly and relevant sequence of attention for the decision maker. For instance, enlightenment is to be fostered by excluding statements and exhibits that are irrelevant to the task of interpreting legal prescriptions in the concrete context of a case. Procedural rules influence the process by prescribing some of the traits required of a decision making individual or tribunal. Rules relating to jurisdiction have a bearing upon the "impartiality" of the forum and many other matters. The rules of jury selection cannot fail, if applied, to influence the pattern of predisposition to be found among decision makers. Taken together the requirements constituting codes of evidence and procedure are likely to influence the enlightenment of the result by affecting the two sets of factors that determine the responses that appear in any human situation: namely, predisposition and environment.

In the United States the outcome is believed to be profoundly conditioned by the great reliance that we place upon two famous institutions: the adversarial system and the jury. We do not believe that a satisfactory conclusion can be drawn at present about either one insofar as they affect the degree of enlightenment displayed by decision makers engaged in sanctioning activities. This scepticism has several grounds. In the light of modern social science we doubt that "blanket" judgments are likely to be correct in the assessment of complex institutions. *The principle of equivalency* suggests what we have in mind. According to this principle—which is differently phrased in several fields of science—the relationship between any two details of a configuration is a function of their relationship to the whole. Applied to "democratic government," for example, it suggests that neither presidential nor cabinet government has "inherent" results; or, to put it another way, it is possible to obtain the same results from each if the contexts are suitable. Another ground of scepticism is simpler: there is an excess of opinion and a minimum of solid research on the jury or the adversarial system.

Limitation of the Adversarial System

We do not doubt, however, that the objections that are often leveled at either institution are sometimes true. Hence we shall refer briefly to some of the many affirmations which, if redefined as hypotheses for investigation, are worthy of serious and extended attention. It has been remarked that " 'Inquisition' is after all practically the same word as 'research' and . . . the only alternative to research in attempting to discover facts . . . is casting dice." In this light, "an investigation into substantial truth involves, in a certain measure, the inquisitorial method," *i.e.*, objective research.[48] "Our mode of trials," in contrast, "is . . . 'contentious' or 'adversary.' It is based on . . . the 'fight' theory, a theory which derives from the origin of trials as substitutes for private out-of-court brawls." [49] In this context "the lawyer aims at winning in the fight, not at aiding the court to discover the facts. He does not want the trial court to reach a sound, educated guess, if it is likely to be contrary to his client's interests." [50]

The adversarial system, it has been repeatedly observed, engenders a "partisanship of the opposing lawyers [and] blocks the uncovering of vital evidence or leads to a presentation of vital testimony in a way that distorts it. . . ." [51] In such a context "an experienced lawyer uses all sorts of strategems to minimize the effect on the judge or jury of testimony disadvantageous to his client, even when the lawyer has no doubt of the accuracy and honesty of that testimony. If . . . a witness happens to be timid, frightened by the unfamiliarity of courtroom ways, the lawyer, in his cross-examination, plays on that weakness, in order to confuse the witness and make it appear that he is concealing significant facts." [52] An observation like this is not unusual among "insiders":

You want to remember that the *facts* in a criminal case do not count. The question is not whether the defendant *committed* the crime. The only point is whether under present rules the people have produced evidence to prove to the satisfaction of the jury . . . that the defendant *did* commit the crime.[53]

In this context confusion appears to be compounded by excluding much that is relevant and including much irrelevancy. Rigid application of the hearsay rule provides a case in point.

But 90% of the evidence on which men act out of court, most of the data on which business and industry daily rely, consist of the equivalent of hearsay. Yet, because of distrust of juries—a belief that jurors lack the competence to make allowance for the second-hand character of hearsay—such evidence, although accepted by administrative agencies, juvenile court and legislative committees is (subject, to be sure, to numerous exceptions) barred in jury trials. As a consequence, frequently the jury cannot learn of matters which would lead an intelligent person to a more correct knowledge of the facts.[54]

The opinion rule, in its orthodox form, continues to accept expert testimony solely when it is initially demonstrated that nothing short of absolute necessity requires the admission of such evidence if the jury is to perform its function of fact finding.[55]

Erratic Admission of Expert Testimony

The trend of decision is toward greater liberality in admitting expert testimony; the "true criterion" for the establishment of such admissibility in an increasing number of cases is—"[*o*]*n this subject* can . . . [the fact finders] from *this* person receive appreciable help?" [56] Nevertheless, the requirement of demonstrated absolute necessity is perpetuated under "the 'orthodox' view of the many courts who depend only on the encylopedias which repeat the formulas of the older cases." [57]

It is standard practice to permit the use of reputation testimony when it bears upon the improbability of the commission of a given crime by a given defendant. Such testimony is a haphazard collection of community opinion. With the exception of one pioneering jurisdiction,[58] the courts have yet to receive the significantly more valid psychiatric opinion to the same effect, *i.e.*, that "the (defendant's) personality structure (is not) consistent with the commission of the offense alleged." [59]

It is not to be overlooked that incompetent individuals are often readily permitted by the rules to cloak themselves within the courtroom with the authority of experts. Claims of expertise are subject to no consistent test of reliability or proof of formal skill or experience.[60]

We are all acquainted with the apparent distrust of the partisan expert who appears in adversary proceedings. Yet it is notable that although expert qualifications can be determined within the broad bounds of judicial discretion it is not customary to subject claims of skill to systematic and searching appraisal. The case of medical and particularly psychiatric expert witnesses is squarely in point. It has been held that an "expert" opinion "in the domain of medicine" is admissible even though the "expert" witness "has not a license to practice medicine" if the court is otherwise satisfied of his competence.[61] An "expert" witness who testifies to the mental state of an accused (or kindred matters) need not have specialized in psychiatry.[62]

A survey of the operations of the since defunct lunacy commissions of New York, covering a period of five years from 1926–1930, portrays a situation that obtained until at least the recent past and is to be found elsewhere to this day.

> In the course of five years, 14,982 felonies and 6,808 misdemeanors were tried. It was also found that 792 lunacy commissions and examiners in mental defects were appointed. Of the 792 prisoners examined, psychiatric conditions were noted in 517 cases. The appoint-

ment of these various commissions required the services of physicians on 1050 occasions. The number of men qualified in psychiatry appointed on these commissions totalled 16. . . . [Q]ualified psychiatrists served on 6 per cent of the cases in which this court had to appoint physicians for a psychiatric opinion.

The qualifications of the physicians appointed by the court were determined by reference to the medical directory, wherein a short autobiography of physicians is recorded, the doctor designating his own hospital affiliations and the branch of medicine he practices. As a result of such an investigation it was found that there were appointed physicians specializing in internal medicine 15; surgery 15; gynecology 5; urology 4; pediatrics 6; ear, nose and throat 5; pathology 3; public health 3; obstetrics 1; hematology 1; orthopedics 1; proctology 2; dermatology 2; and neuropsychiatry 16.

Although these men were physicians in good standing and specialists in various branches of medicine, they did not designate themselves as psychiatrists, and were not qualified to give expert opinion, by either training or experience, on the mental status of the prisoners.[63]

Inadequacy of Present Procedure to Nullify the Prejudicial

One of the tests of a procedure conducive to enlightenment is the nullification of the prejudicial. The Anglo-American system takes it for granted that some prejudicial matter will leak into the proceedings despite the existence of special rules of evidence designed to enhance the rationality of the result by excluding items of the kind. As a means of nullifying the prejudicial the judge is expected to instruct the jurors to disregard it. But there is little ground for believing that instructions of the kind are effective. Motions for mistrial, upon such a basis, are resorted to with great reluctance.[64]

Historically several devices have been used to require the decision maker to sort out the component elements of the problem before him, thereby diminishing the likelihood of "global" rather than "differentiated" responses. Our appellate courts are expected to elaborate a simple "yes" or "no" by written opinions. The decision maker must focus more explicitly than would otherwise be the case upon the relationship between the controversy and the relevant context of legal prescription; and he is induced to consider the relative weight of the evidence brought to his attention. The jury is not disciplined by similar requirements; it is sometimes proposed that they should be. The present system does not compel the jury to account for its decision, in whole, by requiring a detailed opinion, or in part, by requiring special verdicts.[65]

In modern times at least our system sets up a number of barriers intended to protect the privacy of jury deliberations. Clearly the assumption has been that intimidating factors would have less influence under these conditions. Has this policy gone too far? Would prejudice be more effectively nullified if the jury's deliberations were open to limited scrutiny? An examination of existing doctrine indicates that the question is by no means irrelevant. The general rule is: "The verdict, as finally agreed upon and pronounced in court by the jurors, must be taken as the sole embodiment of the jury's act. Hence it stands, irrespective of what led to it in the privacy of the jury room." [66] Today it is

> universally agreed that, on a motion to set aside a verdict and grant a new trial, the verdict cannot be affected, either favorably or unfavorably, by the circumstances: that one or more jurors *misunderstood* the judge's *instructions;* or were influenced by an *illegal paper* or by an *improper remark* of a fellow-juror; or *assented* because of *weariness* or illness or importunities; or *assented* under an *erroneous belief* that the judge would use clemency or have the legal right to vary the sentence; or had been *influenced* by *inadmissible evidence;* or had decided upon grounds which rendered *newly-discovered evidence immaterial;* or had *omitted to consider* important evidence or issues; or had *miscalculated accounts* by errors of fact or of law; or had by any other *motive or belief been led* to their decision.[67]

Under this doctrine, verdicts arrived at by lot have been sustained against challenge by holding jurors incompetent to "impeach their verdict" in that regard in some courts, although contrary results have been obtained in a few others.[68] In 1883, a Missouri court excluded testimony, in impeachment of a verdict, that the rendering of the guilty verdict was preceded by the throwing of a hangman's noose into the jury room.[69] In 1944, a federal court held a Negro juror incompetent to impeach a guilty verdict through testimony that he had agreed to it only as a result of intimidation by the other eleven white jurors.[70]

If the traditional adversarial system of the courts has provided little effective nullification of prejudicial material, the loyalty-security program has provided even less. We are in the process of relearning the dangers of prejudicial irrelevance, exemplified in the loyalty-security proceedings by the haphazard inquiry into associations, musical and literary tastes, sexual habits, emotional health and stability, and political opinion.[71]

The Dangers of Public Agitation in the Course of a Trial

Everyone is aware of the danger to the ideal of impartial justice that arises when there is public agitation during the course of a trial. Mr. Justice Frankfurter has tellingly formulated the ideal atmosphere for a process that aims to produce the most enlightened possible result. "Criminal justice is concerned with the pathology of the body politic. In administering the criminal law, judges wield the most awesome surgical instruments of society. A criminal trial . . . should have the atmosphere of the operating room." [72]

In the United States we have become accustomed to the destruction of a responsible setting in which the serious business of sanction application is carried on. In the name of the "freedom of the press" unbridled comment is permitted to appear in the media of mass communication. As a result it is often exceedingly difficult if not impossible to impanel a rather unbiased jury. The difficulty may go far beyond the borders of the district in which venue is laid to include the region or even the country at large. We know that evidence, inadmissible in the trial, may be presented to actual or prospective jurors through news stories. Although jurors are barred from direct or indirect *personal* contact in the course of the trial, they may be affected through the impersonal contact of news media.[73]

"Trial by newspaper" may not be an idle slogan in the *cause célèbre.*

The Hauptmann trial was attended by 141 newspapermen and photographers, 125 telegraphers and 40 messengers. Other homicide trials have been photographed, and more recent ones broadcast, . . . tape-recorded or even telecast. The average newspaper front page devotes ten to twenty per cent of its space, and an even higher ratio of its headlines, to crime and scandal. Although only ten per cent of radio time is devoted to news, crime is highlighted more in newscasts than in newspapers, to say nothing of dramatic radio programs.

Trial by newspaper begins as soon as the crime is reported with publication of details of its commission and lists of suspects. It continues unabated through arrest, preliminary hearing and indictment of some defendant with disclosure of his confessions, witnesses' statements and comments of police and prosecutor. Usually the unsealed verdict of journalism is reached before the courtroom trial opens.[74]

Against these threats to enlightened judgment our legal institutions interpose no significant restraints.[75] The practice of "some countries," as described by an English judge, is readily identifiable with our own. "There are some countries," declared Lord Denning,

> where in any sensational crime, the newspapers conduct their own investigations and make their own comments. From the time of the committing of the crime to the apprehension of the suspected parties, and thereafter in the course of their preliminary examination and trial, the newspapers publish all sorts of statements concerning facts and suspicions with glaring headlines. These statements purport to give evidence much of which would be inadmissible in a court of law. Hearsay at first hand and second hand is freely printed. A commentator has said that in that way "the mental atmosphere of the entire community is poisoned forever and a fair trial, is impossible." The lawyers themselves often take part in the publicity. They hold press conferences and issue press releases. They make statements for no other purpose than to have them picked up by reporters and printed in large type. This is an evil which in those countries the law seems powerless to remedy.[76]

The impact of public agitation appears to be particularly oppressive in the case of the defendant charged with political crime.

Changes of venue are ineffective devices when the atmosphere of the entire country has been "poisoned." Reversals on the basis of an unfavorable trial atmosphere—confined by existing precedent to the rare, bizarre, and distinctly unsubtle [77]—are not likely to be forthcoming as a practical matter particularly where the situation is as favorable as conditions anywhere in the country will permit.[78] The weapon of "criminal contempt" against offending news media does not seem to be invoked in such cases.[79]

The conditions to which we have been alluding are not inherent in the operating methods of a modern industrial nation. England offers a sharp and refreshing contrast:

> In England there is no such abuse. There is no trial by newspaper [t]here. Lawyers do not give press conferences and press releases about their cases. Once a man is arrested, newspapers carefully refrain from

comment or from publishing anything except that which takes place in court. If a newspaper should temporarily lapse from this high standard, the courts step in quickly to administer condign punishment.[80]

The sanction utilized is that of punishment for "contempt of court." The publication of anything except that which takes place in court in a case *sub judice* is thus treated as a "contempt of court" on the assumption that its "tendency and sometimes . . . [its] object is to deprive the Court of the power of doing that which is the end for which it exists—namely, to administer justice duly, impartially, and with reference solely to the facts judicially brought before it." [81]

"It is difficult" indeed in this light "to conceive of an apter description of such conduct than is conveyed by the expression 'contempt of Court.' "[82]

In our discussion of the connection between the respect value and the sanctioning process we emphasized the fact that many of our procedural rules are supposed to prevent discrimination against defendants. At this point we emphasize the stake of public policy in perfecting procedures that increase the probability of an enlightened outcome. Not only the defendant has a stake in obtaining facts: the community has it. If the private advocate of a defendant charged with crime lacks the necessary material or intellectual resources, or if the office of public defender is understaffed or incompetent, the judging processes of the body politic will be hampered by the lack of the information required for an enlightened outcome.

The adversarial system itself is to be assessed as an intelligence agency of the community, not simply as a simple substitute for violence. And as an intelligence agency it can function effectively only if the "non-rational" factors are nullified. In practice this means that the arena of adversarial controversy can be expected to produce optimum results when the parties are equally influential, and when they have at their disposal in the judicial arena talent of equal intensity of devotion and skill, and with access to equal facilities. The stake that a party has in a controversy presumably increases the chances that he will dig up everything favorable to him. If counsel for one party seeks to conceal or distort available data, only an equally intent, competent and equipped counsel for the opposing party is capable of an effective defense. Can we expect more enlightened outcomes if in place of an adversarial system we had a magistrate system in which the representative of the community had sole responsibility? One may well doubt this as a general proposition, however accurate it may be in various contexts. The magistrate and his staff are not likely to have the intensity of involvement in each case that so often characterizes counsel for contending parties.

Evidently what we need to explore are the possibilities of expanding the role of the judge in the American system in order to make of him a more effective counterweight to the parties. Instead of depending so much upon what the parties allege, the judge can often reach a more enlightened result by independent investigation.

At this place in our examination of sanction law we do not pursue these matters further. We are directing attention to the features of our present practice that require more careful appraisal than they have usually had in the past. The time is overdue for a vigorous and comprehensive examination of our sanctioning arrangements insofar as they affect enlightenment when it is possible for responsible participants to make statements like the following: "Judge Learned Hand, after considerable experience as a trial judge, said in 1921: 'I must say that . . . as a litigant I should dread a law-suit beyond almost anything else short of sickness and death.' "[83]

TRENDS

When we look at the contemporary picture in relation to the past, one conclusion stands out: we have been making relatively less progress toward enlightenment than toward respect. The two trends are, of course, interdependent to a degree; and the long-term drive to liquidate discriminatory practices has at the same time done away with barriers to enlightenment. The cases involving many formerly disregarded groups in the community are receiving more thoughtful and competent consideration than before. Similarly, the growth of enlightenment has contributed to the dissolution of old barriers. As more information becomes available about the operations of man in society, and of the place of America in the world community, discriminations based on lack of access to enlightenment are withering or weakening.

Some Clarifications Among Specialists of the Role of Sanctions

There has been some clarification among specialists, at least, of the possible role of sanctions in a body politic whose ideal goals are embodied in the conception of a free society. The steady expansion of professional concern for sanctioning results has brought about a number of innovations. We shall have occasion to refer to these in another connection. There have been advances in the reporting of violations and in summarizing the manner of disposition. The revolutions in technology, so conspicuous in modern times, have revolutionized the methods of the police and of the offender, with the result that communication networks have been developed among law enforcement officers to encompass the arenas in which illegal activities are carried on. The new gadgets for the gathering of information (*e.g.*, wiretaps, recorders, concealed cameras, "truth drugs") have been used by both sides; naturally, they have posed old questions more sharply than ever.

In view of the great increase in the complexity of modern life it is doubtful that we are relatively as well-informed today as we were a few years ago about the efforts of various offenses upon American values and institutions. Some results of murder or robbery are fairly evident; but the consequences of an intricate net of corporate control are not so easy to gauge.

There is, in fact, a wide gap between our attempts to forecast and influence crops or the level of national income and our efforts to forecast and affect the level of deviation from prescribed norms.

Our sanctioning arrangements have continued to contribute to public confusion about the goals of public policy, the degree to which these goals are realized, the factors that significantly condition them, the prospects for the future, and the available strategies of effective social action to maximize the degree to which our values are realized in the future.

4. SANCTIONING MEASURES AND THE SHARING OF SKILL

EVERY COMMUNITY anywhere on the globe and at any time in history depends for its total success upon the cultivation of the appropriate skills. As a rule we think of skill in terms of the operations required to achieve an effect that depends upon cumulative activity; and we regard a skill as a discernible pattern of thinking and doing that can be deliberately sought and transmitted. Although skills are ordinarily evaluated according to the contribution they make to wealth and other "extrinsic" values, it is worth recognizing that human beings characteristically pursue skill as an "end in itself," and are guided by "intrinsic" relationships. In an elaborate techno-scientific civilization we have become aware of the profound importance of the pursuit of intrinsic as well as extrinsic outcomes. Our study of creativity among children or adults has demonstrated the role that is played by demands to complete a given "configuration" that is perceived as imperfect in terms of the interrelationship among component parts. The mathematical, musical, or poetic imagination, for instance, has this "completion" propensity. It leads to more elegant equations and more subtle compositions.[1]

We raise the question of skill effects in order to give them the prominence which they are often denied in the treatment of sanctioning processes. It is, for instance, obvious that we require a complex structure of interrelated professional and occupational skills if we are to accomplish whatever objectives are prescribed for the whole process. The skill structure includes lawyers, police, prison and other correctional officials; and these specialties are distributed in various concentrations through America. Have our sanction activities to date attracted the talent that is essential to the performance of the tasks involved? Do we have a balanced pattern of distributing the talent at hand?

Moreover, when we look outside the skills immediately implicated in law enforcement and try to assess the impact of the total process upon the skill structure of American society, what do we find? Are we successful in our attempts to deplete the amount of ingenuity that is attracted into prohibited activities?

PRESCRIPTIONS

It is possible to make a number of inferences about the prevailing state of affairs when we analyze official prescriptions that relate to sanctioning. What qualifications and what modes of selection are laid down for judges, prosecutors, defense counsel, police and correctional officials? In the context of our discussion of enlightenment we were interested in the use of experts to increase the chances of an enlightened decision. Here we are concerned with a closely related but separable question. Are the qualifications and modes of selection usually prescribed in our codes likely to encourage the talent presently required to fit our sanctioning methods to its task?

In this country it has been taken for granted, for the most part, that judges, prosecutors, and public defenders are not to constitute a specialized field of professional competence. This is in marked contrast to the situation so often found in other modern countries when those who are qualified for admission to legal practice often divide into private practice and government service. Our higher judiciary under present prescriptions need not be recruited from the lower; nor is there a recognized "ladder" for the upward movement of public prosecutors or defenders. Our prescriptions do not focus public (including student) attention upon the forms of public service relating to the sanction process. Given this lack of differentiation it is easy to see why the idea of equipping a body of specialists to examine the aggregate impact of sanctions upon the public order has received no direct encouragement.

We know from the comparative study of professions that standards of high level performance tend to be set by a few major centers. Subcenters are most successful when they develop, not as a means of protecting access to local jobs, but in response to some of the other advantages of decentralization. Moreover, it is to be expected that local barriers will bring about or emphasize inadequacies in the geographical dispersion of skill, notably in new branches.

An analysis of the qualifications presently prescribed for experts having to do with sanction law is most revealing. It shows a thicket of local residence requirements imposed as a condition of licensing.[2] We agree that these restrictions "in a very real sense, [tend to] inhibit the movement of skills to places where they are most needed." [3] Moreover, statutory standards of qualification, in addition to residence requirements, do not always seem conducive to the raising of levels of skill. Occasionally, it has been noted, irrelevancies in requirements "creep in with a certain careless gaiety, as when Georgia enacted that each applicant for a commercial photographer's license must submit a certificate from the board of health, showing a negative Wasserman test." [4]

Forensic Matters and Public Policy

It is clear from existing prescriptions that forensic matters are not generally recognized as a field of concentration that is capable of contributing to the execution of public policy. Standards of expert qualification for courtroom testimony, for that matter, do not require that a specialist shall be competent within the subfield of the discipline that is relevant. The free use of general medical witnesses in psychiatric matters is a case in point.[5] Nor is any formal educational requirement prescribed for the application of a given discipline to forensic matters. Even when duly qualified under the standards of their discipline, not many expert witnesses are required to be trained in the practical application of their skills to legal problems. Existing statutes, for instance, do not require the establishment of centers for the teaching of forensic medicine. It is not surprising to learn that such centers are few and far between.[6]

APPLICATIONS

The current situation can be best understood if we turn from the relatively fragmentary items found in the codes and look directly at the place of the skilled individual in the whole complex of sanctioning activities.

Professional rewards (and deprivations) are so arranged that many able individuals are induced to cultivate skills that distort or defeat justice. As the late Professor Dession put it, the natural tendency of officials in the contemporary scene

> . . . is to accommodate the community's preferences, and to accommodate special interest groups to the extent that pressures from these are not offset by greater pressures from the community. There is little encouragement in this atmosphere for the long view, be it in planning against future hazards to public order or in inaugurating preventive programs. Police and prosecutors well know that their performance will be measured by the convictions obtained in cases with news value, and legislators are similarly aware that there is little public interest in major legislation short of an actual and generally appreciated emergency.
>
> Under these circumstances, when a disturbing case does occur, the aggressions aroused are likely to focus for their target on the particular offender, rather than on the social processes which evolved him and may be assumed to be evolving others like him. There is more interest in making an example of the particular offender than in abating the patterns and conditions of which he is symptomatic.[7]

Absence of basic skills as well as diversion of talent into wasteful activity is as characteristic of the bench as of the criminal bar and of the prosecutor's office. It is redundant to say more about the elaborate subterfuge by which defense counsel are often able to confuse the issue though remaining within the letter of the law and the spirit of the adversarial system.

It is reasonable to believe—although the point has not been conclusively established—that the low reputation of the criminal bar serves to alienate men of character and ability. Defense counsel too often appears to act as the "mouthpiece" of a dubious client rather than as an instrument of community policy. An aroma —not always faint—of sharp dealing clings to the practice of law in one of the fields of utmost importance for the sanctioning process.

Traditional arrangements do not give the lawyer who is acting on behalf of the criminal defendant an unambiguous status as an officer of the court. Nor does tradition define the role of the prosecutor as that of an official who is as much concerned with legitimate defense as with getting convictions. The public defender concept is too new and weak to help in the task of transforming the "prosecutor's office" into a "Justice Department" in which independent wings and perhaps transferable personnel are engaged.

As seen by at least some observers, needlessly frequent incompetence is tolerated in the judicial sphere "in sharp contrast to conditions which prevail in other countries. There the judge stands at the head of a profession infinitely more learned and of vastly higher culture than . . . the members of the profession who practice in the courts . . ." [8] "In this country," it has been alleged, not without some support in the evidence, "the judges are drawn as a rule from the mediocre members of a mediocre profession. As a result, the average politically selected judge stands dwarfed before the more experienced members of the profession who practice in his court." [9]

Nor does judicial efficiency appear to be enhanced by the prevailing levels of mental health encountered within our courtrooms. "Madness in great ones must not unwatched go." There is, however, no preliminary screening to eliminate the sadistic or paranoid personality among candidates for the bench. Sentencing day, to speak of no other occasion, continues to give striking display of these unlovely human characteristics. Incipient psychotic processes themselves may pass unnoticed in judicial candidates. Evidence of active psychosis is discoverable even in a formal judicial opinion by a federal court.[10]

We have been joining in the common view that men of character and talent are alienated from important branches of legal practice by our sanctioning institutions as they are today. The alienation of skill goes much further. Our system has not yet realized the possibilities of a "third force" entering into the judicial arena and moderating the distorting effects of an exaggerated adversarial system. Today the adversarial pattern often puts the expert in a situation that is offensive to competent and perceptive people.[11] This state of affairs is particularly frustrating for specialists who deal with problems of human behavior which are to a very considerable extent matters of judgment and experience, in addition to specific items of well-authenticated knowledge.

Alienation and Denigration of Expert Witnesses

The plight of the psychiatrist is the most striking case, perhaps. The profession suffers from the image created when the "battle of the experts" seems to depend on who hires them. The following judicial description of the adversarial mobilization of experts for impending forensic battle puts the matter in clear, if unflattering perspective:

[T]he opinion of an expert may be honestly obtained and it may be quite different from the opinion of another expert also honestly obtained. But the mode in which expert evidence is obtained is such as not to give the fair result of scientific opinion to the Court. A man may go, and does sometimes, to half a dozen experts. . . . He takes their honest opinions, he finds three in his favor and three against him, he says to the three in his favor, "will you be kind enough to give evidence?" and he pays the three against him their fees, and leaves them alone; the other side does the same. It may not be three out of six, it may be three out of fifty. I was told in one case where a person wanted a certain thing done, that they went to sixty eight people before they found one. . . . That is an extreme case, no doubt, but it may be done and therefore I have always the greatest possible distrust of scientific evidence of this kind, not only because . . . the mode of its selection makes it necessarily contradictory, but because I know of the way in which it is obtained. I am sorry to say the result is that the Court does not get that assistance from the experts which, if they were unbiased and fairly chosen, it would have a right to expect.[12]

Expert testimony has under these circumstances been known to be given with such zest and abandon, particularly in medical litigation, as to justify, on occasion, as lugubrious a view as this:

In litigation involving personal injuries, death by accident, alleged mental irresponsibility and the like, the medical expert has become a stench in the nostrils of upright judges. He disgraces his own profession and the legal profession which uses and tolerates him. Combinations between crooked doctors and shyster lawyers impose upon honest jurors. . . . Even the generally respected physician and surgeon whose skill is unquestioned frequently shades his testimony to the advantage of the party paying his fee. Alienists are notoriously available for prosecution and defense in sensational criminal trials.[13]

The serious minded members of the psychiatric profession find themselves frustrated and dissatisfied when they are unable to contribute what they have to say in ways that make sense to them. They feel wedged into a legalistic strait jacket. Experts may be limited in presenting opinions based upon data that are satisfactory according to the standards of the experts' own discipline. Often an expert opinion may be validly propounded upon the basis of statements "of a highly reliable kind such as a report of an examination by another physician, or hospital charts and records showing the symptoms, treatment, and progress of a patient. The prevailing view, however, is that a question calling for the witness' opinion upon the basis of such reports . . . is improper." [14]

In New York, for example, it has been held that a psychiatrist is not permitted to propound an opinion as to the mental state of the accused at the time of the commission of the alleged crime on the basis of information he had obtained in the course of the psychiatric interview. Thus, the New York Court of Appeals declared:

The prisoner's declaration in November as to his condition in September was not competent as evidence of his actual condition at that time, nor could it be the basis of a scientific opinion as to whether he was sane or insane at that period. Had the question related to his condition at the time of the interview, the result might be quite different.[15]

We are thus faced with the anomaly that the courts, after recognizing the superiority of expert knowledge, proceed to impose standards resting upon no other basis than judicial opinion. The procedure appears to be about as rational as that followed by the hypothetical judge "who, when medical evidence of poisoning . . . [was] given, . . . [proceeded to] instruct the jury as a matter of law that they must be governed in their verdict by the presence or absence of a particular symptom." [16]

More serious perhaps is the handling of the expert in relation to the case in a manner that precludes him from using his own tools of observation fully, or of making his advice available throughout the contact of the court with the defendant. Once retained or appointed the expert rarely begins his work in the preliminary stages of the case, at least in a criminal proceeding.[17] His difficulties in a criminal investigation are compounded by the dearth of pretrial discovery since the most advanced form of criminal procedure, the Federal Rules, do not permit "an advance comparable to that achieved on the civil side in this respect. . . ." [18] Unlike his counterpart, in the quasi-inquisitorial system of the Civil Law whose "task . . . is set out for him (at the commencement of the case) by the investigating magistrate" [19] the American expert is often without firsthand knowledge of vital aspects of the case relevant to the exercise of his skills. Time and again he will, therefore, propound his opinion, not upon the basis of firsthand observation, but on the hypothetical assumption of discriminately or indiscriminately selected data presented to him in the celebrated hypothetical question. That question, "on principle, *need not include* any particular number of facts, *i.e.,* it may assume any one of more facts whatever, and *need not cover all the facts which the questioner alleges in his case.* The questioner is entitled to the witness' opinion on any comparison of facts that he may choose." [20] Under such circumstances, everything hangs upon the skill and fairness of the questioner. Prevailing practice affords little room for optimism. The abuses to which the hypothetical question has been put have been deemed to have "become so obstructive and nauseous" as to warrant an authoritative judgment "that no remedy short of extirpation will suffice." [21]

Operating in such an atmosphere the skills of counsel are frequently misapplied to the task of misleading the judge, who in turn often devotes much of his own ingenuity to the making of fine though marginally pertinent distinctions.

In many jurisdictions the medical history furnished by a patient to his physician remains inadmissible as an exception to the hearsay rule, *i.e.*, for the truth of the matter asserted. Its introduction in evidence may nonetheless be obtained through the back door, not as an exception to the hearsay rule, *i.e.*, for the truth of the matter asserted, but as the foundation for the medical opinion, elicited by appropriate questioning.[22] In such a context failure or success in securing the reception of vital testimony depends more on the alertness of counsel than the merits of the particular claim.

The woes of the physician and especially the psychiatrist are quite conspicuous. More generally, our sanctioning process appears to carry over into the modern era many uncritical prejudices against expert knowledge of any kind that were current in the days of frontier hardship and mediocre educational levels. In such a setting we do not provide the facilities calculated to draw enough men and women of brains and character into the service of this profoundly important social function. And we alienate promising young people by the denigrating reception given to skill.

For example, scientific expert testimony is often denied the weight it deserves, in contrast to continental practice.[23] "When the testimony of lay witnesses contradicts the testimony of experts, or when experts of the general practitioner type are contradicting experts of the specialist type, the lay witness or the general practitioner may carry the day." [24] An example is the refusal of some courts to accept the results of "blood-grouping" tests as conclusive evidence of exclusion in proceedings designed to determine the paternity of illegitimate offspring.[25]

Insufficient Use of Specialists

Even in the great metropolitan centers insufficient use is made of significant specialties where they are needed in connection with sanctions. The failure to provide psychiatric diagnostic skill in preparing the defense of indigent prisoners who are charged with crime is illustrative. While it is generally conceded that mental and emotional illness is relatively high within such a group,[26] routine psychiatric screening in all such cases is not established. The inherent power of the court to summon its own expert witnesses and the occasional statutory power of the court to effect hospitalization of the accused for psychiatric observation have not culminated in the practice of requiring that all such cases receive routine examination.[27] It is true that a routine psychiatric examination is provided for, though in restricted categories, under the Briggs Law in Massachusetts.[28] A comparable but by no means identical result has been effected by court psychiatric clinics in less than a dozen metropolitan centers.[29] Even under optimum conditions the examination in the criminal case does not receive the care given to its counterpart in, say, Sweden where "the courts now require a mental examination of defendants in an increasing number of cases. . . . [and the] examination is made before the rendering of the court's decision and often requires a period of two months." [30]

Lack of Territorial Balance of Skill

It is common knowledge that forensic talent, particularly in the field of psychiatry, is not distributed according to need.

It is still rather exceptional to make use of psychiatric consultation in aid of disposition after conviction. "Experience has shown that where thorough presentence investigations by a competent probation staff are available to the criminal court (1) there is greater use of probation as disposition, (2) jail and prison commitments are relatively lower, and (3) the rate of recidivism or failure on probation is reduced." [31] However, presentence investigations are not required in many of our states and where required, are rarely sufficiently "thorough" to include psychiatric examination itself. One notes in passing that "a person convicted of murder in Sweden nowadays is rarely turned over to the prisons. When he is subjected to the mental examination required for every prisoner accused of such a crime, he is usually found to be so abnormal mentally that he must be given hospital care instead of prison treatment." [32]

The practice of employing psychiatric talent to assist in estimating the credibility of witnesses has not made much progress to date in the United States. When accepted it is of dubious utility since it is founded for the most part upon courtroom observation. Under these circumstances the physician is able to make use of very few of the special devices of observation upon which he normally relies in establishing a diagnosis. Rule 35 of the Federal Rules of Civil

Procedure now restricts pretrial medical examination to the parties. Efficient appraisal of witnesses also requires pretrial examination.[33]

The present situation is that though "the testimony of witnesses" is conceded to be "affected by their experiences and temperaments," [34] yet courts have availed themselves but little of the methods of objective verification developed in the contemporary behavioral sciences. When applied, the conditions have been far short of optimum.

High Rates of Recidivism Cast Doubt on Sanctioning Skills

When we look beyond the trial to the skill with which our sanctioning system handles prisoners, the results raise grave questions. What are the objectives sought by imprisonment? Almost everyone would agree that one aim, at least, is to change the offender so that he will cease to offend society when he is returned to ordinary life.[35] Now it is impossible for any critical mind to seize upon any one figure relating to the sanction process and assert that the success or failure of the whole system stands or falls thereby. But if there is a single figure that raises a stronger presumption about the effectiveness of the system than the rate of recidivism it is hard to think of it. If the figure continues to rise it suggests that there is, in all probability, some failure of skill—as well as facilities—on the part of those administering the system. A falling figure does not conclusively establish the point that the total operation is successful, since there may be some decline in police effectiveness. But the figures do begin to tell a story: and we need to investigate in detail to learn how to finish it. Table 2 shows that a large percent of persons who are arrested for crime have been arrested before on a criminal charge.

TABLE 2. PERCENT OF ALL ARRESTS REPORTED TO THE FBI THAT HAD CRIMINAL FINGERPRINT RECORDS ALREADY ON FILE[36]

Year	*Percent*	*Year*	*Percent*
1937	42.4	1947	55.4
1942	49.1	1952	60.6

Recent studies indicate a general deterioration in this situation. "The proportion of repeaters received into federal institutions"—

representing the best in our nation-wide prison system—declares an official report for 1958—"rose again to a new record. This year 66.6 percent of the 1,322 prisoners received in Federal institutions with sentences of more than one year had served one or more previous terms in either State, Federal, or local institutions. This proportion was greater than in any of the previous 15 years for which comparable data are available." [37]

Existing figures do indicate that some prisoners do not again come within the clutches of the legal machinery. It is very doubtful that the percentage, low as it is, indicates reformation that can be attributed to the beneficent workings of the sanctioning system. It can in fact be authoritatively asserted that it is "impossible to demonstrate statistically that reformation, when it occurs, is due to institutional treatment." [38] Its occurrence, itself, as has been demonstrated, is disappointingly rare.[39]

If we ask why this paucity of desirable results we must listen to the investigators who have compared the sanctioning institutions of various countries and of various parts of the United States. Apparently the judgments expressed by the most articulate and reputable observers are in substantial accord. They say that the basic approach is unsound. It is said that the overwhelmingly punitive attitude of the contemporary prison system militates against whatever successes might be achieved by the use of such facilities for treatment as are available.[40] On the face of it, the combination of treatment and punishment appears to be a contradiction. In point of fact, the punitive element predominates. The authoritarian mould of prison discipline has not tended to approximate the often asserted ideal for the prisoner of "self-reliance, self-control, self-respect, self-discipline . . . and the *desire* to conform to accepted standards . . . in free society." [41] Instead the dominant impacts "are not conducive to reformation" and "interfere with attempts at treatment." [42] It is notorious that the "good prisoner" is not fitted to be a "good citizen," at least in the democratic, as distinct from the totalitarian social order.[43]

Presumably the prison population has some opportunity in a modern penal set-up to acquire and exercise (and receive some rewards for) socially useful skills. Can it be said, however, that the men and women of a given level of previous education are permitted and encouraged to prepare themselves to play a useful part in post-prison society?[44] Do the existing methods of prisoner classification take sufficient account of these potentialities? Are the facilities made available to prisoners the kind that fit the needs of a training and reorientation program? Is the scale of remuneration harmonized to the requirements of a reeducation plan?[45] It may be only a slight exaggeration to say that the chief skill acquired within the American prison system is a haphazard facility for framing of petitions for writs of error *coram nobis* and habeas corpus.[46] Under present circumstances the conclusion is inescapable that "the prison must necessarily have a low degree of efficiency in reformation." [47]

Dissemination of Skills and Sets of Mind Hostile to Public Order

The position of our sanctioning institutions appears to be even less favorable than the strictures just made might suggest. The system is not only vulnerable for its failure to reform; it is responsible for the affirmative dissemination of skills and sets of mind hostile to public order. The process of criminogenesis has been aptly described:

> An offender entering a prison for the first time is introduced to the culture in much the same way that a child is introduced to the ways of behaving of his elders. The general process by which a child is taught the behavior of his group is called "socialization," and the somewhat comparable process among inmates has been named "Prisonization."
>
> For many men, prisonization does not cease when there is mere engulfment by the rather routine prison life, however. The prison community contains other patterns which are learned and accepted by some inmates. These men learn to gamble, to participate in homosexual activities, and to hate and distrust prison officials and, generally, "outsiders." They not only accept the prescribed prison code, they attempt to enforce it. They not only hear the prison dogma, they begin to spread it. They not only believe that the environment should administer to them, they attempt to control the environment through prison politics and conniving. These and similar changes do not occur in every man, and all of them usually do not occur in any one man. They are, nevertheless, characteristic of the prison community. . . .
>
> Generally, the informal organization of prison social life is conducive to the retention and development of criminal attitudes rather

than to reformation. As a result of the antagonism between prisoners and authorities most long-term inmates become isolated from intimate contacts with anti-criminal behavior patterns and, instead, develop a loyalty to criminals as a class.

Although inmates learn many criminal techniques from each other and often form alliances for the perpetration of crimes after release, retention and development of criminal attitudes in prison do not result primarily from mere contamination and individual tutelage of one prisoner by another. Instead, they occur in response to participation in a community which has *collectively* developed traditions favorable to crime and to the repression of any tendency toward reformation.[48]

The National Commission on Law Observance and Enforcement, reporting in 1931, summarized its findings with this declaration:

We conclude that the present prison system is antiquated and inefficient. It does not reform the criminal. It fails to protect society. There is reason to believe that it contributes to the increase of crime. . . .[49]

There is little reason to believe that intervening years have rendered the report of the Commission obsolete. Hence it is more than a rhetorical device to ask the question: Is the prison more the enemy than the protector of society? It would be an uncritical respondent who would unhesitatingly answer in the negative.

TRENDS

It cannot be denied that the foregoing summary of the skill level and the skill consequences of our sanctioning institutions presents a dismal picture. Not for the sake of facile optimism but in order to achieve an adequate perspective it is useful to consider the historical sweep of change. It is generally recognized that the situation as a whole has been becoming more satisfactory. Men and women of talent and devotion have given themselves to the cause of investigation, exposure, reform and administration; and the skill level has unquestionably risen, whether we think of legal education, the use of forensic aids, or the management of the convicted.

Briefly, it can be shown that the prison is less of a public menace today than formerly. "Classification or differentiation" of prisoners, however haphazard and inadequate, has become "a continuous process of individualizing penal treatment." [50] The diminution of imprisonment by parole and the substitution of probation for imprisonment have become widespread,[51] though it must be noted in this connection that the scope of such corrective devices seems to have been strictly proportionate to the availability of skilled workers and other facilities. Thus, *e.g.*, probation has been used less in the absence and more in the presence of "probation services of a high quality." [52] The minimum security prison, only a few steps removed from the open institution, better equipped than the traditional prison in every respect for the effective eradication of criminal behavior, has made a long awaited albeit isolated appearance.[53] The open or even the closed institution with truly adequate therapeutic facilities still remains to be established; in this regard this country has not yet matched the pioneering efforts abroad, of *e.g.*, the Netherlands at Utrecht,[54] or of Denmark at Herstedvester,[55] to mention but two examples. In the meantime it may be noted that the achievement of this goal is facilitated by the rise in educational standards of more and more of our correctional officers.[56]

5. SANCTIONING MEASURES AND THE SHARING OF WELL-BEING

AN EXHAUSTIVE inquest of the consequences of sanctioning practice for mental and physical soundness would carry us beyond the offenders who are caught in the net of the police and the courts to the men and women who participate in the formation of community norms and in their enforcement (or nonenforcement). How do the prescriptions of sanction law and the outcomes of actual practice affect the level of mental and physical integrity? It is obvious that the well-being of those who become the targets of electrocution, solitary confinement, or heavy labor penalties are decisively involved. But what of the executioner, the prison warden and his staff, the judge, the attorneys, and the police? And what of the potential offenders throughout the community who hear of what is done by and to the current crop of offenders? It is a curious fact that while the concern of the community with health is evident to all, we have no investigations that have tried to connect the processes of sanctioning law with the total context of well-being which it influences and with which it interacts. There are, however, a number of available facts that illuminate various facets of the problem.

PRESCRIPTIONS

In contemporary codes we find express recognition of the fact that mental disease and defect often play decisive roles in the causation of offenses against preferred norms of community policy. And the proper inference is drawn. Treatment rather than punishment becomes the dominant method of correction.

If we are to understand the present state of affairs, however, we must pass at once from the language of official prescription to the facts of administration. And we shall find that the "follow-through" is largely missing. The brave new insights that find articulate form in legislation are largely forgotten on the day of voting taxes and appropriations. Characterizing the total situation, the late Professor George H. Dession summed up by saying that a "minimum is allocated for locating the potential offender and the potential mental case at the stage in their development when the least depriving methods and a minimum of preventive and therapeutic expenditure would provide a maximum result." [1]

APPLICATIONS

We turn, therefore, to consider what happens in fact: the juvenile offender and the mental patient have been insufficiently protected by the community.

"Some extremely ambitious and social-minded policies with respect to the handling of child offenders," it has been noted, "have graced our statute books for many years. . . . But when the smoke cleared away it developed in many jurisdictions . . . that the exacting function of administering the Acts . . . devolved as an incidental and almost *ex officio* duty upon part-time judges or preexisting "inferior" tribunals who had neither the time, training, nor equipment for the novel and highly specialized work.

. . . "[2] A recent case in the Nation's Capital is illustrative. A girl had been charged in the Juvenile Court of the District of Columbia with disorderly conduct. Prior to her trial, her court-appointed counsel moved for her psychiatric examination at government expense. The motion was based upon the uncontradicted assertion that the girl was a persistent victim of visual hallucinations and that she had commenced sexual relations at the age of ten and had been raped at the age of sixteen. Government counsel argued in opposition to the effect that "if such evidence were the basis of full mental tests, most of the females in delinquency cases . . . [would be] also entitled to . . . [them]." The court in turn refused to order a psychiatric examination for the girl.[3] One may add in passing that no full-time psychiatrist had been attached to the staff of the Juvenile Court at the time of a proceeding, which seems otherwise straight out of the pages of *Alice in Wonderland.*

Similarly, the facilities made available to the public mental hospital under the average legislative budgetary grant have been notoriously inadequate. The State of New York, recognized as providing the best in public mental hospitals in the nation, "even in the most halcyon years never came close to meeting the minimum American Psychiatric Association's standards in terms of doctors, nurses, attendants and other personnel needed to operate a well-functioning state hospital system. It remains desperately short of personnel today."[4]

When we inquire into the use to which current therapeutic resources are put, a rather disconcerting state of affairs soon makes itself manifest. It is extremely doubtful that the psychiatric profession, for example, has been kept under sufficient community control. Conditions have been permitted to occur on a large scale that endanger rather than protect the well-being of patients.[5]

It is noteworthy that courts have provided scant, if any, relief against the existing abuse of electric shock therapy. Psychiatrists, administering such "treatment" without consent, have not infrequently been shielded by the assertion of an emergency as justification.[6] Unduly high standards of proof appear to have kept too many patients from recovering for physical injuries sustained in the course of electric shock therapy[7] for which consent was in fact obtained.

Prefrontal lobotomy operations are another source of severe deprivation imposed without adequate protection. The "need for adoption of legislation against promiscuous use of . . . [this] operation by public institutions to which court commitments are sent is fortified by the glaring fact that lobotomy could readily be used as a satisfactory means of controlling obstreperous inmates who are a nuisance to prison wardens and guards, which the emotionally and mentally deranged admittedly are." [8] No preventive legislation of this type has appeared.

Psychiatrists have been remarkably free of malpractice suits when we compare them with fellow physicians. Psychoanalysts, in particular, appear to have been virtually exempt from any effective legal challenge in their professional work. It is not possible to account for this immunity satisfactorily by pointing to the relatively small number of practitioners or higher standards of ethics or professional competence. A more plausible inference is that in the absence of new and adequately certain and objective legislative standards psychiatric malpractice, however flagrant, is by virtue of its subjective characteristics infinitely less susceptible to judicial proof than the malpractice of other medical practitioners.[9] To assume that this immunization from effective judicial scrutiny is not conducive to mischief seems to imply that psychiatrists are uniquely virtuous.

Government Activities have Contributed to the Undermining of Well-being

There is evidence that some of the personnel measures adopted by the federal government have had adverse effects upon mental and physical health. One by-product of the federal loyalty and security program has been to penalize anyone who turns to a physician for psychiatric aid.

The bare acceptance of psychotherapy has been viewed by some loyalty-security boards as evidence of an emotional instability that warrants dismissal from government. It has been observed that "*urgently* needed psychotherapy [for govemnment employees] in instances in which the disorder presents no real problem of inefficiency or danger to government security" [10] has been discouraged as a consequence. It stands to reason that "the fact that treatment by a psychiatrist can cause a man to lose his job will [also] have the effect of discouraging the kind of *early prophylactic* treatment which is one of the important elements in maintaining group emotional health" [11]—at least in areas of widespread government employment and employment connected with matters of governmental concern.

Loyalty and security investigations, which create a "Kafkaesque feeling of isolation" among hits and near misses, account for "an appreciable number of symptomatic mental and emotional illnesses, ranging in severity from anxiety and obsessive ruminative states to paranoid psychotic breaks." [12] In this process the federal loyalty-security program has generated a "demand for excessive conformity," [13] that can be viewed only as obstructive of the healthy emotional growth and development of the individual and hence of a sane as well as a free society.[14] "No psychiatrist," affirmed a recent psychiatric report, based upon an evaluation of the existing atmosphere in the nation's capital under the federal loyalty-security program, ". . . can view with equanimity a state of affairs in which intellectual boldness and curiosity become suspect, in which conformity becomes the only safety, in which the generous and healthy impulses of youth become, long afterwards, evidence of treachery. This is the climate of frightened totalitarian states, not of the open democratic society we wish our country to remain. It is not a climate in which the concept of emotional health . . . can flourish or even be a meaningful goal." [15] If it is recalled that the federal loyalty-security program has been the subject of widespread imitation on the level of local government,[16] these effects can be assumed to be truly nationwide.

Imprisonment Accelerates Deterioration

It is important not to lose sight of the point that imprisonment, which is the most widely used contemporary sanction, has been shown under various circumstances to accelerate the normal process of organic deterioration.[17] Protracted imprisonment often results in loss of ability to concentrate, loss of strength of memory, loss of determination and emotional balance, and development of illusions.[18] ". . . . [T]reatment of delinquents in prison [by psychotherapy]," it has been noted, "has not been successful." [19]

If not contributive to mental deterioration, confinement within the average public mental hospital under court order rarely realizes the recuperative potential of the patient involved. Overcrowding, understaffing, mediocrity in therapeutic skill and occasional brutality in custodial treatment continue to characterize numerous, if not most, public mental hospitals throughout the country.[20] Moreover, it has been noted that "the whole system [of public mental hospitals] has been hamstrung for decades by physical and scientific isolation from the mainstreams of modern medicine." [21]

Present Sanctioning Patterns Do Not Significantly Contribute to Security Against Crime

In connection with our study of sanctions and skill we emphasized the very high rates of recidivism now prevailing in the United States. At this point in our discussion of well-being we want to underline the fact that serious deprivations of well-being are reflected in the figures on recidivism. The totals are high, not because there has been an upswing in mild offenses against people while severe offenses have tapered off. Our sanctioning system has not succeeded in concentrating its fire with indisputable success upon the most violent violations of bodily integrity. The rate of serious offenses is not going down.[22]

How are these results to be accounted for? The following is a succinct reply:

> Too few of the really serious offenders are caught, and of those caught too few are convicted and appropriately sentenced. . . . This is popularly ascribed to criminal procedure, the thought being that the safeguards of the accused operate as unreasonably technical obstacles to conviction of the guilty. The notion is, of course, balderdash, as all who have any experience in the trial of criminal cases well know.[23]

These events are far more readily attributable to politics and false economy and to occasional official indifference to the cause of the meritorious prosecution itself.[24] The existing situation has been strikingly portrayed in these words:

> In the United States so small a percentage of all offenders are caught and convicted that what happens to them can have little effect on the great body of potential and actual violators of the law. Reports of the Federal Bureau of Investigation for 1939, the last prewar year, from

78 cities with populations over 25,000 and a total population of about 13,000,000 show that for every 100 major offenses known to the police there were 27 arrests, 19 prosecutions, and 14 convictions. In some cities the ratios are even lower than these figures; in one large American city for example, the ratio of convictions to known offenses in 1945 was 5 to 100. The odds clearly favor the criminal in such conditions.[25]

It may be worth mentioning in this connection that "organized criminal gangs," often enjoying the direct protection of the police, "are firmly entrenched in our large cities." [26]

Difficulties of enforcement are further maximized by inconsistent sanctioning exemplified by variations in both the *invoking* and the *applying* functions.[27]

The erratic contemporary use of the death penalty is not only incapable of serving any protective function whatsoever but provides immunity for dangerous criminal elements who get the benefit of the doubt:

The available records indicate that in the United States we are executing only a small percentage of the persons who have committed capital crimes. For example, although it is estimated that in 1949 there were 6,990 cases of murder and non-negligent manslaughter and 16,380 cases of rape in the United States, in that year we executed a total of only 119 of which 107 were for murder and 10 for rape, and in the following year a total of only 82, of which 68 were for murder and 13 for rape. In view of this, we can hardly say that our system of criminal law is contributing in a significant way to the elimination of the "undesirable" or the dangerous from our society.

Furthermore, the death penalty may not be imposed equitably upon all offenders. The man of wealth, education, and position can secure able attorneys and use every legal device and technicality, while the poor, the illiterate, and the friendless can avail themselves of no such resources, and so suffer from greater exposure to the death penalty. Thus, factors other than those which make prisoners a threat to society may determine whether or not they are executed.[28]

The Terror Approach Is at Fault

If our sanctioning system is to cope with the threats to our system of public order it will be necessary to understand the factors to be controlled on behalf of community policy. The fact is, it may be added, that in communities "where the all-out Terror Principle [is] sought to be justified [expressed as a policy of maximal deterrence] it is observable that their apparent necessity for recurring purges appears to be enhanced rather than to be diminished," [29] and that in contrast, in communities where the criminal is treated with leniency and even generosity in expression of a policy of maximal reform, their "crime situation" has been authoritatively described as close to "idyllic." [30]

The Lawlessness of the Police Infringe upon the Well-Being of the Public

We cannot leave the consideration of well-being as it is affected by sanctioning practice without paying attention to the topic that immediately rises to public consciousness in connection with the police. We refer, of course, to "the third degree," or more generally to the mental and physical consequences of arrest, detention, and investigation.

The right of arrest includes of necessity the right to use reasonable force to effectuate the arrest in question. Note, however, that reasonable force has been deemed to extend to the killing of a person whose arrest is sought to be effected for at least a felony. "A person has the right to kill," it has been summed up, "if necessary to effectuate the immediate arrest of a felon. It is immaterial that at a later time the felon could probably be arrested without resort to killing." [31] Does this right to kill apply only to the arrest of the actual and proven felon or does it apply as well to the arrest of a person thought to be a felon upon reasonable grounds? One notes with surprise that at least several jurisdictions have refused to recognize the liability of the police for the homicide of an innocent man in the street who was mistakenly thought to have been subject to arrest for felony (albeit upon reasonable grounds).[32]

The widespread and promiscuous use of firearms by the police when engaged in the apprehension of relatively trifling offenders, and the consequent loss of human life including that of "innocent bystanders," [33] raises the question of changing the rule or else of disarming at least a part of the police (in emulation of the English example).[34]

There appears to be general acquiescence on the part of the public in a great deal of police brutality and violation of privacy upon the assumption that only criminals will be made uncomfortable. The "third degree," in particular, shows no evidence of recession.[35] The seemingly dismal failure of the use of existing doctrine [36] to dam the tide of coerced confessions flooding our courtrooms,[37] raises, in turn, the considerably more urgent question of the emulation of the seemingly drastic remedy, prescribed by Indian law, to wit, the adoption as a rule of evidence, if not constitutional law,[38] of the principle of outright exclusion, without more, in any court proceedings, of any "confession made to a police officer . . . [by] a person accused of any offence" [39] and beyond that of any "confession made by any person while he is in the custody of a police officer, unless it be made in the immediate presence of a Magistrate . . ." [40] or some workable variation thereof.[41]

The lawlessness of the law enforcer is well known in the field of "searches and seizures." [42] The courts give erratic application to the federal rule that provides for the exclusion of illegally secured materials, presumably on the assumption that ordinary criminal investigations by the police would be unduly handicapped if the rule were strictly applied.[43] No unqualified exclusionary rule, as it has been observed, prevails as yet in the majority of state jurisdictions. Unlawful searches and seizures are provocative acts by officers charged with law enforcement and contribute to situations in which clashes occur in connection with police action.

One may validly speculate, moreover, as to the extent to which "dangerous thoughts" have become the frequent or consistent objects of police investigation in our age of anxiety,[44] and as to the effect of such a development in turn on existing anxiety levels throughout the nation.[45] It is elementary learning that a volume of legislative regulation of most phases of living has produced a rapid growth of police activity. Today, the policeman in one form or another, is omnipresent. A common burglary, a congestion of traffic, a corporate merger, an issuance of a stock catalogue, a meeting called by a "Communist-infiltrated" group, a disposal of domestic or municipal refuse, a distribution of "subversive" literature, a political oration from a soap-box or any other rostrum, or indeed any confederation to that end, are at present but *some* seemingly legitimate objects of his professional attention. Under the aegis of contemporary "security" legislation, police activity is, moreover, *explicitly* catapulted into the sphere of private beliefs.[46] In this context it was plain long before police activity had run such a gamut that "the police no longer confine[d] their attention to groups and individuals who . . . [were] essentially outlaws . . . [but that] police function . . . [had] come to involve intimate regulation of the day to day life of nearly every person with whom the police officer comes into contact." [47]

The emerging scope of police surveillance in political and non-political matters alike [48] is not readily reconciled with the assumption made by Mr. Justice Brandeis in dissent, that "the makers of our Constitution undertook to secure conditions favorable to the pursuit of happiness . . . [and that in so doing they] sought to protect Americans in their beliefs, their thoughts, their emotions and their sensations . . . [and hence] conferred, as against the Government, the right to be let alone—the most comprehensive of rights and the right most valued by civilized men." [49]

Against a progressive "misuse of the law enforcement process," [50] by which men's "steps are tracked by spies and informers, their words noted down for crimination [and] their associates watched as conspirators . . ." [51] the courts have interposed no significant obstacles. Further studies of this form of "sanctioning," and of its effects on well-being, are overdue.

Possible Contributions of Sanctioning Activities to Community Health

Information is not at hand for drawing a picture of how the level of mental and physical health that prevails generally in the community is influenced by sanction practice. There are, of course, interesting hints obtained from psychiatric theory and observation. It is clear on general principles of psychological analysis that the reporting of criminal deeds and of the punishment of crime appeals to important motivations in the public. The offender may be viewed as performing a "scapegoat" function; and the hypothesis is plausible that the mental stability of the community is safeguarded thereby. Inner tensions created by the contradictory demands of the individual conscience (the super ego) and the instinctual system (the id) may be relieved by "projecting" self-accusations of guilt or shame away from the self and onto the criminal offender. In this perspective sanctioning operations come within the sphere of self-therapy on the part of the community. However, since the therapeutic measures are not rationally thought out they belong to the domain of popular magic rather than medical science.

At present it is impossible to say how important our sanctioning methods have been as a means of relieving tension and presumably of decreasing the amount of neurotic anxiety or of symptom formation in the community. If the scapegoat function is, in fact, important it can be said to provide a substitute response for diffuse anxiety conditions, or for such psychosomatic manifestations as headache, gastro-intestinal troubles, and heart conditions.

From the point of view of social medicine the question arises whether the scapegoat function, if in fact it exists, is the most economical means of conducting therapy.

TRENDS

There is not much doubt that our sanctioning systems are becoming more focused as a result of the discovery of how mental and physical factors influence deviational conduct. Correctional measures are being adopted, especially in dealing with serious offenders. We note this, for example, in the use of probation in place of imprisonment. "Adult probation," it has been observed, "must be considered as part of the general trend in criminal procedure which has been most completely developed in dealing with children. It implies humane and intelligent supervision of a maladjusted individual, assisting him in reconstructing his personality." [52] Estimates suggest "that the criminal courts throughout the country are using probation in about 35 percent of felony cases and in less than 10 percent of misdemeanor cases. Where [on the other hand] probation services of a high order are available courts use probation as a disposition in more than 65 percent of their cases." [53]

The appropriation of more funds to the agencies of law enforcement has "paid off" in the increasing "substitution of brains for brutality" at the federal level. Correspondingly, the situation in the more impoverished areas has failed to change.[54]

Medical facilities for prisoners have undoubtedly improved even though so much remains to be done.[55]

If we think in terms of ideal standards it cannot be denied that a profound discrepancy exists between what is prescribed in words and what is implemented by money and talent. We are far from a "healthy penal adjustment," *i.e.*, an adjustment characterized by "professing policies looking toward the rehabilitation of offenders, and employing such professed policies as a premise, *only to the extent* to which we may be willing at the same time to assume collective responsibility for that whole segment of human subnormality, wreckage and underprivilege, which we experience as crime and delinquency." [56] As the deprivational potential in all matters of socially imposed "rehabilitation" or "therapy" has been observed to be particularly high in the absence of truly adequate facilities for such ends, random contemporary extensions of "rehabilitative" or "therapeutic" individualization in the disposition of the deviate, in line with the "most advanced penological objectives," continue to serve no significant rehabilitative or therapeutic end while providing for the possibility of abuse, inherent in a system of arbitrary power, like the one symbolized by the *Lèttres de Cachet* of the *Ancien Régime*.[57]

"The professing of [such] policies" (of rehabilitation and therapy), *failing* such an adjustment, however, it may then be validly concluded "can mean, nothing more nor less than a scrapping of the rather precious, if imperfect, guarantees of individual liberty . . . summed up in the maxim *'Nulla Poena Sine Lege,'* " [58] significantly without any compensating gain of any kind. Certainly there are no gains in well-being for the offender or the offended.

6. SANCTIONING MEASURES AND THE SHARING OF AFFECTION

ONE OF the most neglected areas of investigation is the effect of sanctioning practice upon intimate human relations. Altogether insufficient attention has been paid to the impact of the system upon the family, for example. Do our sanctions fall upon targets that we intend to reach or upon others whom we do not want to injure? Are we doing gratuitous damage to a primary social institution?

Modern research into child development—or, more generally, the formation of personality—is emphasizing the fundamental importance of love in the shaping of a human being at once willing and able to play a mature role in society. But "love" is not a simple impulse or a simple idea. When we say that human beings are deeply affected by love we are not saying that everyone perceives an act of loving in the same way.

Research on the "incorrigible" child provides a convincing demonstration of the point. At first any gesture of friendliness as ordinarily understood—is interpreted, not as friendship, but as a trap. Similarly any gesture that looks like friendship on the part of the child is not the expression of a friendly impulse but a ruse of battle. It is a means of putting the other person—invariably perceived as an enemy—at a disadvantage. The enemy may let his guard down. These "incorrigible" children can, however, be taught to love by persons who combine loving impulses with knowledge and capability. It is possible to create an environment in which the hostile child eventually comes to believe in the underlying good will of the other person, and begins to model himself in the same mould of benevolence.

This fundamental point applies in varying degree to human beings at every stage. Research is gradually corroborating the teachings that have been uttered by the moral leaders of mankind. And research is clarifying the situation by filling the gap between soundness of intention and appropriateness of execution. Even today the efficacy of many of our sanctioning measures can be challenged on the basis of the new knowledge.

PRESCRIPTIONS

Several points can be made by examining the text of official prescriptions.

It is clear that statutes and regulations do not give enough consideration to the integrity of family life. The provisions regarding the dissolution of marriage are singularly inept. They concentrate upon a few details and fail to provide a means of assessing a whole context of relationships. Emphasis is put upon considerations that carry all the connotations of a dispute over the applications of negative sanctions.

Divorce is characteristically authorized upon a finding of "fault" exemplified by adultery; on the face of it the finding of "fault" appears the sole goal of judicial investigation in divorce proceedings; this finding, when made, closes the door; no amount of evidence of basic compatibility and therapeutic possibility or probability of improvement of the marital relationship can then bar the divorce demanded by the "aggrieved" party. Conversely, no amount of evidence of basic incompatibility and the therapeutic improbability or impossibility of improving the marital relationship can effect a divorce, absent a showing of "fault." The "fault," to justify divorce, must be one-sided. "To obtain a divorce one must," as a general proposition, "be the 'injured and innocent' party." [1] If husband and wife "are equally at fault, or the one seeking a divorce by reason of conduct of the other materially contributed to or induced such conduct, relief [in the form of divorce] will be denied." [2] No amount of evidence of incompatibility and of the therapeutic improbability or impossibility of improvement within the marriage relationship will bar such a denial. Nor will evidence of mutual consent.[3]

In brief, marriages with favorable prognoses may be dissolved; marriages with unfavorable prognoses may be held to be indissoluble.

Preoccupation with "fault" exacerbates already existing ill will and reduces the likelihood of reconciliation.[4] Problems of child custody and property settlement in particular tend to become more and more complicated as the passions of the parties rise in the heat of inquiry into fault.[5] It is not surprising, therefore, that adequate conditions of custody have not been arranged for the children of divorce.

If the welfare of the child is taken as the standard of disposition in a custody dispute, what is necessarily involved "is a determination of personality and emotional attitudes as they affect relationship between the parents and children." [6] For this determination

> present procedures are inadequate . . . for three principal reasons. The first is that the adversary method is a painfully slow way of developing the mass of factual detail out of which such attitudes can be made apparent, and it may often fail to produce significant data. Second, the conduct of adversary judicial proceedings intensifies the hostilities and further obscures the picture, whereas there should be maximum effort to quiet hostilities and broaden the area of agreement. Third, the court needs the advice of experts in the field of human emotions to assist him in making a determination that in law, and in fact must deal with emotional problems.[7]

This, too often, is not forthcoming.

It can only be concluded that present procedures often work

erratically and produce custodial arrangements that work unnecessary mischief.

The limited approach exemplified by divorce prescriptions is characteristic of statutes which affect the family. Needless interference in family relations is tolerated, for example, whenever the courts continue to enforce leasehold agreements barring the presence of children on the premises.[8]

But the often unfortunate impact upon the family of various statutory requirements becomes especially apparent when we look into the testimony of those who are acquainted with what happens at the administrative level.

APPLICATIONS

Safeguards, secured to the creditor in the interests of private investment, sometimes work avoidable and excessive hardship not only upon the debtor but upon his family. In a leading code jurisdiction such "provisional remedies" as the "arrest" of the defendant,[9] and the attachment of the defendant's real and personal property [10] as security may be had at the behest of the plaintiff at the commencement of civil litigation, albeit upon restricted grounds. In less typical jurisdictions "attachment of the property of the defendant may be had as a matter of course at the beginning of a suit for money damages." [11] Execution of judgment is enforceable in the leading jurisdictions, not only against the personal and real property of the defendant [12] but even against the person of the defendant himself in what is but "a form of imprisonment for debt." [13] The consequences for the defendant's family are entirely overlooked.

The imposition of monetary damages upon loss of a civil suit may threaten the continued existence of the affected family. Even the model insurance immunization,[14] occasionally extended by a legislature, provides but a mild palliative.

Imprisonment is itself one of the great disrupters of the family. The withdrawal of the principal income earner may be fatal to the continuation of the group. It has been demonstrated in several countries, notably in Sweden,[15] that with care the cohesion of the family can be given a great deal of protection. Imprisonment can be more sparingly and selectively used; and shorter terms, when coupled with *adequately* remunerative prison labor and the granting of leaves for the formation and maintenance of family units can minimize the disruption in this field.

Imprisonment tends not only to distroy existing families, but to prevent the formation of healthy family units. Heterosexual adjustments are made more difficult, if not impossible, by prolonged incarceration particularly in the case of the younger male.[16] It is observed "that many confirmed homosexuals become so because of institutional experience." [17] The incidence of homosexuality in our custodial institutions appears far above the national level.[18] Hence the courts may be appropriately advised to "keep in mind that the penal or mental institution to which . . . [they] may send the male has something between 30 and 85 per cent of its inmates engaging in . . . homosexual activity. . . ." [19]

TRENDS

The trend in sanctioning method is toward giving greater consideration to family relations. Courts that deal with domestic relations are provided with a wider range of more skilled staffs. As time goes on the adversarial character of the proceedings fades away.

The enforcement of creditors' rights is modified in some jurisdictions with the welfare of the family in mind. New York has immunized third persons who are beneficiaries of insurance policies from creditors' claims that are directed against the assets of the insured.[20] Agreements that forbid the presence of children on the leasehold premises are increasingly refused enforcement.[21]

Exploitative forms of child labor have withered away under the impact of negative sanctions.[22]

Although we have begun to make use of probationary devices to reduce the traditional dependence of our system upon imprisonment as a sanctioning measure, imprisonment itself continues to be employed with minor rather than major consideration given to affection values and institutions.

7. SANCTIONING MEASURES AND THE SHARING OF RECTITUDE

ONE OF the most spontaneous sanctions against any deviation from a norm is moral disapproval. This is evident in small group relationships; and it is noteworthy that the sanctioning systems of complex societies continue to rely to some extent upon moral condemnation. We see this in the terminology of "guilt" or "innocence," of "wrong," and of many other key symbols of public and private law. The sophisticated jurist and the seasoned practitioner may use these words as counters in a game of analysis or persuasion, and forget all about the halo effect that terms of the kind enjoy in popular usage. But any competent observer of what happens in a courtroom or in any other sanctioning situation recognizes that ethical overtones are frequent. This is most obvious in an ordinary crime or tort in which one party appears to have taken advantage of a weaker and well-intentioned individual.

The connection between sanctioning and standards of right and wrong goes much deeper than the formal or informal condemnation of particular targets. It is generally understood among jurists that if a code is to be effective a positive relationship must exist between its sanctions and the norms of the dominant elements of the community. Among these norms are included the conceptions of right and wrong which we call rectitude. Our system of public order has many features which are protected because they are accepted as right; sanctions must not themselves offend if they are to be applied with effect on behalf of primary norms.

In a social order that affirms the goal of human dignity one of the purposes of the legal order is to reduce the need of coercion and to increase the number of individuals in the body politic who conform by voluntary choice from a sense of responsibility. Plainly this positive support can occur only when the prescriptions of the legal system appeal to the consciences of most—or all—the members of the body politic.

A corollary of what we have been saying is that a system of sanctions employed to defend a public order which is not wholly accepted, or which contains sanctioning requirements that are not regarded as morally justified, has a problematic position. It is true that the community may be transformed through the years to harmonize with the perspectives of the dominant elite. But the system itself may be changed.

Among the questions, then, pertinent to the examination of the interplay between sanctions and rectitude are the following: to what extent are the primary prescriptions of the legal system supported or opposed by conceptions of rectitude found in the body politic? To what extent are the sanctioning prescriptions supported or opposed? If prescriptions contradict one another, how frequently? To what extent is the administration of the sanctioning code supported or opposed by the conceptions of rectitude current in the body politic? Are the trends toward greater harmony or less?

Only sporadic research has been conducted for the purpose of answering these questions. At the moment we are therefore compelled to satisfy ourselves with fragmentary and inconclusive indications of the true state of affairs.

PRESCRIPTIONS

When we examine the prevailing doctrines of our sanctioning system several contradictions appear at once.

Doctrinal Contradictions in Requirements of Personal Guilt versus Vicarious Criminal Liability

The "fundamental principle of Anglo-Saxon jurisprudence that guilt is personal" [1] is inconsistent with the practice of imposing strict and vicarious criminal liability in the administration of welfare and regulatory legislation, under the "felony-murder" doctrine or in the law of conspiracy.[2] Guilt continues to be declared "personal"; nevertheless punishment is authorized for "wrongs" quite apart from any demonstrated awareness of "wrongdoing," and also for "combinations" toward the effectuation of "wrongs" that involve no more than "conscious parallelism" among the "wrongdoers." [3] The conspiracy doctrine has been most far-reaching in effecting such results and hence seems most seriously subject to challenge as ethically indefensible.[4] While the "summary" character of some adjudications can be defended as essential to effective enforcement, it is impossible to justify the language of moral obloquy in the context of welfare and regulatory action where the moral stigma of criminality is not widely present in the perspectives of the community. An obvious escape from the existing dilemma would be the removal by legislative authority of the body of precedent in support of strict and vicarious liability from "criminal" sanctioning to the noncriminal clauses of regulatory and enterprisory codes.[5] In the meantime, however, the history of the type of precedent referred to has been affected by the predominantly remedial nature of the proceedings which gave it birth, and in practice it has been extended to the prosecution of serious crime.[6] This produces the paradoxical result that moral condemnation is formally possible without moral blame. Such conflicting standards are in no sense unique in our system.

The rise of the modern corporation has confronted traditional modes of sanctioning with problems whose solution remains for the future. Traditional sanctions designed to influence conduct in the market were originally aimed at highly individualized targets. They were expected to operate in a setting in which specific entrepreneurs were well known to competitors and customers, and where indignation could be directly expressed against unfair practices and practitioners. Moral condemnation was believed to be a potent instrumentality in the hands of the community in its collective capacity as umpire of the market. The rise of giant corporations has subdivided functions and fostered impersonality to a degree that deprives individual condemnations of its former applicability. Business decisions are the outcome of complex processes that have more in common with the deliberate procedures of government than the summary judgments of a captain of industry.

The Absurdity of Many "Ethically" Formulated Sanctions

It requires no extended research to perceive that many "ethical" connotations conveyed by the language of sanctioning codes are absurd. They invoke a moral sentiment only to direct it toward a blank, expressionless visage; and they end by extracting a small fee which functions as a license to continue the deviation which was originally condemned. A leading jurisdiction has restricted the punishment to be meted out to a corporation for any "offense for the commission of which a natural person would be punishable with imprisonment" to the exaction of a fine of no more than $5,000,[7] *i.e.*, to an easy licensing fee for crime, at least as far as financial giants are concerned.[8] For small businesses these exactions constitute an additional hardship in competition with larger business units.

The jurist is aware of the historical context which alone enables the observer to account for the extraordinary confusion among the standards that formally prescribe for such fundamental matters as sexuality and the family. Our civilization was once entirely dominated by norms that were regarded as possessing much more than ethical significance. These normative prescriptions were imputed to the transempirical world, the province of theology and metaphysics. During recent generations the voice of religious authority has lost the unified sonority of the Middle Ages and become a babble of clashing pretensions. Hence sex and family matters have been approached in an increasingly secular spirit. And this has emphasized the diversity of outlook that now prevails among cultures, classes, and personality types. Under these circumstances the legal system has come to reflect tension between past and present, and within the present. As of this moment, at least, we are not able to say that the prescriptive sanctions relating to intimacy can long be accepted either on the basis of alleged transempirical derivation or of consensus regarding their usefulness among responsible-minded participants in the social context. One aspect of the situation is highlighted in the apt words of Sir A. P. Herbert:

> The trouble is, you see, that our law is an attempt to combine two irreconcilable notions. It's possible, and honest, to hold, . . . that marriage is a holy sacrament, and therefore cannot be terminated by men or the courts of men: . . . It is possible, again, to hold that marriage is a civil contract, a practical arrangement by which two reasonable beings agree to share certain rights and duties, an arrangement made by men and dissoluble by men. . . . What is impossible is to combine the two—to say that marriage is both a sacrament and a civil contract, governed at one moment by the principles of Common Law and at another by the remnants of ecclesiastical tradition—enforceable by one set of rules but not avoidable except by another. . . . If you claim your just rights under a contract of marriage you're supported by the doctrines of the civil law. . . . But if you want to surrender your rights under the contract of marriage—or partnership—you're impeded by obstacles which have a purely ecclesiastical origin.[9]

Disharmonies among Formal and Behavioral Norms

The codes governing sexual conduct and domestic relations have in several respects failed to develop "according to the practical and ideological needs" of an increasingly secular culture in a democratic society. Statutory prohibitions of sexual conduct continue to embody early Puritan conceptions of depravity. The primary theme, now as then, is that of sexual restraint, exemplified in the extant law against fornication.[10] Typically, sexual conduct that has been penalized includes activities engaged in, by "more than 95 per cent of the total male population." [11] The moral claim of various prohibitions to acceptance has been undercut by the manifest lack of relationship between the act condemned and the social dangers resulting therefrom. "Imaginary offenses," viewed by

Bentham as "acts which produce no real evil but which prejudice, mistake, or the ascetic principle have caused to be regarded as offenses" [12] may be punished with greater severity than real ones involving a serious manifestation of social destructiveness. Deviant sexual practices, including those of the heterosexual variety, voluntarily engaged in between adults,[13] may, in some states, be punished with greater severity than the sexual misuse of a child.[14]

In all phases of life, the steadfast refusal of the common law to recognize the principle of active benevolence for appropriate cases has reflected a conception of social and personal responsibility singularly out of touch with the realities of twentieth-century interdependences. As Bentham appropriately observed, however, "the limits of the law on this head seem . . . to be capable of being extended a good deal farther than they seem ever to have been extended hitherto. In particular, in cases where the person is in danger, why should it not be made the duty of every man to save another from mischief, when it can be done without prejudicing himself, as well as to abstain from bringing it on him?" [15]

Vengeance, moreover, continues on the books as perhaps the chief anachronism of contemporary sanction law. Since the majority of our jurisdictions retains the death penalty in the absence of proof that it possesses any significant deterrent effects, and indeed in the presence of some evidence that it "has little if anything to do with the relative occurrence of murder," it is difficult to resist the conclusion that it "seems to mark the survival of the vengeance theory of punishment, of exacting 'a life for a life.' " [16] The death penalty, moreover, has not been restricted to murder and to serious crimes against national security. Only recently, in the face of the fact that the application of this mode of "repression" has been shrinking throughout the Western World,[17] federal legislation, though lacking plausible evidence of the social utility of such a measure, extended the death penalty to narcotics violations,[18] thereby satisfying, if not the needs of the nation, a possible blood lust on the part of some legislators.[19]

Although justified on humanitarian grounds,[20] the obvious suffering inflicted in the maintenance of the time-hallowed rule governing the administration of the death penalty, to wit, that "if a party under sentence of death becomes insane after conviction execution is to be deferred," [21] presumably until such time as the "party" has sufficiently recovered to appreciate the significance of the grisly ritual, suggests the possibility of at least unconsciously sadistic motivations in that context as well.[22]

In the light of available knowledge of its antisocial effects, in its present form, the employment of imprisonment, the most widely used of contemporary criminal sanctions, suggests that motives of crude and primitive revenge combine with ignorance to keep such atavistic measures alive. In this context, it may be observed, as expressed by Judge David L. Bazelon in commenting upon such attitudes that: "our personal resolution of the issue of vindictiveness seems to be achieved at the cost of our human capacity to identify with the offender." [23]

Nonetheless, the law, as expressed by such innovations as Juvenile Court Acts, does give increasing recognition to society's responsibility for crime and criminogenesis. It has, however, continued to allow for the collective expression of *ad hoc* emotional reactions in dealing with many forms of criminal activity. Thus "social factors precipitating criminal behavior are seldom considered" in the general legislative penalization of the "heinous" crime. The "gravity of the offense is more frequently the basis of establishing the penalty." [24]

The legal system as a whole has been notoriously indifferent to a controlling concern for economy in the use of coercion, notwithstanding the fact that "given a democratic orientation and a legal system which places a prime value on the individual," negative sanctioning seems subject to rational application only "with the least possible infliction of severe deprivations upon individuals." [25] The subjection of the "criminal" to the "Justice of Punishment" under the "categorical imperative" of the "Penal Law," [26] tends to serve the end of social catharsis rather than epidemiology. The dominant preoccupation is nemesistic; hence "the criminal law stands to the passion of revenge in much the same relation as marriage to the sexual appetite." [27]

APPLICATIONS

When we allow ourselves to go beyond authoritative language to consider what happens in fact, the most salient point for the present purpose is the gap between professed ideals and actual performance. No one doubts that the moral impact of a sanctioning system depends to no trivial extent upon a dependable positive relationship between what is proclaimed and what is done by public authorities.

Gaps Between Professed Ideal and Performance in the Public Control of Business

In some of the most conspicuous and significant areas of American life the requirements of the sanctioning system seem singularly out of touch with what goes on. Consider the structure of the American economy in the light of our long professed policy of protecting competition in the market by controlling trusts. Have our anti-trust measures accomplished the purpose?

In this place we do not propose to pass judgment upon an issue of such complexity. We do, however, take cognizance of the widespread opinion among farmers, workers, and small business men at least, that competition is vanishing. Small units are continually swallowed up by larger units; and to the "man in the street" such cannibalism does not look like competition. We note further that widely publicized observers, many of whom are scholars, share this common view.[28]

The enforcement of the antitrust laws, says Thurman Arnold, has often been transformed into "pure ritual." [29] "Nearly every important 'commodity' " is "controlled by a few great corporations or by a single holding company or by an association of large-scale producers." [30] The "phenomenon known as 'price leadership' became the dominant factor in establishing control on the part of great organizations. . . . [T]he anti-trust laws, instead of breaking up great organizations, served only to make them respectable. . . ." [31] Whether or not the moral atmosphere of such a development is reminiscent of that of the Prohibition Era, it is too readily identified with a "double standard" to be conducive to a healthy regard for contemporary justice through every level of the economic system. Moreover, the situation is not helped when the prosecution of corporate crime, as distinct from the crime of an ordinary criminal defendant, is often flagrantly haphazard. It has been noted by the late Professor Sutherland that "a poor man was . . . sentenced in Indiana, to serve one to seven years in the state prison on conviction of false pretenses; he had listed with a finance company household goods, which he did not own, as a means of securing a loan . . . [and that the] same law applies to corporations but [that] it is seldom used when corporations misrepresent their assets." [32] "Those who are responsible for the system of criminal justice," wrote the late Professor Sutherland, "have been afraid to antagonize businessmen. . . . [T]he most powerful group in medieval society secured relative immunity from punishment by 'benefit of clergy' and now our most powerful group secures relative immunity by 'benefit of business.' " [33]

Perhaps it is not irrelevant to refer to a change that seems to have taken place among economists who analyze the functioning of our institutions. Today we hear less of "competition" or "monopoly" than of categories like "monopolistic competition." A literature has begun to appear that minimizes the importance of any one criterion of competition, such as price flexibility, and emphasizes the improvement of quality, or the multiplication of new products, or the improvement of labor standards.[34] How are these developments to be interpreted? Are we redefining the free market or are we the victims of an intellectual smoke screen that fosters acquiescence in the "silent and implacable march of monopoly capitalism"? Do the books about countervailing power tell us what *is* or what the author *prefers?* Do the books about responsible capitalism tell us what *is* or *ought* to be?

No appraisal of our system of sanction law can side-step the responsibility for confronting these issues. Certainly it cannot be said that the combined efforts of lawyers and economists have provided a picture that clearly justifies the prevailing activities of our sanctioning agencies.

Contradictions Involved in Divorce and Sexual Problems

The appraisal of antitrust is peculiarly treacherous; the assessment of divorce practice is not. Here we are treading on ground that appears solid enough, and that enables us to characterize the current state of affairs without much reserve. To put it bluntly, contemporary divorce practice is characteristically founded upon fraud, collusion, and connivance, and the knowing employment of perjured testimony, if not the actual subornation of perjury. A New

York Grand Jury report is reflective of conditions in many jurisdictions throughout the nation:

> The investigation confirmed what had long been suspected: widespread fraud, perjury, collusion and connivance pervade matrimonial actions of every type. In short, the grand jury is of the opinion that the present practices exude a stench and perpetuate a scandal involving the courts and the community.[35]

Nor is the contemporary criminal prosecution of the sex offender calculated to inspire confidence in our system of justice. It is noted as characteristic of this phenomenon that the

> police force and court officials who attempt to enforce the sex laws, the clergymen and businessmen and every other group in the city which periodically calls for enforcement of the laws—particularly the laws against sexual "perversion"—have given a record of incidences and frequencies in the homosexual which are as high as those of the rest of the social level to which they belong. It is not a matter of individual hypocrisy which leads officials with homosexual histories to become prosecutors of the homosexual activity in the community. They themselves are the victims of the mores, and the public demand that they protect those mores. As long as there are such gaps between the traditional customs and the actual behavior of the population such inconsistencies will continue to exist.[36]

More fundamentally, however, the basic framework within which existing criminal law enforcement proceeds is open to condemnation as morally derelict. As a result of generations of neglect it has ceased to allow for the adequate accommodation of new goals to changing conditions. "To a greater or smaller extent . . ." it is now indisputable, "the criminal law has in essential parts become out of date. Instead of being a living organism, supported by the confidence of all sections of the community and developing according to the practical and ideological needs of the time, it presents itself as a petrified body, unable to cope with the endless variety of problems, created by an ever-changing world and kept alive mainly by tradition, habit and inertia." [37]

The Disrepute of Law

Increasing criminality assumes full meaning only when seen as a function of the cumulative disrepute acquired by law in contemporary society. Crime, particularly when engaged in by "criminal syndicates" can and does make "tremendous profits."[38] Such profits, in turn, can and do pay dividends in political power. It can be said to be common knowledge "that the alliance between politics and the underworld . . . yields not only money but also strong support at the polls."[39] In too many parts of the country this "alliance" remains a going concern to this day.[40] Continued usage seems almost to have endowed such practices with an aura of superficial respectability.

At all events, an authoritative survey of the national scene[41] convinces one in short order that one has "seen corruption boil and bubble till it o'er-run the stew."[42]

The increasing incidence of popular dependence upon our penal system reflects, in its own way, the self-same disrepute.

Our prison population, we have cause to observe, is steadily mounting, far in excess of anything proportionate to the increase in population throughout the country.[43] In the words of a federal prison report the significance of the problem of overcrowded prisons "lies in the fact that the prison populations are increasing at a greater rate than the increase in [the country's] population would warrant."[44] As we have previously observed, the rate of recidivism registered by return to the prison, is startling. In federal institutions, representing the best in the American prison system, for a more or less average year prior to 1955, the rate of recidivists among prisoners receiving sentences of more than one year has been in the neighborhood of 60 percent.[45] It has since risen to 66.6 percent by 1958.[46]

TRENDS

In view of the moral confusion of the current sanctioning scene it is a relief to turn to the past. It has been grim enough to make the present situation look progressive. The principal point can be recapitulated briefly. Our conception of the theological and moral position of the criminal has been undergoing vast redefinition. This transition from the earlier unity of evaluation is substituting new standards of rectitude for old; but older conceptions are deeply embedded in folk culture and enshrined in the legal system.

The modern interpretation of social responsibility toward the offender accepts the duty of care and cure as well as punishment of the "criminal." New institutional machinery has arisen to achieve these ends. The accent is to an increasing extent upon rehabilitation. Actually the system of probation (the suspension of criminal punishment on condition of good conduct) made its first appearance in Massachusetts in 1869 and spread rapidly throughout the industrial world. It went hand in hand with the development of the new philanthropy of social worker guidance under court auspices.[47] Further social preoccupation with the rehabilitation of the individual is expressed in such new institutions as juvenile courts for young offenders and of parole officers intended to aid as well as to keep tab on convicts who are conditionally released. Probation has been coupled in some jurisdictions with state- administered extramural medical and psychological treatment.[48]

Whatever the divagations may be, the trend appears to be toward the recognition that all punishment is "mischief," tolerable only insofar "as it promises to exclude some greater evil," [49] and the consequent repudiation of vengeance or retributive justice in any form.

Divagations are sufficiently glaring, however, to warrant the raising once more of an ancient question: "A man may see how this world goes with no eyes. Look with thine ears. See how yond justice rails upon yond simple thief. Hark, in thine ear. Change places and, handy-dandy, which is the justice, which is the thief?" [50]

8. SANCTIONING MEASURES AND THE SHARING OF WEALTH

SANCTIONING MEASURES cost money. How large is our investment in courthouses, jails, and other institutions specialized to the correctional process? What does it cost to administer our sanctioning system each year? The answers to these questions give us the "out of pocket" cost, as it were, of sanctions. As an offset on the income side must be entered the value of the commodities and services sold in markets outside the court and detention system. We must also take into account the public (and private) funds devoted each year to the support of dependents whose income has been reduced by the withdrawal of an earner from employment. A further item in the balance sheet would include the number of days or productive employment that are lost by the prison population and by those who lose time as litigants or witnesses in criminal proceedings. An additional item is the cost of legal aid to the defendants and of prosecution by the community. We must add to the sanctioning process the capital equipment of all our police forces and the annual expenditure on police work.

It would certainly be desirable to bring these figures into relation to the economic advantages (and disadvantages) that flow from the total outlay on sanctions. What does the community get in return for the resources diverted into the sanctioning system? Obviously the direct damage perpetrated by the current crop of prisoners was done during a previous time period. Our sanctioning system imposes present deprivations upon the deprivers—and also upon all in society who pay the cost of the system. Are there economic gains to offset the burden to the economy as a whole?

We do not typically require that offenders devote themselves to useful work of a kind that would provide restitution to those who suffered direct original damage. However, by incarcerating offenders, we presumably prevent them from committing new violations in the community at large. How significant is this item? Shall we assume that the offenders would repeat their violations at the same rate as formerly? Or that a certain percentage would increase or decrease their rate? In any case what are the economic magnitudes involved? Further, we may estimate the degree of deterrence (or provocation) that current sanctioning activities exert during the immediate time period (and later). Completeness would require us to estimate the economic significance of the deterrence that is operative during the current period as a result of past sanctioning measures.

The discussion to this point has dealt exclusively with the direct economic costs and gains of our system. This does not, however, exhaust every economic repercussion. Failures to enforce conformity are part of the sanctioning process. A comprehensive account of economic consequences would include an estimate of the results of non-enforcement or partial enforcement. Does illegal gambling, for instance, influence living standards and the flow of saving, investment, production and prices? Do failures to enforce antimonopoly legislation affect production, economic concentration, foreign economic relations? These questions are indicative of the problems that arise when a serious attempt is made to consider the impact of sanctions upon our economy.

We have yet to mention what may be the most profound economic effect of all, namely, the influence of sanctioning arrangements upon voluntary conformity. A vast amount of business is directed into new channels (or is conducted in novel ways) as a result of statutes sustained by sanctioning provisions. These measures are not invariably negative. On the contrary many kinds of inducements are written into our codes in the hope of influencing conduct. The affirmative measures are as much part of sanctioning policy as the traditional deprivations in the form of fines and imprisonment. Makers of economic decisions in the processes of production, distribution or consumption are continually adapting their market policies to positive and negative sanctions (like tax write-offs or penalties). An inventory of economic impacts would proceed by sampling the vast stream of economic activity in order to arrive at an estimate of these readjustments.

PRESCRIPTIONS

By examining statutes, regulations, and court decisions we can make ourselves aware of the contradictions that characterize sanctioning policy in economic matters. Such affirmative contradictions and omissions can be expected to breed uncertainties among investors, entrepreneurs and their advisors. Who benefits from such ambiguities as are found in the public control of business? In the absence of appropriate research we cannot answer this question. However, when we turn to the discussion of applications it will be possible to suggest some hypotheses.

Ambiguity of Regulating Standards in Interstate Commerce

The American system puts the responsibility for maintaining a truly national economy upon the Congress. It is unnecessary to read far into the existing body of authoritative prescription to recognize that neither the Congress nor the Supreme Court has gone far toward clarifying primary norms in the regulation of interstate commerce; nor have they perfected an unambiguous body of sanction law in this domain.

Constitutional limitations upon the state regulation of economic activities do not provide explicit and comprehensive guidance for state legislatures. In fact, the basic judicial doctrine is essentially vague. In interstate commerce, "what is ultimate," it has been authoritatively affirmed, "is the principle that one state in its dealings with another may not place itself in a position of economic isolation." [1] In intrastate commerce, state regulation in turn must have a reasonable relationship to a valid legislative purpose,[2] *i.e.*, it must have some rational basis,[3] and must not be "administered by public authority with an evil eye and an unequal hand." [4]

"Since the Constitution vests the power to regulate interstate commerce in the Congress," it can be accurately stated that "there cannot be—or at least there should not be—any doubt as to the overriding authority of Congress to determine what the states may or may not regulate in the field subject to congressional control." [5] No definitive demarcation, however, has been made by Congress on this subject.

Unceasing adjudication has failed to provide state legislatures with concrete and readily applicable standards for their use.[6] Characteristically, deference to local interests has been considerable.[7] The trend of decision, in fact, has been toward "sustaining state regulation formerly regarded as inconsistent with Congress' unexercised power of commerce." [8]

The uncertainties of legislative generalities have long been celebrated in the antitrust field. Providing for the prohibition of every contract, combination, and conspiracy in "restraint of trade or commerce" and beyond this for the prohibition of the monopolization, attempt, combination and conspiracy to monopolize of "any part of the trade or commerce" [9] of the nation, the Sherman Act has been authoritatively viewed as designed to "maintain . . . [the] appropriate freedom [of interstate commerce] in the public interest, [and] to afford protection from the subversion or coercive influences of monopolistic endeavor." [10] Attributed to fear of the "curse of bigness" and the "desire to put an end to great aggregations of capital because of the helplessness of the individual before them," [11] it has won judicial endorsement as a "charter of freedom," appropriately endowed with the requisite "generality and adaptability" to secure its ends.[12] Challenged as devoid of an ascertainable standard of wrongdoing and hence violative of due process of law, it has been sustained as a constitutional exercise of the police power,[13] "although it is safe to say no business man knew what . . . [its standard] was or for that matter, after . . . years of [judicial] interpretation can even now be sure as to what he can lawfully do although he has been advised as to much which is forbidden." [14]

Neither "restraint of trade" nor "monopoly" is defined by statute.[15] The establishment of the illicit practice, moreover, is subject, in each case, to the Rule of Reason, *i.e.*, the requirement that the act sought to be penalized be one involving an interference with commerce which could be characterized as an "*undue* restraint" in the light of all of its effects.[16]

Applied to Section 1 of the Act, a "*per se*" doctrine of illegality has been invoked to establish an apparently certain and conclusive presumption of "unreasonableness" for "business arrangements which fall into the categories of price fixing, market sharing, or boycotts growing out of joint action among competitors. . . ." [17] Whether or not the adoption of the "*per se*" doctrine for a given category of business transactions automatically forecloses inquiry into the reasonableness of the action in an individual case is something on which informed opinion has differed.[18] Whatever the answer, however, such action has served significantly clearer notice as to the bounds of the forbidden than the case law of the unvarnished Rule of Reason, to the point, in fact, where "it could readily be argued that the trouble with Section 1 is not that it is unclear, but that it has become painfully clear, and that the hope of prospective price fixers is not to clarify the trend but to reverse it." [19]

Recent clarification of Section 2 has been provided by making the effects of the business arrangement on the market structure determinative of illegality, rendering inquiry into subjective state of mind irrelevant. "[N]o monopolist," declared Judge Learned Hand, "monopolizes unconscious of what he is doing." [20] A conscious acquisition of the market power to exclude competitors, even if no actual exclusion is effected, suffices to establish illegality under Section 2.[21] Mere size, accordingly, appears as a significant if not controlling criterion. Beyond this, existing doctrine provides no guidance.

Prediction is complicated by the fact that the "vacillation" of the Court in the interpretation of Section 2 has indeed been "considerable." [22] The practitioner, it has been observed, is "often confused in his study of the cases." [23] "What is the amount of business that must be controlled in order to have a monopoly and to have the power to exclude competition?" [24] While it is known that control is measured by the volume of business in a given community, regardless of territorial coverage, the legal safety limits of such "volume" appear unknown. "We do not undertake," declared Mr. Justice Reed, in a response, characteristic of the Supreme Court in this field, "to prescribe any set of percentage figures by which to measure the reasonableness of a corporation's enlargement of its activities by the purchase of the assets of a competitor. The relative effect of percentage command of a market varies with the setting in which that factor is placed." [25]

Is the law, as expressed in Section 2, moreover, designed to protect against restraints, effected by oligopolistic, as distinct from monopolistic business practices? Absent a showing of conspiracy or an attempt to monopolize, the existence of effective legal curbs against oligopolistic practices appears uncertain. It may be said that "[p]ractically speaking there is no law on oligopoly as such." [26] It is plausible, however, to observe that the American Tobacco Company case,[27] affirming convictions for the acquisition of the market power to exclude by the "Big Three" in the tobacco industry, under circumstances no more suggestive of collusion than of the "rational pursuit of individual, oligopolistic interests" may have gone "far in bringing normal oligopoly behavior, hence oligopoly itself, within the compass of the antitrust laws." [28] But essentially we do not know.

Designed to nip the evil in the bud by outright prohibition of the acquisition of all stock or assets whose "effect . . . may be substantially to lessen competition or to tend to create a monopoly," the latest version of the Clayton Act (§ 7) [29] has found occasion to secure authoritative recognition as an effective bar against vertical as well as horizontal mergers of sufficient dimensions,[30] while appearing to continue to suffer from the familiar infirmities of the earlier antitrust laws discussed above. It remains true that "[t]here is great controversy over what prospective anticompetitive effect needs to be shown to establish a violation." [31]

Business and government alike would appear to need more, simpler, clearer and more concrete criteria of such concepts as "restraint of trade," "anti-competitive behavior," "monopoly," and "monopolistic tendency" for optimum functioning.[32]

The field of antitrust legislation is in no ultimate sense of the word the only happy hunting ground of ambiguous standards for primary or sanctioning activities relationg to government and business. "The law," remarked Mr. Justice Holmes (in an antitrust case), "is full of instances where a man's fate depends on his estimating rightly, that is, as the jury subsequently estimates it, some matter of degree." [33] The pattern of judicial response to the passage of legislation regulatory of economic activities is "full of instances where a man's fate depends on his estimating rightly, that is, as the jury subsequently estimates it, some matter of degree," and therefore presents a bewildering and erratic maze.[34]

An extended scope for absolute or strict liability in economic activities has been justified, it appears, upon the assumption that while the maxim "*actus non facit reum nisi mens sit rea* may be admirable in a state of nature, . . . it will not fit the facts of a complex social order." [35] Significantly, however, the specific circumstances under which a more or less absolute or strict criminal liability will be imposed for economic activities, not perceived as "mala in se," has remained uncertain, and in too many instances, a business man must speculate at his peril as to the legality of contemplated economic action. Even reliance upon assurance of the legality of the contemplated economic action, furnished by competent counsel, will not secure his exoneration, if the estimate turns out to be wrong, that is, not "as the jury subsequently estimates" the "matter of degree" involved.[36]

A split of opinion has appeared as to whether reliance on erroneous administrative interpretation of the law will have the same deprivational results. Some courts have viewed acts that objectively violate regulatory legislation but which have been committed with bona fide reliance on administrative assurances of legality as devoid of criminal responsibility in "complicated phases of modern commercial life." [37] Others, however, have viewed such situations as endowed with the requisite quantum of "guilt" to justify criminal prosecution, declaring that the maxim "*ignorantia legis neminem excusat*" constitutes "a stern but inflexible and necessary rule of law that . . . [allows] no exceptions in judicial administration." [38] The "lack of binding effect" of an advisory opinion upon agencies in "non-criminal" matters appears no less oppressive.[39]

In the absence of legislative prescription the uneven pattern of judicial precedent in many state jurisdictions has too often left potential investors in a limbo of uncertainty. The "Reasonable Use" Rule, applied to water litigation, to take one example, has often failed to provide *any* worth-while criteria for prediction. It can be fairly and accurately asserted that in the absence of new legislation or judicial action "no one can say for sure just what rights Michigan irrigators do have." [40]

We have been calling attention to gaps and contradictions in the language of authority, for the most part; but there are other problems. If some legislative prescriptions are lived up to they display the wrong kind of certainty. They constitute barriers to a national economy. An example is the practice, which is on the increase, of imposing residence requirements for the exercise of various occupational skills.[41]

The character of such laws has been well described:

> Restrictions of this sort are not related to the public health, safety, and welfare—the ostensible objectives of licensing laws. Rather, they are, calculated to protect local interests against the competition of persons debarred from being licensed, not because they lack qualifications, but simply because they live on the other side of the highway. The ultimate consequences are at once apparent. No longer can ear be given to the advice "Go west, young man"—or east or north or south. If a young man is hopeful of engaging in a licensed occupation, he must remain right where he is in order to satisfy residence requirements. Especially is this true when apprenticeship is a necessary preliminary to achieving licensed status, for the apprenticeship must be served under one who already possesses the coveted local license. Even a man already trained and licensed in one state may have to cool his heels for a long period if he has the temerity to move to another.[42]

Erratic measures in the field of tax policy constitute deprivations of a nationwide economy, if they are at all effective in operation. Existing statutes impose high personal income taxes on persons of moderate as well as high incomes; [43] and since "[i]n their very early stages new businesses frequently have to depend primarily on the personal resources of the individuals directly interested . . . [h]igh personal income taxes, by curtailing the funds available to these individuals, may effectively prevent the organization of some important new businesses and delay the progress of others"; [44] and present revenue laws provide not only for the high taxation of corporate profits [45] but give "the government a second and substantial bite out of earnings already subjected to the corporate tax," [46] *i.e.,* out of the earnings of the shareholders.

APPLICATIONS

The evidence clearly indicates that uncertainty as to the boundaries of state regulation has resulted in the multiplication of subtle but effective trade barriers by state legislation that has been enacted under the aegis of the state welfare and police power. The sharp division of the Supreme Court in cases in which an overt establishment of a trade barrier by state law has been struck [47] down has tended to create an atmosphere increasingly favorable to the protection of local interests at the cost of varying degrees of economic isolation from other states. State laws, ostensibly designed to secure legitimate local interests without infringing upon the national interest, have too often tended "to operate to the disadvantage of persons, products or commodities coming from sister states, to the advantage of local residents and industries." [48] In practical effect, if not in contemplation of law, "practically every state has placed restrictions and regulations on interstate trade. Every farm product is affected. These regulations and restrictions include discriminatory inspection fees, licenses and taxes, conflicting food grading, labelling and packaging laws, a maze of quarantines, embargoes and other impositions." [49]

It may be asserted, in fact, that "unintentionally, we have been reverting to the establishment of trade walls between states in the fashion that existed at the beginning of our country's history." [50]

Licensing in particular, has often effected irrational interferences with normal business practice, and fostered the exclusion of lawful competitors. The wide latitude allowed by the Supreme Court to the states in the protection of local interests in this context has at times seemed particularly susceptible to bizarre results. In *Kotch* v. *Pilot Commissioners,*[51] experienced pilots had been excluded from the exercise of their skills in navigation through the Mississippi River under a Louisiana law requiring the service of a six months' apprenticeship with a duly certified pilot, appointed by the governor. Incumbent pilots, having "unfettered discretion under the law in selection of apprentices" appeared to have "selected with occasional exception, only [their] . . . relatives and friends. . . ." [52] Speaking through Mr. Justice Black, the Supreme Court, viewing this exclusion "within the framework of . . . [a] long-standing pilotage regulation system," [53] tolerant of such practices, could not "say that . . . [it was] the kind of discrimination which . . . [violated] the equal protection clause of the Fourteenth Amendment." [54] It appeared, therefore, as stated by Mr. Justice Rutledge, in dissent, that "[t]he result of the decision . . . [was] to approve as constitutional, state regulation which [made] admission to the ranks of pilots turn finally on consanguinity." [55]

Opportunities for politically motivated or personally spiteful discrimination in licensing have remained inherent in the general judicial practice by the state courts of sustaining "[a]n ordinance which merely discriminates between different localities of the municipality according to the advantage they may present for the business for which a license is sought, . . . making . . . distinction . . . between places only . . ." [56] and of resolving a doubt as to the existence of unreasonable discrimination in favor of the licensing ordinances under attack.[57] Further opportunities for the abuse of licensing enactments have been inherent in the sporadic and haphazard character of the judicial supervision accorded to licensing practices and hence the basic ineffectiveness of judicial controls, specifically in licensing situations involving necessary judgments as to general proficiency.

The pattern, in brief, has too often flouted the obvious requirements of productivity.

Imperfect Control of Corporate Structure

In general, the result of private scholarship and public inquiry has appeared to support the conclusion that the "development . . . of effective methods . . . for the control of . . . great corporate structures is still very imperfect." [58] In point of fact,

> more than half a century . . . [after the enactment of the first antitrust law], there is pretty general agreement that monopoly is more common and concentrations of economic power more prevalent than at any time in [our] history, and that the trend is gaining momentum. . . . It is true that of the seven or eight industrial giants against whom the Sherman Antitrust Act was aimed in 1890, only two remain in the same form today, but it is also true that America's 250 largest nonfinancial corporations control two thirds of the total industrial wealth of the country.[59]

The antitrust laws have been described in this connection as almost ritualistically directed at the "curse of bigness" and yet as tolerant of combinations, necessitated by the adoption of "specialized techniques essential to producing goods in large enough quantities and at a price low enough so they could be made part of the American standard of living," [60] permitting "men to look at a highly organized and centralized industrial organization and still believe that it was composed of individuals engaged in buying and selling in a free market." [61]

An analysis of what professional economists have to say on the structure of the American economy does not provide a clear answer to questions that can be raised about the impact of government action upon the shape of the economy. We shall not summarize this voluminous literature in this place; rather, we shall reiterate our regret at the failure of scholarship to arrive at a more definitive consensus on processes that have been more exhaustively studied than any institutional relationship in American civilization. Whatever the disappointment, however, it does not make sense to give up the attempt to obtain more thoroughgoing analyses and results.

One conclusion, at least, is beyond serious challenge: the existing situation has been aggravated by the lack of consistent enforcement of such admittedly imperfect sanctions for the public control of business as are at hand.[62]

Another conclusion appears to arise from the study of our efforts to use the courts as agencies of regulation in many fields of economic life. Planning, which is essential to the conservation of such primary and interdependent resources as oil and water, has not in general been capably carried out under the courts. It has long been apparent that the national interest in this field could not be "safeguarded without a long-term program that assigns production quotas, changes production costs, superintends production methods and generally interferes with market procedures." [63] Since our courts as constituted are incapable of engaging in resource exploration and in the protracted supervision of "long-term programs," conservation would seem to call for the substitution of administrative for judicial processes.

Though appropriate administrative bodies, charged with such functions, have received authoritative recognition "as the permanent representatives of the [sovereignty's] regulatory relation to the . . . [resource affected] . . . [possessing] an insight and aptitude which can hardly be matched by judges who are called upon to intervene at fitful intervals," [64] the extension of administrative control over resources has proceeded by fits and starts, and as a rule only in the isolated context of state rather than national action.[65] In the meanwhile, the use of available judicial sanctions has been so unwieldy that present and future interests in production have not been rationally balanced.

The points we have been making about the impact of regulative and sanctioning operations upon economic life are admittedly fragmentary in the extreme. But they point up the vast gaps that exist in the systematic, comprehensive, and objective study of this vital matter. We shall use but one further example; this one we select from the area of direct expenditure for sanctioning activities.

It is possible to supply a few scattered details about the cost of our vast apparatus of courts, correctional institutions, police facilities, and prosecution and defense.[66]

We can, of course, give a few scattered bits of data about the annual cost of known criminal activities.[67]

It would be possible to challenge the existing allocation of resources to sanctioning (and criminal) operations, and to suggest how it can be changed. This enormous task of sanction law will not, however, detain us here, since it requires the prolonged study by competent personnel for which we are pleading. We shall, however, offer one positive comment in the words of the late Professor Dession:

> But perhaps the most conspicuous error in our allocations of resources consists in the disproportionate amount invested in medium and maximum security prisons in contrast with minimum security and outpatient clinic facilities; and in the meager provision in the construction and the budgets of reformatories and prisons for adequate classification and segregation of the different categories of offenders, and for vocational training and productive work. These things affect sentencing, since courts like the rest of us must make do with the resources at hand; and, of course, they affect the development and subsequent careers of those sentenced. Practical prison administrators in the United States seem agreed that a very substantial percentage of those committed to their custody require no such drastic handling. As one advocate of the more extensive use of outpatient clinical treatment of offenders remarked, on contemplating the cost to the community of keeping one offender in institutions for the greater part of his adult life: "That would buy an awful lot of therapy." [68]

It has been observed in this connection that according to "current cost estimates compiled by the Construction Section of the Federal Bureau of Prisons, camps for minimum-custody offenders in rural areas can be constructed at a ceiling cost of $2,000 per inmate. But a maximum-security prison will cost $15,000 per inmate. An average penitentiary, housing 1,200 inmates, will cost approximately $8,500 per inmate, while a medium-security correctional type institution can be constructed for about $5,000 per inmate." [69] Adding to the cost of the prison system "is the widespread failure to provide productive employment for prisoners." [70] Beyond this, our prisons, in their failure to diminish criminal destructiveness "are piling up costs beyond reckoning." [71]

In contrast, it has been noted that open institutions of the type adopted by Sweden for an increasing number of offenders "are far cheaper to establish and operate." [72] and their curb upon criminal destructiveness has seemed significantly more effective.[73]

TRENDS

The diversified and permeating impacts of sanctioning devices upon the national economy cannot be summarized with assurance at present. In part the perplexity arises from the problems that appear when an attempt is made to sum up the main trend relating to the balance between monopoly and competition. Depending upon the historical cross section chosen our results fluctuate sharply. We are aware of the role of concentrated governmental and private control in the colonizing of the Atlantic seaboard. And we are conscious of the continuity of economic influence that has been exerted through the years by various families and institutions.

In the absence of a balanced picture of the fluctuating currents of economic concentration and of the role of sanctions in affecting the processes of production, distribution and consumption, we shall make no effort to characterize the facts. The inference is that more deliberate attention to the development of a body of knowledge in the field of sanction law is necessary if we are to introduce intellectual order into the present relatively chaotic picture.

9. THE IMPACT OF SANCTIONING UPON POWER

THE DISTINGUISHING mark of power is the capacity to impose severe deprivations. Hence we think of the imposition of severe deprivations as a proper monopoly of government and recognize that the public order is undermined to the extent that power gravitates into private hands. We have emphasized the point that all sanctions are not negative; and we can also make the point that all sanctions, even when deprivational, are not necessarily severe. Although power is the distinctive mark of the government there is no implication that institutions which are conventionally called "governments" at any specific time or place limit themselves to the prescribing of norms that are backed by the sole use of severe sanctions. The conception of power is given a restricted "functional" definition in order to preserve its usefulness as a tool of social analysis. Among other things we are able to separate the functions of any conventionally recognized government into power and nonpower components; and, also, to discover the power activities carried on by unauthorized private individuals and agencies.

Severe sanctions are officially used internally against violators of community prescription; and they are also used against external targets in the name of norms shared by the world community. We have limited the scope of the present discussion to the internal sanctioning process in the United States. It is important, however, to recognize what this leaves out. A comprehensive examination of sanction law would look directly at the world arena as a whole and explore the effect of sanctioning arrangements upon the shaping and sharing of values throughout the world. Such a treatment would reach up to and embrace the law of war, and of measures short of war directed by unilateral, multilateral, or organized action against nation states. It would require us to describe the growth of "international criminal law," among other forms of authoritative prescription. We are leaving this vast topic to one side because it is our present intention to focus as sharply as possible upon the national scene in this country and to underline the connection between national norms and the value process occurring among us. In another context we propose to deal exhaustively with the issues that arise when we take the entire world arena as our frame of reference.

It is within the scope of any study of power effects to examine the position of the nation state in the world setting. The internal devices employed for sanctioning purposes have repercussions upon the power position and the power potential of the national unity. Sanctions may function as means of consolidating the strength of the nation or, on the contrary, sanctioning arrangements may sow discord, alienation and weakness. To what extent have the sanctions in the hands of government contributed to the solidarity of the body politic? To what extent have these devices kept alive fundamental divergencies or fanned the flames of disaffection? Do we find that in the present or the past the instruments of public policy employed for sanctioning purposes have fostered civil cleavages and created minority groups receptive to other ideologies than the traditional ideology of the United States?

Another fundamental set of questions relates to the democratic process. Power is widely shared to the extent that popular government is endorsed ideologically and applied in action. Do our santioning methods defend and extend democracy or not?

PRESCRIPTIONS

When we inspect the language of formal authority we find that sanctions are being applied to naturalized citizens in such a manner that they are partially excluded from an equal voice with other citizens. This state of affairs is new. Undoubtedly it is to be interpreted as an effect of the continuing crisis in world affairs upon the traditional hospitality of the nation toward aliens (traditional, that is, until the influence of organized labor, taking advantage of its rising political weight and the insecurities of world politics, began to foster barriers against further immigration).

Restrictions on the rights of naturalized citizens appear to have been effected through the direct and indirect operation of present laws to the point where naturalization cannot be deemed to confer upon the "stranger" a status of full equality with the native born, but effectively only a form of second class citizenship, significantly inferior to that of the born American. While, despite the explicit constitutional establishment of the ineligibility of the naturalized citizen for the presidency, it may well be doubted "that the framers of the Constitution intended to create two classes of citizens, one free and independent, one haltered with a lifetime string tied to its status," [1] subsequent judicial and legislative action appears to have produced just such a result. In the light of contemporary law the judgment of naturalization cannot in fact be taken as final and conclusive; it is subject to nullification at any time during the life of the naturalized citizen on a showing of nonfulfillment by him of at least the statutory conditions precedent to the granting of citizenship on the assumption that "naturalization is a privilege presumably to be given or withheld on such conditions as Congress sees fit." [2]

Fraudulent concealment of the nonfulfillment of such conditions precedent as attachment to the Constitution at the time of the taking of the oath of citizenship has thus repeatedly constituted the basis of revocation of citizenship.[3] Although it has been held that in such cases the government "must sustain the heavy burden which . . . rests upon it . . . by 'clear, unequivocal, and convincing' evidence which does not leave the issue in doubt," [4] fraud in the naturalized citizen's declaration of attachment to the Constitution at the time of admission to citizenship has been allowed to be established by the showing of statements and conduct, indicative of disloyalty, significantly *subsequent* to naturalization.[5] Under such circumstances operative doctrine, notwithstanding occasionally articulate and vigorous judicial opposition,[6] has in fact tended to give a zealous officialdom a *de facto* power of "surveillance of . . . the souls and minds of foreign born citizens. . . ." [7] Prudence, accordingly, will compel a naturalized citizen to shy from action or speech which may rouse official ire or suspicion. The native born citizen is under no comparable disability.

Contemporary legislation has even provided for the revocation of citizenship on a showing of nonfulfillment by the naturalized citizen of what can but be regarded as conditions subsequent. Congress has thus only recently recognized as constituting ground for revocation of naturalization a "refusal on the part of a naturalized citizen within a period of ten years following his naturalization to testify as a witness in any proceeding before a congressional committee" inquiring into allegations of his guilt of subversive activities, provided that such citizen is subsequently "convicted of contempt for such refusal" on the theory that the naturalization must be presumed to have been "procured by concealment of a material fact or by wilful misrepresentation." [8] Congress has further provided in this connection that if any person naturalized after the effective date of the law, assumes, within the five years following his naturalization, membership in an organization which, during alienage, would have barred his admission to citizenship, "it shall be considered prima facie evidence that such person was not attached to the principles of the Constitution . . . at the time of naturalization, and, in the absence of countervailing evidence, it shall be sufficient . . . to authorize the revocation . . . of the order admitting such person to citizenship." [9]

Under such circumstances, too, operative doctrine, until such time as it may be struck down by the courts as unconstitutional, has tended to give a zealous officialdom a *de facto* power of "surveillance of the souls and minds of foreign born citizens" and prudence will compel a naturalized citizen to shy from all manner of actually or potentially hazardous association. The native born citizen is under no comparable disability.

Last, the right to foreign residence by the naturalized citizen has been explicitly limited by providing for forfeiture of nationality for the naturalized citizen who maintains "a continuous residence for three years in the territory of a foreign state of which he was formerly a national or in which the place of his birth is situated . . ." [10] or "a continuous residence for five years in any other foreign state. . . ." [11] The native born citizen is under no comparable disability. Such legislation, moreover, has been sustained over dissent, as a reasonable exercise by the sovereign of the "natural and inherent right" of "expatriation." [12]

The failure by the courts to establish the judgment of naturalization as final and conclusive for all purposes has favored the developing pattern of restrictions on the rights of naturalized citizens. As expressed by Mr. Justice Rutledge, dissenting, in *Knauer* v. *United States:* [13]

> The act of admission [to citizenship] must be taken as final, for any cause which may have existed at that time. Otherwise there cannot but be two classes of citizens, one free and secure except for acts amounting to forfeiture within our tradition; the other conditional, timorous and insecure, because blanketed with the threat that some act, or conduct, not amounting to forfeiture for others, will be taken retroactively to show that some prescribed condition had not been fulfilled and be so adjudged.

The Burden upon Ethnic Minorities

The language of authority gives abundant indication of the historic struggle to maintain the superior position of the white caste in the South by excluding Negroes from the franchise. The sanctioning devices at the disposal of the federal government have been slowly or inadequately applied by judicial tribunals when antidemocratic measures of the kind are challenged. "The most dramatic and probably the most significant, restrictions upon actual exercise of the franchise have been those which exist in the southern states. . . ." [14] The best known form of restriction of this type is probably the poll tax—"a device which had its genesis as an expansion of the suffrage, which was reenacted to bar the Negro from the polls, and the retention of which serves to exclude the poor white." [15] Judicial decision, holding the equal protection clause not to "require absolute equality," [16] has sustained the poll tax against attack as constitutional: "To make payment of poll taxes a prerequisite of voting is not to deny any privilege or immunity protected by the Fourteenth Amendment." [17]

Another form of restriction of this type is educational qualification, ranging from the requirement of mere literacy [18] to that of satisfactory demonstration of skill in constitutional interpretation.[19] Literacy tests have been sustained as constitutional by the courts.[20] The status of tests of constitutional interpretation appears uncertain despite the fact that one federal court decision has invalidated an Alabama provision on a showing of a manifest legislative intent to effect the exclusion of Negroes from the polls and of the subsequent administrative discrimination against prospective Negro voters in reliance on a requirement, deemed vitiated by vagueness, that "only those persons who can 'understand and explain' any article of the Federal Constitution can be registered as electors." [21]

Limitations upon Freedom of Association

Besides access to the franchise an operating essential of democracy is freedom of association. This is at one with the ideology of popular government at many points. There is a presumption in favor of the choices made by individuals; and there is a presumption on behalf of a pluralistic rather than a monolithic structure of society. At the same time the interdependent processes of contemporary civilization often require the curbing of individual and private group initiative. In view of our traditional regard for outspokenness, American policy has been to defend the organizing of private efforts to propagate ideas. We have tried to draw a line between "speech" and "deeds" that damage the public order. There are indications, however, that the constitutional protections of "speech" are not as jealously safeguarded as they were; [22] and, further, that restrictions on the right of association are multiplying.[23]

State legislation, highlighted by the California penalization of "[a]ny person who . . . [o]rganizes . . . , or is or knowingly becomes a member of, any organization . . . to advocate, teach or aid and abet criminal syndicalism" [24] has been sustained as constitutional.[25] Although, in the majority view, the act for which the conviction was obtained under this legislation was "of the nature of a criminal conspiracy," [26] it seems nonetheless that the crime created by the legislature was, in the words of Mr. Justice Brandeis, concurring, "very unlike the old felony of conspiracy or the old misdemeanor of unlawful assembly. The mere act of assisting in forming a society for teaching syndicalism, of becoming a member of it, . . . [was] given the dynamic quality of crime. There . . . [was] guilt although the society . . . [might] not contemplate immediate promulgation of the doctrine.[27] The novelty in the prohibition introduced . . . [was] that the statute . . . [aimed], not at the practice of criminal syndicalism, nor even directly at the preaching of it, but at association with those who propose[d] to preach it." [28]

Perhaps the best known federal legislative action in this sphere is the "Smith Act." This proscribes the knowing and wilful advocacy of the teaching of the duty of "overthrowing or destroying the government of the United States . . . by force or violence," the printing or circulation of written or printed matter to the same end "with the intent to cause the overthrow or destruction of any government in the United States . . . by force or violence," and the organizing or helping or attempting "to organize any society, group or assembly of persons who teach, advocate, or encourage the overthrow or destruction of . . . government by force or violence." [29] Coupled with these prohibitions in the Smith Act is the further prohibition of all manner of conspiracy directed to such ends.[30] The conspiracy clause, coupled with the clause proscribing advocacy have been sustained as constitutionally valid by the Supreme Court in the Dennis case.[31] Faced subsequently "with the question whether . . . [these enactments prohibited] advocacy and teaching of forcible overthrow as an abstract principle, divorced from any effort to instigate action to that end," the Court significantly held "that . . . [they did] not." [32] Thoughtful spectators at contemporary "Smith Act" trials could not help wondering whether this distinction could be effectively maintained in the mind of the jury in the stress of day to day litigation, and whether, therefore "under the Court's approach [as thus formulated] defendants could still be convicted simply for agreeing to talk as distinguished from agreeing to act";[33] whether, in sum, the "Smith Act" trials of the future charging in essence the crimes of organizing or conspiring to advocate would largely resemble the "Smith Act" trials of the past, at least insofar as they would continue to be "prolonged affairs lasting for months. . . . [characterized by] the routine introduction in evidence of massive collections of books, tracts, pamphlets, newspapers, and manifestoes, discussing Communism, Socialism, Capitalism, Feudalism, and governmental institutions in general, which, it is not too much to say, . . . [would continue to be] turgid, diffuse, abstruse and just plain dull . . . [with the live] testimony of witnesses . . . comparatively insignificant."[34] "Guilt or innocence," under such circumstances, one might conclude, with Mr. Justice Black, might well continue to "turn on what Marx or Engels or someone else wrote or advocated as much as a hundred or more years ago."[35]

One might observe that it would seem doubtful, as Mr. Justice Jackson remarked, that convictions obtained under such a law would succeed in sending "Communism . . . to jail with . . . [the] Communists."[36] One might observe too that a continued quest for such convictions might come to depend on the instrumentalities of massive surveillance, more at home in the garrison or garrison-prison state[37] than in the open and free society.[38]

Another prohibition (still part of the Smith Act)[39] addresses itself in its "membership clause" substantially to the penalization of "[whoever] . . . is a member of . . . any . . . society, group, or assembly of persons [organized to] (teach, advocate, or encourage the overthrow . . . of . . . government by force or violence . . .), knowing the purposes thereof."[40] No less dependent than any antecedent clause on turgid and tedious disquisitions upon the politico-literary tracts of by-gone years to secure the necessary proof, the "membership clause" gains distinction from the fact that it marks "the first time that guilt by association was," overtly and without equivocation, "introduced into a federal criminal law. Neither the Sedition Act of 1798 nor the Espionage Acts of 1917 and 1918 included such a conception." [41] In brief, the penalization thus undertaken by the Congress in this instance has at least thus far brought "into our federal criminal law," an acceptance without effective qualification of "the European principle that a man is known by the company he keeps." [42]

The concurrent expansion of the law of conspiracy by federal and state courts alike has, moreover, tended to blur the bounds of permissible activity and association beyond all previously countenanced precedent, "the modern crime of conspiracy . . . [having in this process become] so vague that it almost defies definition."[43] These consequences have been felt with particular rigor in the field, described above,[44] though we have been once again assured on the highest level of judicial authority that henceforward the courts "will view with disfavor attempts to broaden the already pervasive and widesweeping nets of conspiracy prosecutions." [45]

In the same vein is the recent federal law which, whether intentially or otherwise, effects an indirect yet nonetheless unprecedented ideological and political policing of the membership of labor organizations. It does so, ostensibly in the interests of interstate commerce, by denying the benefits of existing labor laws to labor unions whose officers do not file a "non-Communist" affidavit.[46] It has been sustained as constitutional by the courts.[47]

The fact that notwithstanding the intensity of existing legislative preoccupation with security, legislation in this sphere can at times seem peculiarly haphazard is highlighted by the Internal Security Act [48] and the Communist Control Act.[49] Jointly these two enactments have focused upon "Communist-action," "Communist-front," and "Communist-infiltrated" organizations (which, incidentally never emerge from the miasma of legislative verbiage for clear and concrete identification) for a plethora of penalization of their members including the forfeiture of passports, of access to government work and defense facilities, and even employment in "any labor organization as that term is defined in section 152(5) of Title 29" [50] upon the required registration of the groups. Determination of the operative facts of such consequences by administrative "hearing" has been made available. The hearing in turn is subject upon demand to judicial review [51] although significantly under a rule that "the [administrative] findings . . . [that a group fits one such designation], if supported by the preponderance of the evidence shall be conclusive." [52] To say that the end product, decisively more astringent than the Alien and Sedition Act of 1798, reflects more legislative haste than wisdom, is to remark the obvious,[53] though it may be worth noting in passing that what is in essence the "outlawry" of "subversive" groups appears to have advantages to the individual defendant in the form of "notice" of the forbidden not possessed by the conspiracy prosecution under the Smith Act.[54] Both the Internal Security Act and the Communist Control Act are still in the process of challenge in the courts.[55] Their retention in whole or in part will speak for itself. It is safe to assert, however, that the atmosphere of political repression that they have helped to generate will linger long after their invalidation or repeal.

The nationwide institutionalization of the loyalty-security inquisition,[56] previously described, involving—at least in terms of some contemporary consequences—a not inconsiderable impetus toward conformity, completes the picture.[57]

What is then seen in perspective is the "erosion of civil liberties" [58] under law.

"Under ordinary circumstances," it was observed in the late Professor Dession's lucid analysis of this process, "the common criminal is the low man on the social totem pole, and as such the most eligible scapegoat; but in these situations of exceptional tension he does not suffice. Is it any wonder, then, that the unpopular minority group is substituted for the common criminal, and the hard core of the community's attitudes and practice toward the latter is turned on the new scapegoat?" [59]

No effective sanctions appear to have been prescribed to bar the establishment of excessive obstacles against the formation of new parties, or the unfair apportionment of voting districts, by gerrymandering or other means.

The requirement, interposed by state legislation, that political candidates for a "state-wide office" should, regardless of the sum of actual supporters in the State, demonstrate "support not limited to a concentrated locality" as a condition of candidature in an election, appears widespread [60] and is viewed by the courts as "allowable State policy"[61] devoid of remedy[62] despite the apparent "dilution of political rights"[63] of minority parties which may be involved.

The apportionment of voting districts in the interests of ruling political parties, to the prejudice of political minority groups, through the disregard of the principle of "equality in population of districts" as well as by other means under state legislation is a widely recognized abuse. Regardless of the apparent extent of the loss of political rights incurred in such a context, the provision of relief has been viewed by the Supreme Court as "beyond its competence. . . ."[64] "Courts," it has been authoritatively declared in this connection by Mr. Justice Frankfurter, "ought not to enter this political thicket. The remedy for unfairness in districting is to secure State legislatures that will apportion properly or to invoke the ample powers of Congress."[65] In the meantime, such unfair practices continue in the protected "thicket" of politics.

We note nonetheless an increasing popular participation in the power process on the formal level, exemplified by a widening franchise. In contrast the power process, above and below the level of formal authority appears increasingly beyond the bounds of popular control.

Where "only a generation ago advocates of 'pluralism,' . . . pleaded for more recognition of the social groups within the State . . . the question must [now] be raised in all seriousness whether the 'overmighty subjects' of our time—the giant corporations, both of a commercial and noncommercial character . . . have taken over the substance of sovereignty."[66] Certain it is that these " 'overmight subjects' of our time" have exercised increasingly frequent influence and even control over the formal machinery of government,[67] and that they have done so without necessarily reflecting majority interests.[68]

There is no evidence that the growth of such power, buttressed by control of contemporary technology, has been significantly inhibited by legislative or judicial action. It follows that "together with the superficial trend towards democracy and the greater participation of the people in political and international affairs, the technical means by which small groups of people can guide and rule the masses have grown immensely, in quantity and quality."[69]

APPLICATIONS

On the basis of existing research it is not possible to arrive at a satisfactory assessment of how sanctioning methods have strengthened or weakened the position of the United States in world affairs, or affected the effective sharing of power inside the nation.

There are, it is true, some indications of the connection between domestic policy and repercussions abroad. The notorious restrictions against the Negro constitute one of the most vulnerable spots in the armor of the nation during this historical period. The colored peoples of China and Southern Asia, of Africa, and the Pacific Islands are coming into their own as they move toward modernization and toward the rejection of white supremacy in any shape or form.

It is clear that the American people are in rapid transition on matters affecting the power position of ethnic elements. The Negroes in the Northern States are not going to be disfranchised; and they are not going to desist from using their political power to reward the friends of Negro equality and to punish their foes. The eventual outcome will undoubtedly consolidate the nation. Meanwhile there are internal difficulties that add nothing to the immediate strength of America. A serious question is whether we have engineered this transition with as much skill as we are capable. Has the timing of sanctions of various kinds been optimum? Have the courts and other officials waited too long? Have they acted prematurely in various arenas of public policy? Such are the questions deserving of more informed analysis than they have been receiving up to now.

No competent observer of any body politic denies that the institutions specialized to the administration of justice affect the destiny of the whole community. The fragmentary studies now at hand disclose abundant evidence of the frequent failure of our sanctioning arrangements to protect the poor, the obscure, the uneducated, and other rank and file elements in the nation. These findings can be coupled with the uneasy concern of many scholars and men of affairs with the alleged alienation of Americans from modern life. Often this is at the relatively superficial level of concern at the failure of eligible men and women to go to the polls. (There are plausible if not sufficient grounds for arguing that our voting record is an accurate index of general satisfaction.) More penetrating commentators are disturbed by the lack of involvement of broad classes of the population with civic responsibilities. Recently the shocking results of Communist "brain washing" in Korea have given a new sense of reality to those who view the situation with alarm. Why did so few American prisoners try to escape? Why was it possible to guard so many American prisoners with so few soldiers? Why did so many American prisoners cooperate with the enemy against fellow Americans?

We do not ignore the importance of more obvious failures of our sanctioning process, that is to say, our lawlessness. We have referred to the magnitude of the "take" from such illegal activities as gambling, narcotics, prostitution, and racketeering. When it is realized that the income from such illegal activities goes in part to buying protection from political leaders, legislators, executives, judges, police, and other participants in the political process, we begin to sense the magnitude of corruption in American life. Can we say that corruption contributes to democracy at home or to our national security in world affairs?

TRENDS

The same reserve that we have shown in examining the historical impact of sanctions upon other values must be exhibited in regard to power. The record of lawlessness in the occupation and settlement of the continent is of truly fantastic proportions. The critical assessment of these trends is a problem for the future consideration of scholars concerned with sanction law.

PART II. *The Possible Scope and Method of Sanction Law*

10. THE BASIC PROPOSAL

THE PREFERRED values and practices of the American system are sufficiently well understood, whatever the marginal difficulties of definition, to leave no doubt about the principal conclusion of our survey of the sanctioning system. Granted the provisional character of the findings they nevertheless provide ample grounds for the assertion that sanctioning policies are confused, contradictory, and full of danger to the basic goals and institutions of the American community.

SUMMARY OF PROVISIONAL FINDINGS

When we examined the sanctioning system in terms of the criterion of shared respect we came across some explicit denials of basic human equality of right, and a number of discriminations stemming from contradictory doctrines of responsibility. Summary proceedings are resorted to in an unnecessarily large number of instances, and in many cases procedural arrangements have discriminatory consequences. Attention was centered upon the neglected rights of various groups, not only the rights of prisoners or the poor, but of the middle-income—the "average"—American.

In a body politic that aspires toward freedom, shared enlightenment is a crucial value, since decisions depend upon the clarity, comprehensiveness, and realism of available information and estimates of the future. Our appraisal of sanctioning arrangements in matters involving enlightenment produced a notably disturbing result. The language of penal codes lacks self-consistency; and when we investigate the interpretation given to such commonly used terms of art as "criminal" or "civil" it is apparent that these words are misleading guides to public officials and to the community at large. Among other matters our summary drew attention to nondisclosure of pertinent evidence, erratic admission of expert testimony, doubtful results of jury privacy, and dangers resulting from public agitation during the course of trials.

Everyone concedes in theory that in a complex modern commonwealth it is important to draw into government men and women of sufficient skill to cope, with a reasonable expectation of success, with the gigantic problems of the time. When we look at contemporary sanctioning arrangements we discover that our system erects many formal and informal barriers against attracting competent persons into these services. Furthermore, many able individuals are induced to cultivate skill in distorting or defeating justice. High rates of recidivism cast grave doubts upon the level of skill at the disposal of the American sanctioning system.

Americans are committed to attain high levels of safety, comfort, and health throughout the commonwealth. Our examination of the sanctioning system calls attention to the fact that the most violent offenses are precisely the ones with which we cope least successfully. Many standard methods of sanction are administered in ways that contribute to the mental and physical deterioration of those whom they touch.

High among the proclaimed goals of the American society is a community characterized by congeniality and love in immediate personal relations, and in the larger social context by love of country and of other socially contributory groups. We believe in freedom to choose friends and found institutions devoted to fraternal activities. Above all, we are concerned with the family; hence any useful survey of sanctioning informs us of the impact of sanctions upon family relations. To sum up our conclusion: the present system does not give enough consideration to the integrity of family life. Creditor safeguards, for example, often endanger the family unnecessarily; and imprisonment is gratuitously disruptive.

In the American civilization we have a great tradition of concern for rectitude, for the individual's sense of responsibility. We recognize that unless the individual demands of himself that he consider the consequences of his acts for all who have been or can be affected, the whole community is likely to suffer damage. Do sanctioning prescriptions win the approbation of the most responsible members of the American community? The survey emphasizes the fact that we are not united concerning proper standards. We are aware of discrepancies among proclaimed norms of conduct—in sexual matters, for instance—and between public declarations and private practice. Statutory and doctrinal prescriptions often have little support in the community and flagrantly deviate from the actual norms of the American civilization. Do applications of sanction succeed in awakening a sense of responsibility among the targets? The relative failure of the sanctioning system to build responsible character is evident in the subsequent history of so many of those who have been exposed to its ministrations.

The emphasis upon wealth as a value is by overwhelming consent a principal characteristic of the American way of life. At the same time, many national policies aim at sustaining "a healthy middle class" and obviate the possibility that a few rich families will float in splendid isolation in a sea of poverty-stricken fellow citizens. Sanctioning arrangements designed to curb monopoly are in accord with national goals. Nevertheless, any competent survey reveals the gap that separates effective application from broad declarations of purpose. When we look at the economic assets employed in constructing and sustaining our vast apparatus of sanction—courts, police, penal establishments—and try to estimate the result by counting the cost of "crime" and other deviational activity, the balance sheet is neither clear nor, so far as can be ascertained at present, gratifying.

We sum up the investigation reported in Part I in two generalizations about the American system of sanctioning: (1) Many characteristic features of the system contradict the proclaimed goal values of the American commonwealth. (2) Many social consequences of the system are incompatible with the protection and fulfillment of our system of public order.

The purpose of the Part II is to suggest that as a step toward narrowing the gap between value goals and the facts of life it is important to employ the tools of social theory and empirical observation on a scale and with a strategy that has not been sufficiently relied upon to date.

To this end we underline the advantages of viewing sanctioning arrangements contextually as a system within the legal system, which in turn is a component of the American system of public order.

THE INTELLECTUAL TASKS IN CONTEXT

The advantage of seeing the system as a whole is indicated by the picture described in Part I for the intellectual tasks to be performed by anyone who concerns himself with problems of science or policy.

The Clarification of Goal

An advantage of examining a total context is that many situations are disclosed for which general conceptions of goal have received insufficient specification. The interplay between general categories and concrete situations is invariably present in any serious intellectual undertaking. Gaps always remain since no specific enumeration can be sufficiently detailed to provide for all the varied tapestries of human experience. The discipline of confronting generalities with concrete circumstances is itself an important contribution to the attempted solution of any problem pertinent to science or policy.

The act of searching for a specification is a two-way procedure. It may begin with a broad definition and look for specifics, or more technically, "operational indexes" of conceptual terms. Or it may start with a concrete term and consider the clarity with which general definitions enable the detail to be classified.

Perhaps the widest opportunity for misunderstanding arises in interpreting the rectitude value. This comes in part from the practice of "arguing" rather than "designating" when terms are introduced which carry a load of religious, ethical or metaphysical connotation. By rectitude we refer to such subjective events as occur when an individual's ego demands that he take a "responsible" attitude toward the consequences of his own conduct, hence striving to take into account all who are affected. We include such operations as using terms like "right" and "wrong" in stating general standards or in passing judgment on concrete actions. Besides words we include the making of gestures which are recognized as equivalent to uttered or unspoken words that express judgments of right or wrong. Rectitude patterns also refer to acts of conformity or nonconformity with norms of right and wrong.

Although some of our value categories are not in common use as we define them, they present relatively few difficulties of specification. Enlightenment, for instance, in the sense of giving or receiving information about the past and present and of estimating the future, presents few problems; nor do skill, affection, respect, or power.

We referred above to the two-way interplay between concepts and specifics. The examination of goal values also poses another question: how are our preferences "grounded"? For instance, our over-all term for preferred events is "human dignity." How is this justified? In our civilization it is a well-established pattern to "ground" general affirmations of preference for social events by referring them, for example, to God's will or to a metaphysical generalization. It does not come within the scope of the present inquiry to engage in theology or metaphysics. We delimit our task to viewing the sanctioning system from the angle of a set of values which we *postulate* for purposes of the investigation. We postulate human dignity—which we characterize in ways that are widely current in American civilization—and confront these norms with the facts of sanctioning. At the same time we believe that ethicists and moral theologians may be stimulated to consider the panorama presented in Part I from the standpoint of their professional competence.

The Description of Trends

Our inspection of trends in sanctioning calls attention to many areas in which important data have not been gathered by legal and social historians. It is especially surprising to see how little scholarly effort has gone into the study of sanctioning arrangements and their impact upon the evolution of economic institutions. Similarly, it has been more common to declaim about ethical improvement or degradation than to focus upon specific topics such as the historical impact of civil and criminal sanctions upon the general rectitude practices of society. In spite of the recent expansion of professional interest in the study of "the communications revolution" little has been done to relate sanction law to the structure and functioning of mass media or to the trend of serious research.

To go no further in this recapitulation, we make the point that one advantage of a comprehensive picture is that it challenges attention to neglected areas of historical study which, if cultivated, would not only add to general enlightenment but could not fail to provide some guidance to public policy.

The Analysis of Conditions

In this preliminary summary of the sanctioning system we did not single out for systematic treatment the present state of scientific knowledge concerning the principal factors, and factor combinations, which explain the state of the sanctioning process at any given time, or which enable us to account for its consequences. It is, however, impossible for any social scientist to review even this cursory record without taking note of indications that refer to factors which he is accustomed to investigating. Many features of our sanctioning process continue the predispositions regarding sanction that were brought to the New World environment from Europe. Subsequent developments have been influenced to some extent by a later impact of change—or stability—in Europe. Research questions include: under what conditions has the impact of Europe been greatest? When have indigenous conditions had their greatest effect upon sanctioning? For instance, our consideration of respect consequences could not fail to note the shock effect of totalitarian ideologies and techniques upon America, and further, to emphasize the differential responsiveness of communities (*e.g.*, northern, southern, metropolitan, small town) within the United States.

Likewise, it was impossible not to take note of the interplay between sanctioning and social class (and caste). A great many investigations have documented the impact of high, middle, or low degrees of control over such values as wealth, power, respect, rectitude, or skill. More subtle class factors are the "class myths," that is, the comparatively stable images of the self (and others), the conceptions of social practice regarded as advantageous to the self, and sanguine or alarmist expectations regarding the future of the self. Common identities, demands, and expectations are the perspectives current among members of a class; they cannot but influence the prescriptions and applications of any sanctioning process. The confused myth current among middle- and lower-class Americans (in terms of wealth) is a major factor that accounts for the peculiar features of sanctioning in regard to economic values and institutions.

In Part I we often drew incidental attention to the effect of interests upon sanctioning. We understand by an interest a group that does not coincide with a community or a class, and may therefore be smaller than either, or possibly cuts across them. Interests, too, can be divided for classificatory purposes according to dominant value. For instance, each skill group is an interest that includes a great many subgroups possessing somewhat distinctive perspectives. In this context we have ample indication of the significant part played by the bar as a whole, and by the special bars which touch the sanctioning process. A comprehensive inventory of those who play specialized roles in the sanctioning system would include prosecutors, defense counsel, judges, court attendants, officials and staff of penal and correctional organizations, plaintiffs, defendants, witnesses, and many more, including jurors in general, and those who become "professional," thanks to their amenability to the prosecutor's office.

In addition to interest factors our survey alluded on occasion to personality factors. Personality structure is a major constellation of variables, since it refers to the "myth" of the self plus the practices and mechanisms constituting the "technique" of the self. As with a group, an individual's myth is composed of the comparatively stable images of the self (and others), of the practices which are interpreted as preferred values, and of sanguine or apprehensive expectations concerning the self. The self-system is organized at various levels of waking or marginal awareness or of unconscious process. For instance, we referred to "persecutory agitators," and mentioned the unconscious demands present in all personalities—such as destructive aggression—which are held in check in varying degrees, though subject to activation toward collective targets by the sanctioning process.

Any factor enumerated thus far—community, class, interest, personality—can be usefully examined according to the significance of crisis level for impacts upon sanctioning. The continuing crisis in the arena of world politics is a conspicuous instance of how a high level of community crisis can influence sanctioning prescriptions and applications.

The preceding discussion of conditioning factors has made almost no mention of the elements in the total situation with which lawyers and jurists are best acquainted. We refer, of course, to the language of legal discourse, which includes the phrasing of statute and doctrine, of decision, of claims advanced by contending parties, and of justifications offered to and by community decision makers. In a word, it is a question of the "power myth," embracing political doctrine, legal formula, and popular lore. Before we conclude our examination of the sanctioning process it will be abundantly obvious that we attach no little importance to such factors.

In fact, one result of this survey, so far as the authors are concerned, has been to underline the significance of ensuring perpetual interplay between jurisprudential and conventional legal conceptions in the sanctioning system. Hence our recommendation that the field of "sanction law" be distinguished for purposes of teaching, research and policy.

The Projection of Future Developments

One advantage of a comprehensive picture of the sanctioning system is that it challenges the imagination of the observer to anticipate the course of future evolution, assuming for the moment that he himself has no influence over the future sequence of events. Will past trends toward greater or lesser contradiction between goal and performance be continued?

As stated in Part I many past trends have been most gratifying, notably in terms of values and institutions relating to respect, and to some components of well-being, affection, and skill. The situation in regard to enlightenment and rectitude, and to wealth and power, is less satisfactory. When we remind ourselves of the total context of national and world development the future is unmistakably overcast. The most conspicuous doubts refer to the arena of power and the continuing threat of the garrison state as a form of adaptation to the arms crisis in the world arena.

Our review has emphasized the role of factors which as a rule receive insufficient consideration in projecting future probabilities. Perhaps less attention is given to enlightenment variables than to any other category of significant influences, despite the fact that the flow of information provides the basic intelligence upon which all judgments rely, particularly in a complicated and far-reaching society. An "attention framework" is interposed between participants at every successive phase in the endless chains of interaction that comprises the social and hence the sanctioning process. Attention frameworks are among the factors most open to change; and this helps to account for the confusions and contradictions we observe in the sanctioning system. Our mobile and subdividing civilizations diversify attention frameworks, and the result is that the nation is probably less informed today than in simpler times about the impact of deviational conduct upon values and institutions. Unless the flow of comprehensive, timely, and realistic enlightenment is increased during coming years we see little ground for a sanguine view of the future contribution of sanctioning to the realization of American value goals.

We believe that projections into the future enable jurists, policy advisors and policy makers to arrive at more disciplined evaluations of the alternatives open to them.

The Invention and Evaluation of Policy Alternatives

This carries us to the last of the five intellectual tasks which we identify in connection with every problem, hence in regard to sanctions. It is almost impossible for able and well-instructed minds to consider the system of sanctions in context without thinking of new alternatives of policy or of revaluating the relevance of policy alternatives previously proposed. Many practices current in a limited area deserve to be generalized; and many standard policy proposals need to be downgraded, often drastically. As an instance of the latter we take the ancient custom of imprisonment, which fares less and less well as we get acquainted with the impact of prisons upon well-being, affection, rectitude, wealth, power and other values. The survey shows that terms of legal art, like "criminal" and "civil" carry connotations that confuse the sanctioning process. The findings point to the importance of improving intellectual tools to the point that enables policy evaluations to relate expectations to fundamental value demands. Our examination of the context casts doubt upon the adequacy of many established practices which figure in the specialized work of decision making and execution; and, as we shall presently propose, lead to various possible courses of reconstruction.

We believe that the discrepancy between American values and the sanctioning system can be reduced by providing for a comprehensive, accurate, and continuing reappraisal of the total picture. We stress contextuality because of the improvement of judgment in problem solving that comes from subjecting judgment to the discipline of exposure to an inclusive map of goal, trend, condition, projection, and alternative. Hence our basic proposal in the field of sanctioning is to develop the conception and the implications of sanction law as a recognized specialty.

11. THE SANCTIONING PROCESS

THE FIELD of sanction law as we understand it is the entire process of sanctioning. In this chapter we propose an outline of the principal features of the process. It will be unnecessary to begin with a detailed definition of the term *sanction* since it seldom gives rise to controversy save in the marginal cases which are always with us. Sanctions are *patterns of conduct employed in a social context with the expectation of influencing conformity to a norm of the context.* In applying this conception we distinguish among sanctioning processes. First, we consider the "official process" in the United States which is concerned with sanctions conventionally regarded as "legal." Second, we examine "effective" sanctions, including the measures used to maintain norm conformity whether the norms are perceived by the community as official or not. Third, we outline the "authoritative" sanctioning process which is focused upon norms that are both authoritative and controlling. These sanctions are what we mean by "law" in the functional, rather than the conventional sense.

The three sanctioning sequences which concern us will be referred to in terms that bring them close to the complex configurations recognized by lawyers, criminologists, and commentators. Many thousands of social interactions are alluded to in the most cursory fashion in these outlines. It is, however, important to keep in mind the possibility that it will prove rewarding for scientific or policy purposes to concentrate upon the exhaustive examination of specific interactions. Hence it is perhaps initially useful to call attention to the fundamental categories that we have at our disposal for analyzing any interaction in a social process.

SOCIAL INTERACTIONS

A social interaction is an instance of men seeking to maximize values through institutions affecting resources.

Participants (with perspectives)

IDENTITIES

By the expression identity we have reference to the primary ego of any person or group, to the egos which are included with the primary ego to constitute a self, and to the egos that are perceived as other than self. The reader can consider himself: you have terms to designate the "I" "me"; you bracket the members of your family with the "I," "me" as comprising "my (our) family"; and you perceive other families. All who use parallel symbols of reference comprise the group identity.

DEMANDS

The term demand covers all general categories of preferred events (affection, respect, etc.), and all specific practices interpreted as constituting these events.

EXPECTATIONS

We extend the word expectation, or matter-of-fact assumption, to include past, present, and future.

MYTH

The relatively stable components of a system of perspectives are the myth. Individuals have relatively distinctive myths concerning the self as a whole; and individuals share group myths with others.

Doctrines. The most general beliefs are doctrines; they may be theological, metaphysical, or simply personal.

Formula. This term covers the "musts" of conduct, the demands prescribed by the individual to himself alone or by a group source; when the primary prescriptions are violated, the sanctioning prescriptions take over. We refer to the "conscience" of the individual or the "mores" of groups.

Lore (*or miranda*). Lore includes the less formal components of the myth, such as anecdotes.

Base Values

The demands of a participant referred to above are the "scope" values of an individual or group. A base value is an asset (or liability) available to a participant for use in seeking to influence outcomes. Thus an individual or a group occupies an upper, lower, or middle position in a social context in terms of each value.

Strategies

A strategy is a means of using base values in pursuit of value maximization.

Outcomes

The commitments made by an individual or group choice (or decision).

Effects

Short range, middle and remote consequences of an outcome.

THE OFFICIAL PROCESS

We distinguish sanctioning activities at every level according to the seven-fold classification of decision phases which we substitute for the traditional triad of legislative, executive, and judicial.

The Intelligence Phase

We expect the Congress, the legislatures of the fifty States, and the legislative bodies of local government to keep themselves informed of situations in which members of the community suffer value deprivations of sufficient importance to challenge the overriding objectives of American life; and, having established the facts, to consider the probability that such deprivations will occur in the future if present statutes remain unchanged. These projections of future developments depend upon the examination of past trends in the deprivations referred to, and upon the analysis of factors conditioning their occurrence. If future deprivations seem likely to continue on a disturbing scale the legislators are expected to act by "passing a law" which will reduce the future incidence of deprivation or which will provide some amelioration to the lot of the victims. Besides these demands relating to the future it is also customary to expect the legislature to impose counterdeprivations upon the deprivers simply to make them suffer (vengeance).

The formal authority of legislative organs to investigate deprivational situations varies according to the level of government. The investigative competence of the Congress is usually regarded as very broad indeed whenever legislation is alleged to be in view. Under our system a constitutional convention presumably has the widest latitude in seeking information required for constitution making; however, it cannot be truthfully said that constitutional conventions have pressed very far in this direction.

The formal authority of Congress to receive whatever information is offered to it is limited by the shadowy restraints of the separation and division of powers, and by whatever deference is paid to confidentiality.

Among the questions that might be raised, at every level, are: what officials are under an obligation to provide legislatures with information regarding deprivational situations? What members of the community are so obligated? Who, if anyone, has a claim upon the legislature to receive information, or to obtain information? What limitations, if any, bear upon the sanctions that may be employed by legislatures against those who obstruct the gathering of information regarding deprivational situations?

Not only are legislatures empowered to participate in the intelligence process as a possible prelude to legislation, but at the federal level the President reports on the State of the Union; and other executive officials may concur in, or veto, proposed statutes. Questions parallel to those raised in regard to legislators can be asked for other officials.

In the present book our attention is almost exclusively directed to sanctioning problems internal to the United States. However, we take note of the fact that the United States is part of the world arena and accepts many authoritative prescriptions on behalf of systems of public order that go beyond the shores of this country. Among questions pertinent to the internal intelligence function of the United States which also involve the larger scene: what limitations, or facilitations, relate to obtaining information regarding deprivations within the territorial United States? What limitations, or facilitations, relate to the obtaining of such information outside the United States?

The Recommending Phase

Recommending means the promotion of policy. Legislators are officially expected and empowered to go beyond the gathering and assessment of intelligence to advocacy. The President and some other officials, too, are authorized to campaign actively on behalf of sanctioning measures. Private individuals—speaking as independent persons or as spokesmen of organizations—also have wide latitude under the United States system.

The Prescribing Phase

The laying down of general authoritative requirements regarding sanctions is within the province of legislatures, though the scope of sanctioning competence varies sharply by level of government. Several constitutional limitations were explicitly designed in order to narrow the range of policy alternatives open to officials. These limitations are legacies from past struggles with military and despotic power in the history of America and Great Britain.

Historically the United States has directed its greatest sanctioning efforts against other Powers in the arena of world politics. In this connection key questions include: do international prescriptions limit the sanctions that American officials may direct against members of their own community, or other communities? Are there international prescriptions that oblige the United States to prescribe sanctions against members of their own community, or other communities?

The Invoking Phase

Within the prescriptive framework at any given time the American system of sanctioning obliges and permits various participants to make provisional application of prescriptions to concrete circumstances. The invoking function includes the provisional application of sanctions by administrators and administrative agencies subject to review by judicial tribunals.

Any competent examiner of the regulations that fill the gap between statutes and administrative acts learns that regulations often lay down general rules and are therefore prescriptions.

The sanctioning activities of administrators are hedged by devices designed to protect the targets of action from unnecessary value deprivation.

The Application Phase

By this phase we mean the relatively "final" application of prescriptions to concrete circumstances. The situation most closely conforming to this definition is the decision of a court of last resort. However, even more "final" actions are open to "political" officials who are expected to serve as safety valves to relieve protest against the working of the judicial machinery. All courts are structures belonging primarily to the application phase of sanctioning.

The Appraisal Phase

Appraisal is closely connected with intelligence, and it is often economical to consider these two phases at the same time. Strictly speaking, we understand by intelligence the gathering and evaluation of information about deprivational situations which are not yet covered by primary or by sanctioning prescriptions. Intelligence also includes planning which involves projection and policy evaluation. The main thrust of appraisal is retrospective, the task being to weigh the evidence for the success or failure of past sanctioning policies. It is illuminating to regard appraisal as a separate phase of the total process because of the intense resistances that are so often met and which have provoked special authorizations intended to protect the integrity of the process.

Are the sanctions invoked and applied by government officials during a given period in harmony with technical prescriptions and also with the overriding objectives of policy? This is the question to which appraising activities are addressed. Hence appraisers deal with questions of legality, efficiency, and impact. In the strictest sense they do not "invoke" since, for example, they do not issue tickets to individual violators. Rather, they investigate the incidence of deviation from prescribed norms, and summarize the aggregate situation.

Among the many functions legislatures are expected and authorized to discharge is the appraisal of past performance in sanctioning. The main burden of legislative committees is to ride herd on administrative and judicial officers, and to obtain information pertinent to judging degrees of conformity and of success in the implementation of official policy.

Within an administrative structure self-appraisal receives varying degrees of emphasis. Inspectors may be used to obtain pertinent information; and inspectors may operate overtly or covertly. In democratic politics we are especially apprehensive about covert activity, since there are historical grounds for viewing secret police, and particularly political police, with suspicion.

The reports which are formally required of most officials have this in common: they tell what has been done; they say something about results. Both are components of appraisal.

The Terminating Phase

Termination brings sanctioning prescriptions to an end, and puts a final date upon arrangements made in pursuance of prescriptions. The former activity is usually merged among the many tasks of legislative bodies, although special agencies are sometimes empowered to declare an end to a body of rules and to dissolve themselves. The largest network of special organs dealing with termination handles the specific arrangements made within the framework of community prescription. Parole boards are conspicuous examples.

THE EFFECTIVE PROCESS

The official process of sanctioning provides a sketch of what government officials are supposed to do when they act within the limits of formal authority. Informed persons are well aware that official prescriptions are not necessarily reflected in the actual process. Sanction law, as we conceive it, goes beyond formalities to actualities. Hence, the next step is the effective process of sanction since in investigating any concrete context the problem is to discover how the formal process is related to wider contexts.

The Pre-arena Stage

By pre-arena events we refer to events that occur before the formal decision makers of the community are involved in a sanctioning sequence. An exhaustive study would trace these sequences in detail for representative cases leading up to the involvement of government officials at every stage of the seven phases mentioned previously. It must suffice at present to provide brief indications of how the process can be fruitfully examined.

PRE-INTELLIGENCE

The Original Situation of Alleged Deprivation. The situation referred to as "original" is a state of affairs which is subsequently called "deprivational" by someone in an official arena.

We consider the intelligence phase of the sanctioning process first, taking a single example in the exposition. A legislative committee is told that the disposal of radioactive waste constitutes a health hazard against which existing prescriptions provide neither protection nor remedy. Situations may be cited in which factories located at the edge of metropolitan areas or lying upstream have discharged radioactive waste in forms that contaminated the water used by thousands of people. By "original situations" in this context we mean the factual circumstances called to the notice of the legislature, as these circumstances are viewed from the standpoint of a scientific observer properly equipped for observation. For example: who first felt that he or someone with whom he was identified was subject to potential or actual deprivation from radioactive waste? In terms of what value, if any, besides well-being? Inflicted by the use of what practice, such as the pouring of waste into running streams of water which brought about contamination?

The Preparation of Presentations. The scientific observer who studies pre-arena events sees the significant part that is often played in the careful preparation of statements addressed to community decision makers. Before appearing before legislative committees, for instance, private parties may have turned to lawyers who in turn consulted with physicists and public health experts. Probably the experts provided information about past and potential dangers resulting from faulty disposal methods, and proposed standard regulations for the disposition of radioactive residues, including prompt sanctioning measures in case of nonconformity.[1]

Parallel Situations. An important question in connection with the pre-arena stage is whether situations of deprivation exist which are practically identical with the original situations mentioned above, save that they initiated no sequence of activity that eventually brought the alleged deprivations to the notice of community decision makers.[2] Scientific study may show, for example, that many individuals and communities which were threatened or overtly damaged by radioactive waste did not appeal to legislatures.

Other Salient Features. The purpose of this seemingly catch-all category is to provide a place for the study of conditioning or trend factors pertinent to the sanctioning process. Why did community A or individuals A, A′ . . . reach the legislature with a demand which others did not carry that far? Perhaps the culture of the community was important, since community A may have been native American; other communities, perhaps, were recently populated from south of the border. Community A may have had more upper class physicists and physicians, and more enlightened community leaders than neighboring areas. Community A may have had potent industrial interests concerned with protecting their personnel and their investment. The personality factor may have been significant since strong, self-confident public spirited democratic individuals may have been relatively abundant in community A.

Possibly, too, crisis factors mattered greatly, since community A might have been especially sanguine of its future, unless disturbing developments—like health hazards—put road blocks in the way.

Trend analysis may show that radioactive hazards exhibited an explosive curve in recent years; thus the burst of "social control" activity at a particular time becomes more intelligible.

PRE-RECOMMENDING

The Original Situation of Alleged Deprivation. We keep to the type of situation mentioned above. We are now interested in what led up to promotional activity before the legislature, or by officials, *e.g.*, agitational speeches to or by legislators.

The Preparation of Presentations. Students of human affairs know that those who experience what they consider to be deprivation, or who become aware of situations that they believe to be deprivational, often leap over the intelligence phase and at once begin to denounce and demand. The history of legislation often shows that pressure group and political party programs are developed long before an issue becomes a burning question on the calendar of the Congress or of state legislatures.

Sanctioning policies have often had agitational histories extending over many years before legislators became seriously concerned in getting results. The spread of probation and juvenile court facilities are familiar instances. The revision of the Federal Administrative Procedure Act, by contrast, was accomplished with a minimum of public agitation, the whole enterprise being conducted by bar and bench in the course of a low-pressure campaign.

More familiar are sensational campaigns to impose penalties of great severity upon sex offenders, kidnappers, saboteurs, or other groups who have recently figured in the headlines.

Parallel Situations. An interesting problem in this context is why seemingly identical circumstances fail to ignite chains of agitation.

Other Salient Features. The sets of factors referred to above can be explored to account for the differences mentioned.

PRE-PRESCRIBING

The point of interest here is, for instance, legislation; and the study of original situations, preparation, and parallels will show that nearly identical sequences may or may not lead up to actual legislation. Hence, it is worth while to search for the factors that account for the difference.

PRE-INVOKING

The Original Situation of Alleged Deprivation. In view of the vast network of prescriptions nominally in effect in any jurisdiction a major question relates to the original situations out of which come acts of invocation. It is easier to follow the successive steps within the process once an official act has occurred than to describe original situations. Thus we can describe the drop-out between the traffic tickets initially issued—or complaints against debtors, landlords, and other groups—and later stages of administration.

From the standpoint of public policy the most illuminating question is "who complains?" And especially who utilizes a form of complaint that, if accepted by a community decision maker, will carry a sanction with it that is high—or low—if compared by a scientific observer with original circumstances.

The Preparation of Prescriptions. When private associations take the first step in litigation and file a complaint or instigate public officials to act, the case has often gone through elaborate preparatory stages. At the opposite extreme are initiatives taken by police officers who act promptly in the presence of an act which unexpectedly occurs before their eyes, and which also takes the other party by surprise.

Parallel Situations. Experienced observers make various estimates of the number of fact-situations which involve deprivations that lead to no official acts of invocation. In the absence of systematic research we can only say at present that not more than 10 percent and often not as many as 1 percent of certain kinds of situations are carried to the invoking arena.

Many cases are settled by private negotiation or by private arbitration. In other instances, however, the deprived party feels too weak to ask for a sanction which might deter or prevent future deprivations. From medical sources we learn, for example, that many more women suffer from acts of physical—to say nothing of mental—cruelty than initiate formal complaints against a depriving husband or child.

Systematic study of all value-institution contexts would provide the base line for any given period from which the entire legal, and especially the sanctioning system could be appraised.

Other Salient Features. Although such factors are present in all contexts we lay special stress upon "expectations and demands regarding sanctions" as factors affecting what is done or left undone by participants in pre-invoking activities. Intensive study of individual cases often shows that the demand to proceed against a particular party is strongly motivated by a demand for vengeance; or, more broadly, for demands to see that a particular kind and magnitude of deprivation is imposed. It will probably be possible in the course of scientific investigations to isolate the parties who when examined at the pre-arena stage are more sanction-oriented than they become at a later stage. Probably, too, we can isolate—especially among parties experienced in litigation—individuals having a minimum concern for punitive action, and showing great concern for sanctions which are related to deterrence, restitution and the like.

PRE-APPLICATION

Original Situations of Alleged Deprivation. Typically we are here focused upon the background of the litigation that reaches a judicial tribunal, or a controversy that comes before administrators.

Preparation of Presentations. At what stage, for instance, does a party turn to a lawyer for assistance? By what sequence of events does he choose a legal counsel? What other professional or unprofessional individuals are consulted first? What is the interplay between client and counsel prior to formal invocation?

Parallel Situations. The usual problems come up here: How many situations do not lead to litigation, even though in the beginning they appear to be substantially identical with those that do?

Other Salient Features. What are the significant perspectives that client and counsel have of one another, and of the judicial process, and how do these influence their early relationships?

PRE-APPRAISAL

Original Situations. We are interested in a somewhat wider range of situations in the pre-appraisal context than in previous parts of the analysis. Pre-appraisal of official sanctioning activities does not necessarily begin, even among private persons, with the experiencing of alleged deprivation. Sanctioning appraisals are often initiated by civic organizations who begin with no intention of studying sanctions, but who find that sanctioning is a highly pertinent part of a general investigation of efficiency in government.

Preparation of Presentations. In some metropolitan areas private "crime commissions" have hired competent staffs to prepare reports that assess the integrity, competence, and impact of the police, the courts, and the agencies concerned with penal or corrective activities. At the other extreme are "letters to the editor" or other denunciations—or fulsome endorsements—of sanctioning officials which rely upon little observation and much private fantasy.

Parallel Situations. It is highly pertinent to our understanding of the sanctioning process to match those editors, reporters, or civic figures who do engage in appraisal activities with "identical" individuals and groups who take no part in operations of the kind.

Other Salient Features. Because of our present emphasis upon the importance of private appraisal we offer some suggestions to help account for the fact that sanctioning machinery receives less systematic professional and academic attention than one might suppose in view of the significant role that it plays in affecting the tension level of the body politic. We have very few criminologists; and schools of law do not regard it as part of their task to conduct regular surveys of the local state of sanction law administration. Presumably the bar associations recognize a responsibility in this connection. But it is well known that systematic and competent surveys of sanctioning operations are not typically made by these associations.[3] We cannot at this point summarize all the explanations that have been offered of the laxity of the bar. In general it can be said that there appears to be some reluctance to become concerned with "criminal" matters. It is no secret that lawyers, by and large, respect other branches of practice more than the criminal area, and no doubt some of this disesteem acts as an obstacle to the mobilization of bar committees to probe into prisons and related institutions. Field work is essential to a reliable report on conditions; and many lawyers prefer types of committee work where preparations can be made in a law library without sacrificing the time required for visits to remote locations. It is also obvious that the facts are not always on the surface since prison authorities, for instance, are not invariably willing to disclose everything freely to "snoopers," especially if much of the evidence reflects against them. Prison authorities are fully cognizant of the dangers connected with a brief inquiry conducted by amateurs. The inexperienced person often "falls for" the complaints of glib individuals who have private scores to settle with public officials. Lawyers with a narrow experience handling criminals may themselves fall victim to these stories. Lawyers are often keen enough to recognize that unless they have subpoena power they may be victimized; and no attorney feels comfortable in such a position. Moreover, the lawyer is not professionally trained to use the methods of investigation that have been devised by social anthropologists, sociologists, psychologists and other students of behavior. Typically he does not want to invest the man hours required to make a thorough exploration by all the methods available to the scientists of behavior.

Despite the importance of such obstacles it should be pointed out that in many jurisdictions bar association committees have performed invaluable service in exposing deplorable conditions and introducing a healthier state of affairs. Often counsel has learned to work in harmony with experts from other fields who supply the skills or motivations that are lacking among local lawyers.

PRE-TERMINATION

Original Situations. The pre-arena stages that culminate in terminating a prescription or a specific arrangement do not necessarily begin in a situation perceived as deprivational. For instance, scholars who are reviewing legal codes may give publicity to obsolete statutes and propose repeal, or call attention to the end date of agreements which have been overlooked. However, it often happens that appraisals are undertaken because someone believes himself disadvantaged by a sanctioning prescription, or by a concrete application such as a prison sentence.

Preparation of Presentations. Requests that are brought before parole boards vary at the preparatory stage from the masterpieces produced by the "Philadelphia lawyers" among prisoners to the sketchy offerings by potential parolees who take little interest in the procedure.

Parallel Situations. Attention is occasionally called to the fact that many obsolete or obsolescent prescriptions come to the attention of lawyers, legal scholars, and others without precipitating any action on behalf of termination. It is also true that many individuals fail to take even the minimum of initiative required to put an end to sanctioning arrangements that in many ways work to their disadvantage.

Other Salient Features. As we shall have occasion to state with more emphasis presently, the seeming reluctance of individuals to take even the tiny steps that in some circumstances would presently terminate the burden of a negative sanction can often be explained by a fully contextual investigation of the "hidden indulgences" that they obtain from what formally appears to be a state of deprivation. Imprisonment, for example, brings the convict into a subcommunity that constitutes a minority culture that may presently become as attractive to the participants as many patients find the environment of a hospital to be.

The Arena Stage

The arena stage includes events that occur during the time when community decision makers are primarily involved in a sanctioning process.

PRE-OUTCOME

The first series of events extends from the time when the decision maker is brought into the picture until his decision is made. At a representative intelligence phase, for instance, this might extend from the time that a commission of factual inquiry begins to hear testimony to the moment when hearings are terminated and the committee considers its final report. A typical *pre-outcome* recommending sequence begins when the committee on platform of a political party receives proposals—concerning antimonopoly sanctions, for instance—and the beginning of the committee's final deliberations. When the outcome is a referendum vote by an electorate the pre-prescription phase may be dated from the filing of the signatures requesting a referendum and the calling of a special election. The pre-outcome period in connection with invocation can be very short, indeed, as when the traffic officer flags one down and tolerates a minimum of explanation. Administrative and court proceedings are very formal in receiving complaints and moving through successive steps to the consideration of the ultimate decision. An official inspection, as part of pre-outcome appraisal, may go forward in a methodical manner; and the applicant for a pardon may be granted sufficient time to present arguments for executive clemency.[4]

Intra-arena. Some events impinge directly upon the focus of attention of decision makers during the pre-outcome phase. For all the official role players mentioned above—members of the electorate, and so on—*intra-arena* events are those brought to their notice in a formal setting. Since the interactions in some of these contexts are of highly specialized interest to lawyers it may be useful to indicate how to apply more intensive interaction analysis.

Participants. In each situation we distinguish between decision makers and others. Often roles are numerous and explicitly named, as at the application phase when plaintiff, defendant, counsel, and witnesses, for example, are recognized members of the cast. Besides such identification terms there are many informal labels that occur in local usage; and participants can be meaningfully distinguished by the scientific observer according to scope and base values.

Claims. Plaintiffs and defendants put forward formal demands upon decision makers to make values available to them or to cut down the values of others. Although the intelligence phase is concerned with factual statements and future estimates, it is not to be overlooked that more than the transmission of enlightenment is at stake. If the declarations of one set of witnesses concerning the effect of fluoridation on tooth decay are accepted by a legislative committee, the value consequences for the witnesses whose testimony is rejected may be more than trivial. The rejection may be regarded as a substantial deprivation of respect, and there may be repercussions upon income and other values. Promising political careers may be blocked. None of these are sanctions in any formal sense of our definition, yet a realistic account of the total decision process will not fail to bring them into view.

Justifications. Whatever the demands made upon decision makers it is presented in a context of justification. Because of the role of the legal formula in community myth we expect to find legalistic *arguments* cropping out at all phases of sanctioning. Intelligence activities can be involved in controversies over the proper limits upon the subpoena power of Congress. Recommendations having to do with sanction, such as demands to modify the definition of treason and to add severity to penalties, will invariably touch upon constitutional provisions. Prescriptive functions are open to the argument that some procedural error, such as failure to require a proper majority, has been made. At the application level the appeal to legalistic argument is at its climax, although pre-outcome conflicts are frequent at the invoking, appraising, and terminating phases. Besides arguments, participants put forward *supports* of a factual nature purporting to corroborate the chief assertions upon which they rely. Some of the participants present *factual summaries* of original situations. The summaries given to decision makers are not to be relied upon for scientific accuracy. It is generally taken for granted that plaintiffs and defendants, for instance, "tell the truth optimistically" about the past, optimistically, that is, in the hope of influencing the eventual response of judge and jury. Deliberate or inadvertent distortion is particularly common among the propagandists who figure in the recommending process.

Co-arena. The *co-arena* event is any event that acts upon the decision maker outside official arenas. A marginal situation is the judge's chambers. But we have in mind all the events presented at the focus of attention of judge or jurors up to the time that they "make the decision." Included are all the people whom they see outside the courtroom; and all the content of the communication media to which they are exposed.

Co-arena events pertinent to litigation embrace pressure group activities designed to influence the outcome. Obviously progaganda and public relations manipulations can affect the content of media read or viewed by judges, even though the latter are unaware what lies behind the news or editorial items. The scientific observer who is searching for factors that may in fact explain what happens in a sanctioning process will not omit to take possibilities of this kind into consideration.

OUTCOME

The final commitment by decision makers is the "outcome." A commission of inquiry votes to accept a specific document as its final report; a committee on platform agrees upon its recommendations and adds a vigorous argument for its proposals; votes are cast on referendum measures; a grand jury returns an indictment; a court makes its decision; an inspector writes and submits his report; the executive issues a pardon.

For many purposes it is important to go outside the final event and to use the conception of outcome to include all deliberative acts from the time that inquiry is closed to the vote. The Supreme Court, for instance, may interpose months of delay between the pre-outcome stage and "decision day" for a given controversy. During this time the justices may consider their decision privately, or in discussions that include all members of the tribunal. Clerks may prepare tentative drafts of opinion and argue the matter among themselves, with results that filter into the total flow of deliberation.

One of the most dramatic outcome stages in the sanctioning process is jury deliberation; and research has been steadily closing in upon this institution. It is clear, for example, that the relative value position of the jurors in the larger community has an important bearing upon the influence that each juror exerts upon the final result. The image that women jurors have of themselves, and that male jurors have of women, affects the role of the sex groups in the process.[5]

Outcomes are sometimes analyzable into the *decision* in the narrow sense of "yes" or "no" to the claims advanced by parties to a controversy, and *opinion* which elaborates the justifications alleged for the decision. Intelligence reports, for example, may be able to sum up the essential facts in a few sentences, and devote the main body of a report to evaluating the credibility of the sources. Recommendations as finally formulated may make no direct mention of rejected alternatives, since the recommenders may think that the acceptance of their own proposals would be jeopardized by giving further prominence to the opposition. The same tactic is commonly used in the language of constitutional documents and statutes, although the introductory matter may declare intentions that are indirect rebuttals of the arguments put forward for defeated viewpoints. Documents that invoke a prescription in a set of concrete circumstances often detail at great length the alleged violations perpetrated by the party against whom action is taken. When direct bargaining breaks down eventual invocations may present arguments and counterarguments in profusion. At the application stage the decision may be blunt: "guilty," "not guilty." "Judgment for the plaintiff (or the defendant)." Appellate courts are usually expected to justify themselves in an opinion; and the result is a rising tide of judicial rhetoric that presents a formidable problem of assimilation to our digesting services.

The decision and the opinion are responses that indulge or deprive all who have demanded one outcome rather than another, or have urged one justification over another. Since we are speaking of public officials the response is always an act of value indulgence or deprivation in terms of power, since the decision places power as a base value at the disposal of some parties while refusing to make it available to others, or actively employs power to the disadvantage of certain parties. The claims put forward by a political party, a pressure group, or a party to litigation may be phrased in terms of a single value. It is common to allege that the aim is to elevate public morals (rectitude); but detailed examination usually shows that all values are sought in varying degree. Hence the true outcome is not fully expressed in the formal decision for or against the defendant.

We also distinguish among those who are indulged or deprived by taking note of the directness or indirectness of their participation in pre-outcome activities. Campaigns to promote legislation, for instance, may involve thousands of contributors who provide money and other forms of assistance. The spokesmen of a movement who appear before political conventions or legislative committees are more directly involved than the rank and file; but the rank and file of the organization do not necessarily include all members of the community who are in favor of a given legislative proposal, or against it. These unorganized and indirect participants are also among those who are indulged or deprived by the result.

To the legal specialist many complex inferences may be made

about the future effects of a case upon the predispositions of a court to accept or reject various arguments for or against types of claims which may be put forward on behalf of particular kinds of parties. For instance, the analyst will observe that some arguments advanced in the briefs may be passed over with no mention whatsoever. The judges of a court may in fact add justifications which they impute to the parties but which are in fact their own. The presence or absence of citations to certain previous cases, or to social and economic sources, may be construed by the trained lawyer as reflecting the orientation of specific justices or of the whole court.

In assessing the factors that help to explain the response of a given set of decision makers particular attention is given to the final alignment, and to positions taken at successive stages of pre-arena and pre-outcome events. Comparative studies indicate the importance of the "initiating role" and also of the "pivotal role" in decision sequences. Initiators may, for instance, handicap the prospective success of a given outcome because of the negative evaluations that prevail toward them. Pivots are especially significant, since some constituencies or officials occupy "swing positions" among the shifting membership of various coalitions.

Only when one looks back at a closed incident can one say that the final outcome stage has been reached, since any contemporary situation may be stretched through many new arenas. Our governmental and legal system is peculiarly rich in opportunities for appeal, retrial, and pardon; for "further study" by agencies of intelligence and appraisal; or for postponement and reconsideration at any decision phase. In connection with "criminal" or "corrective" cases the following captions suggest the "outcomes within application outcomes" that may multiply situations of interaction between officials and various parties: *Sentencing, Probation, Clemency*. Earlier in the sequence are "outcomes within invocation outcomes": *Accusation, Arrest, Detention, Release, Prosecution, Defense,* each of which may be split into component interactions capable of being described in terms of the basic categories (participant, base values, strategy, outcome, effect). As our presentation makes clear, the significant social reality is composed of interactions, and the conventional labels used to designate them require continual revalidation or amendment before they can be used for scientific purposes.

The Post-arena Stage

We are concerned with events occurring after the outcome stage which are "effects" of the sanctioning process to date. (As implied above, further official stages may be regarded as complications of the arena stage.) Post-outcome effects do not include the immediate activities precipitated by a decision, such as release from incarceration or assessment of costs against a loser. Post-arena effects can as usual be described in both value and institution terms, and for specific participants or the social aggregate. So far as specific participants are concerned it is important to trace the impact of sanctions upon their pre- and co-sanctioning value position. Sometimes so many specific participants are affected that we can identify an aggregate impact rather quickly. For instance, it is possible to date the changed position of Negroes in reference to respect, skill, and certain other values from a few leading decisions.

We are more accustomed to think of institutional practice than of value effects. Lawyers, for example, have a high professional stake in anticipating the way in which such specific patterns as vulnerability to a particular legal doctrine is affected by one or by a run of decisions. Careful examination shows that institutional structures may be modified as a consequence of decision. It is commonly believed, for instance, that many judicial institutions are becoming more "investigative" as a result of giving more scope to the testimony of experts. Some administrative tribunals, on the other hand, seem to be becoming more "litigious" as conventional rules of evidence seep into their deliberations, and as they create "precedents" which are more and more referred to.

What is ultimately involved is the entire system of public order and the ever-present question about the sanctioning process is whether it protects or fulfills the principal goal values of the system and maintains and adapts the preferred institutions by which values are shaped and shared. Called for is combined intelligence and appraisal functions which confront the conventional image of sanctioning with images that have been disciplined by appropriate methods of inquiry.

THE AUTHORITATIVE PROCESS

In the light of the preceding outlines of official and effective sanctioning it is possible to clarify the meaning of the legal process of sanctioning which, for shorthand purposes, we call authoritative. Obviously we agree with all who reject the idea that "law" can be usefully studied as a branch of linguistics or of literature. Not words alone suffice; words must be related to deeds. A law is here conceived to be an authoritative and controlling practice. We refer to a pattern of action as authoritative when it is regarded as formally required. A pattern is controlling when it is effective. Hence we do not assume that the sentences found in the Statutes at Large are "law," although we may very well agree that they are "authoritative." The final classification depends upon an inquiry into the concrete situations to which a statement nominally applies. Obviously there is "no law" if the authoritative rule is disregarded. If it is important to be precise an operational definition can be adopted which specifies how many instances of conformity must be discovered before the term "law" is applicable. The broad gradation is:

1. Obsolete. No one expects the words to be invoked.

2. Obsolescent. The words have not been invoked, even in private argument, for many years, but it is admitted that a slight possibility exists that they might be appealed to once more.

3. Superannuated. The prescription is not complied with, but is occasionally appealed to, or even enforced, despite general surprise or even shock.

4. Enforced. Patterns of compliance, enforcement, and approval.

Much noncompliance combined with little effort at enforcement; also (1) noncompliance is approved (by the population as a whole, or by people segregated in particular territories; by the elite classes, mid-elite or rank and file), or (2) noncompliance is disapproved (as above), or (3) enforcement is approved (as above), or (4) enforcement is disapproved (as above).

Much noncompliance is combined with much effort at enforcement; also (1), (2), (3), (4), as above; or

Little noncompliance is combined with little effort at enforcement; also (1), (2), (3), (4), as above; or

Little noncompliance is combined with much effort at enforcement, or (1), (2), (3), (4), as above.

5. Compliance. Total compliance with no efforts to enforce (substantial unanimity).

Our definition of law has clearly shown that we look upon the legal process as part of the decision process. Power, we emphasize, is authoritative or controlling. When power is authoritative and controlling it is law; when power is controlling and not authoritative it is "naked power"; when it is authoritative and not controlling, it is "pretended." [6]

SANCTIONING AS A SYSTEM

To speak of a system means that the parts of the whole reciprocally affect one another in regular ways. Changes may be introduced from outside the system; or changes can be "built in" to the system. In either case the modification of a "part" gives rise to regular sequences of adaptation which are characteristic features of the whole.

There are many indications that American sanctioning arrangements can be fruitfully considered as comprising a system, at least during any selected cross section in time.[7] For instance, it can often be demonstrated that innovations occurring at any phase of the total process are regularly followed by innovations in the same phase elsewhere in the nation.

Consider the intelligence phase, for example. Inquiries into subversive activities at the federal level usually spark a sequence of similar inquiries at the state and local levels. Investigation may show that initiatives that arise in the metropolitan centers move horizontally to one another, and upward to state and federal jurisdictions. Even more detailed investigation may identify other paths within the system such as East-West or West-East for special categories of sanctioning investigation.[8] Of particular interest to us is how research in the historical, social, and behavioral sciences enters into the stream of intelligence regarding sanctions.[9] The fact is that the American sanctioning system is part of a larger system that includes Western Europe, and more recently Eastern Europe.[10] Legislative reference bureaus, including the Library of Congress, are specialized structures that speed the tempo of modern intelligence activities that relate to sanctions.[11]

Regular patterns of response to innovation can be traced at the recommending phase of the American system. This is especially true since the growth of organizations that promote uniform codes dealing with many topics. Bar associations are an established network of relatively "low pressure" promotion of change. Among the most active centers for new projects appear to be the American Bar Association, the Association of the Bar of the City of New York, and the American Judicature Society. Channels of diffusion for promotional activity are closely related to intelligence networks; but they are modified by the many factors that give distinctiveness to local jurisdictions.[12]

Since the prescribing function is presumably less responsive to immediate changes than either intelligence or recommending, the characteristic pattern of innovation is relatively slow. Nevertheless, the tempo has probably become more rapid in recent years. There are in fact some rather startling instances of speed.

Waves of indictment and arrest often begin in a great metropolitan center, receive vast publicity, and spread throughout the nation.[13]

Similarly the news of convictions obtained in one major jurisdiction regularly precipitate convictions elsewhere for the same alleged offenses.

The spread of appraisal activities in the sanctioning field follows fairly discernible channels. "Hoover Commissions" on the efficiency of government ignite a blaze of "Little Hoover Commissions" at state and local levels.

Terminating activities fall in line with the broad pattern previously referred to, as when "codification" movements lay emphasis upon the elimination of inapplicable prescriptions.

The foregoing reminders relate to phase by phase relations at the intra-system level. Research also suggests that similar connections can be demonstrated for inter-phase patterns. We alluded to this in connection with the publicity given to arrests and convictions. More generally it can be shown that some regular patterns of change begin at one phase and move through one or more remaining phases of the sanctioning system.[14]

A comprehensive analysis of the sanctioning component of the decision process would ultimately relate to the entire social context. Relevant to sanctioning is the interaction between officials responsible for the administration of community coercion and nonconformists. A rough equilibrium exists between official sanctioning activity and the level (and kind) of nonconformity. When deviational acts increase, "crime" news often becomes more sensational, agitation mounts on behalf of new legislation, and complaints are made to enforcement officers. Detentions, arrests, convictions, and imprisonments go up; then presently the tide recedes. The result may be that acts of nonconformity return to former levels (which may be high). When such relations are stable the public order system must be described to include a regular pattern of violation of norms. This is the sense in which community institutions can be said to include both the norms (mores) and the counter-mores (that is, an expected level of deviation).

Special equilibria are established between sanctioning activities and each value-institution component of the public order system. Such a relationship exists between the subdivision of power institutions specialized to sanctioning and power institutions as a whole. When intelligence media report that "subversive" activities instigated by foreign powers are increasing it is usually safe to predict that protective action will be demanded, and that this will take the form of recommending the adoption of more prescribing, invoking and applying activities.[15]

Changes in the economic system often precipitate a flurry of activity in the sanctioning field. It is well known that when industrial concentration is rising rapidly (big mergers and trusts) sanctioning activity typically rises, and is directed against the new combinations.[16]

Since it will probably be agreed that special equilibria are likely to be approximated, we shall not review all eight value-institution categories. Rather we turn to the point that system changes are *cyclical* or *structural*. Several of our examples have referred to cyclical movements, such as the demand for "honest law enforcement" followed by a flurry of activity at other phases of sanctioning.[17] Other examples have been structural, since significant institutional practices were rather permanently altered. For instance, the trend of sanctions relating to marital infidelity has been toward less rigidity and less severity in prescription and application.

A sanctioning system is not fully explained until it has been related to hypotheses inspired by the maximization postulate. The postulate tells us that people seek to maximize their value gains while minimizing their losses. The implication is that cycles occur on the basis of different, though complementary, expectations about the conduct that maximizes the values of those who are interacting with one another. Plausible as this hypothesis is, we cannot say that research has been systematically directed to its confirmation. Or, for that matter, that systems of changing perspectives have been systematically investigated to account for structural modifications in sanctioning. Some researches on trend can only be satisfactorily explained if we adopt the hypothesis that influential elements in society have come to regard a new pattern of sanctioning policy as more contributory to their net value position than the pattern that has been superceded. Modern capitalism, for example, is said to encourage leading social groups to think in terms of production, and therefore to decry forced labor or idle manpower. It is true that imprisonment and mutilation, for instance, have given way to fines in nontotalitarian industrial nations, and that economists and politicians can be quoted who give voice to the expectations required by the hypothesis. The variables called "fines" or "imprisonment" are described statistically, with the result that local and short-range variations around the central trend can be located.[18] Modern techniques of quantitative semantics have not yet been employed to describe the variations to be found in the contents of communication relating to sanctions. In all probability the use of quantitative semantics would confirm the broad hypothesis concerning economists and politicians. The data would also make it possible to investigate more refined hypotheses, revealing the channels of diffusion and restriction of expectations and demands pertaining to sanction. Comparisons can be made to show "lead-lag" relations among various media, such as articles and books dealing with criminal and civil sanctions, editorials and commentary in popular media, programs of pressure group and party organizations, legislative debates and statutory modifications.[19]

In general the pattern of sanctions employed in the United States has coincided with what appears to be the general trend in European countries to shift the emphasis from deprivational measures to less deprivational or more positively indulgent practices in the whole field of sanction law. If we examine the prescribed sanctions in the United States criminal code at various cross sections through time the direction is toward mildness and away from severity. Close study also reveals many divagations around the central tendency of sanctioning measures in the United States and elsewhere; and quantitative semantics, coupled with elite studies, promise to pinpoint the most significant factors making for or against the structural transformation of earlier systems.

We sum up by saying that our sanctioning arrangements comprise a system not because they have been thought of as a unified whole, but because the component parts do in fact affect one another in regular ways. It is the special task of the scientific appraiser to consider the system in its entirety and to discover the significance of any component for the basic objectives of the American system of public order. This brings us to the strategies of sanction law.

12. THE STRATEGY OF SANCTIONING

PRINCIPLES OF sanctioning are generalizations that stand between the over-all propositions that apply to every problem and the particularities of a concrete situation. The intellectual tasks to be performed in coping with any problem we have summarized in terms of goal, trend, condition, projection and alternative. The principles of sanctioning emphasize relationships within this special field.

Before moving toward details we underline a few conspicuous characteristics of our fundamental approach to all decision processes. The first is *futurity,* or orientation toward the future. Decisions are steps into the future. This proposition is true irrespective of the fact that discussion is often carried on in a language in which explicit references are to past events. Only the future is open to change; only the future can be affected by decision.

The second characteristic is *contextuality*. Orientation toward future events can be implemented by contextuality, which is concerned with locating future events in the manifold that includes, not only the future, but the past. Past events provide grounds of inference about coming events; and the inspection of historical trends and scientific interdependencies is provocation to create new ways of seeking to bring the future into closer harmony with fundamental preferences.

A third characteristic is *economy*. In terms of overriding goal values the task is to accomplish as much as possible with as little as possible; as little, that is, in terms of cost, which is calculable according to ideal aim.

Fourth, and finally for the present, is *realism*. This is the adaptation of policy to the factors that condition decision. Policy is always confronted by configurations in which some components can be modified at bearable cost, though others cannot. Decisions are realistic when they work within the limits set by conditioning factors. Among these limits are base values at the disposal of community decision makers.

Strategic principles can be employed by scientific observers or decision makers as guides in explaining the relevant context. These principles are reminders of the considerations that are most appropriately kept in view. In this sense they are guides to the "content" of what is worth thinking about, of what needs to be brought to the decision maker's focus of attention at some phase of the total process. Strategic principles are also modes of "procedure," since they can be used as an agenda for the orderly consideration of related matters.

THE OBJECTIVES OF SANCTIONING

When sanctions are properly chosen, they are selected according to objectives which are intended to narrow the gap between the ideal goals of the public order system and the current or anticipated state of affairs.[1]

The objective of *prevention* is pursued within the limits set by an existing system of public order. In the civic arena of the United States it is rarely necessary to take into account the possibility of widespread armed resistance to a decision made by authorized officials. In the world as a whole, however, the situation is much different, since the expectation of violence continues to exercise a profound conditioning effect upon the conduct of politics. Hence the strategy of prevention is a much more complex and uncertain operation than when it is conducted within the national arena. It cannot be taken for granted that the effective decision makers of nation states will expect to be better off by preventing breaches of peace than by provoking them. Clearly, one prerequisite of voluntary support of preventive measures is the expectation on the part of significant figures that they will be better off—in terms of all their value goals—by giving, not withholding, support.

The objective of *deterrence* is one of the most widely agreed upon aims of sanctioning. Since the transition from prevention to deterrence is not abrupt, it is largely a matter of convenience where the scientific observer, at least, draws a line. Prevention is largely oriented toward precrisis policy; it also plays a prominent part in postcrisis periods when the task is to realize the potentiality of the social context for the obviating of further crises. Hence prevention emphasizes the positive inducements that come from living in harmony with norms, aiming in this way to build up expectations in support of conforming conduct. But all preventive measures are not offers of indulgence nor do they emphasize the positive gains of conformity. Prevention has its negative side, since part of the strategy by which challenges to public order are sought to be obviated is by making preparations to impose prompt deprivations upon all who deviate. The preparations are intended to influence the expectations of potential deviators by making it clear that prompt and severe deprivations will follow any substantial violation. Moreover a minimum degree of threat or of imposed loss can be described as a deterrent measure, from the standpoint of the scientific observer, when such a measure is taken by a decision maker who is attempting to bring nonconforming conduct to a speedy halt, and who entertains the expectation that there are at least moderately sanguine prospects of success. Such perspectives are in great contrast to the use of minimum measures by decision makers who regard their action as a tactical step toward general violence. In order to distinguish the fact situations which in the main are preventive from those where the dominant objective is deterrence, we sum up the former by saying that the accent is upon positive advantages, including the removal of provocative conditions; in the latter case, the accent is upon precluding acts of nonconformity by underlining the cost of deviation. In both cases sanguine expectations for the immediate future are current among decision makers even though it may be recognized that in the long run or even in the immediate situation, acts of nonconformity are by no means entirely precluded. Sanguine expectations are subjectively estimated probabilities of a certain degree.

The objective of *restoration* is pertinent in fact situations where norm-violations have occurred or are occurring. By intervening promptly, community decision makers may bring violations to a halt, possibly "rolling them back," or even restoring the initial state of affairs substantially intact. In many circumstances however official sanctioning policy cannot immediately bring about the restoration of a former situation. There may be long delays; and the damage done in the meantime may diminish the chances that specific restitutions can be made.

The objective of *rehabilitation* typically applies to factual circumstances in which nonconformity has already appeared. Rehabilitation refers to a wider context of destruction than does restoration; in regard to nations, for instance, rehabilitation is a problem when productive equipment and other forms of social capital are destroyed to a degree that makes it impracticable for the society to approximate its former level of operation. Individuals are rehabilitation problems when they have been so damaged in destructive situations that they are unable to resume their former level of activity.

The objective of *reconstruction* differs from prevention in the scope of the changes sought. Preventive strategies take a public order context for granted and seek to keep deviations at a minimum within it. Reconstruction strategies are more ambitious; they set out to transform the public order itself. Conspicuous instances are the attempts, notably at the end of World Wars I and II to transform the world arena. These efforts are signalized in the League of Nations and the United Nations, and in related movements.

The strategic principles reviewed in the foregoing paragraphs have the merit of drawing attention to important components of the context where scholarly or final decisions must be made. Since no single sanctioning objective is designed to be exclusive, it is essential to recognize the interconnection of all objectives, and hence to consider their degree of applicability in every concrete case. We phrase this as the *principle of dominant though interconnected objectives.*[2]

The previous enumeration of strategic principles is as important for what is left out as for what is put in. For instance, it is not compatible with the ideal conception of human dignity to seek vengeance or the imposition of suffering for its own sake. The blood baths of history and the destructive depths of the unconscious revealed by psychiatric investigation are enough evidence to show that vengeance and sadism are recurring motivations within each human being and hence in collective situations. The urgency of these impulses varies enormously from time to time and place to place. Ubiquity, however, does not justify including them among the *objectives* of sanction; they are factors which *condition* policy and need not dominate it. We have indicated that our interpretation of human dignity as an ideal aspiration excludes the cultivation of coerciveness; on the contrary the long-range goal is to reduce or eliminate coercive human relations. In the short run we have no doubt that the effective demand to coerce both the primary ego and other egos will continue. But the problem is not to eradicate motives. A motive can remain potent without coming to expression since it is open to the impact of countermotivation within the personality, to negative social consequences when expressed, and to positive social rewards for failing to find expression.

If the assertion is that suffering is "good," the discussion turns upon the rectitude value. We regard people as "good" when they think and act responsibly, that is, when they take the consequences for all concerned into account, and conform their conduct to the ideal of a free man's commonwealth. Responsible people learn from their failures, since they voluntarily engage in a continuing audit of the relation between aspiration and performance. They voluntarily endure regret and grief for errors of omission and commission. It is true that we support sanctioning policies on occasion that expose individuals under various circumstances to the moral opprobrium of the community. But we do not justify the condemnation sanction as an end in itself, a scope value; rather, we regard it as justifiable to the extent that it is a means, a base value, that brings about such effects as a growing sense of responsibility on the part of a target of sanction. And this is an empirical matter to be ascertained by proper methods, and not settled "by definition." Without pursuing the subject further at the moment we say flatly that research has already shown that exposure to the condemnation sanction does not always have a moralizing effect; on the contrary, in circumstances, some of which can be generalized, the impact is to encourage immorality.

If the justification for making others suffer for their own good is religious or metaphysical, we concede—and assert—the freedom of the justifier to make these allegations; but we insist upon empirical tests of whether socially imposed suffering contributes to moral responsibility. We do not test the transempirical proposition; we test alleged empirical consequences.

If it is argued that the community at large will be indignant if people are not mutilated, boiled in oil, flayed alive, and the like, our answer is that community standards need to be brought to the level required by the ideal of human dignity; and that the smallest concessions possible are to be made to the community's outbursts of immorality. The limits of necessary concession are more questions involving the power than the rectitude value. We are in favor of candor in recognizing when a decision maker violates the demands of rectitude in the interest, for example, of well-being and power, as when he permits the court to hang a man rather than let the mob do it, in the expectation that otherwise the mob might also burn down the courthouse, and kill the judge.

THE IDENTIFYING OF DISTURBING SITUATIONS

Sanctioning decisions require that disturbing situations be identified which conform to existing prescriptions of the legal system, or which need to be the subject of new prescription. The latter task—the preparation of new statutes, regulations, or doctrines—is the explicit function of all decision making organs that engage in legislation. Some strategic problems that arise in this connection are also present at the decision phases of intelligence and recommendation, appraisal, and termination; in fact, it would be a mistake to assume that they have no bearing whatsoever at any particular phase of the decision process.

Undoubtedly it will be agreed that the simple fact that a deprivational situation occurs, even when precipitated in contravention of an authorized norm, is not enough to justify intervention by the community's decision process. *Avoid triviality* is the principle that sums up common experience. How trivial is trivial? In a formalistic sense the reply is: where the net advantage of dealing with a situation is less than the advantage of leaving it alone. But this formula provides no satisfactory clue to the limits within which inaction is justifiable. It is not entirely empty or ritualistic to add that a decision maker, before arriving at a judgment of triviality, is well advised to make a rapid survey of the context with several questions in mind. Does the situation appear trivial because it has not been seriously investigated? Or because it concerns subcultures within the wider community which are poorly represented in the decision process? Or affects social classes that suffer from the same handicap? Or interest groups? Or because a claim has been put forward by a personality regarded by decision makers as disagreeable? Even a cursory application of the contextual mode of thought will suffice, on occasion, to challenge a fixed though dubious stereotype of "triviality." [3]

Another principle helps to make explicit the ground of many judgments of triviality or significance. We phrase the strategy this way: *de-emphasize highly improbable repetitions.* This is a counsel of economy. It is designed to discourage the building of redundant statutory, doctrinal, or administrative structures.

In this connection it should be recalled that highly improbable events are not impossible; in fact, formulas are at hand for the predicting of such occurrences.[4] However, the expedient way to handle these rare deprivations is by social insurance, since such events are properly counted among the hazards of living which are unforeseeable by ordinary standards of prudent expectation.

THE IDENTIFYING OF ELIGIBLE TARGETS

A principal task of every sanctioner is to identify eligible targets for the application of sanction. Assuming a destructive situation, or a class of destructive situations, the next question is whether any participant, or class, should be made the object of community supported action on the assumption that community policy can influence future levels of conformity. In a society that aspires toward freedom in human relations the continuing bias is in favor of allowing individuals, acting in their private roles, and private groups, to settle their own problems with a minimum of action by the authorized sanctioners of the community. To put the point negatively, the ideal is that human affairs should be conducted with minimum resort to coercion; either privately, or through agencies of public authority. In fact one of the chief occasions on which public coercion is justifiable is when it is expected to keep net resort to coercion at the lowest level.

When a destructive situation is identified, as we indicated above, it is judged that two conditions have been fulfilled, assuming that a community standard exists: 1. a prescription has been violated; 2. deprivations have been experienced by one or more participants. Since we regard human conduct from a scientific standpoint as a response to determining factors, a question that arises is whether these determining factors are isolable in such a form that they can be singled out for policy action that will affect them in the future; in particular, affected in a way that diminishes the probability of the occurrence of future deviations.

The maximization postulate when applied to human conduct holds that human responses are to be explained according to expectations. That is to say, we respond by using pattern *A* rather than *B* since we expect to be better off in terms of all values by invoking *A*, not *B*. Expectations are in terms of *all* values as they are interpreted by the chooser. Expectations occur within a setting that affects capability, and that always includes limitations upon the potential range of action. It may turn out, as indeed it frequently does, that expectations are more sanguine than is warranted by capability for the control of future events.

In this view, subjective events (expectation, value demands, identifications) are among the determining factors that affect response; and responses include patterns of subjective events which in turn are more or less tightly related to nonsubjective events, such as bodily movements. In social interactions the subjective events occurring among participants may affect one another; in this case the effects are mediated by the nonsubjective events of gesture, writing, and the like. Mediating events which are specialized to communication are *signs.* A "nonsign" event, for instance, is hitting another person, or the coordination of activities in pulling a load.[5]

Given this picture of social interaction, what do we mean by freedom? Freedom occurs to the extent that certain categories of subjective events are the determinative components of interaction. These events are the problem solving activities that we have described in terms of the intellectual tasks (goal clarification and so on). For instance, the sequence that we call "taking future consequences into account" is part of free choice when the individual has a range of alternatives open to him which he can perceive, and which are within the potential capability of the base values at his disposal.

The implication for the sanctioner is that his task is to influence future acts of conformity by affecting future perspectives in the community; furthermore, the problem is to accomplish this result within the fundamental objectives of sanctioning policy which we summarized in the terminology of prevention, deterrence, restoration, rehabilitation, and reconstruction. It is also to be assumed that sanctions will themselves work within the basic principles of futurity, contextuality, economy, and minimum coercion.

We now approach the fundamental distinction in the sanctioner's choice of eligible targets. Assume that he has identified a participant or class of participants in a destructive situation as those who contributed to the value destruction that occurred. Among these contributors shall the sanctioner seek to reach each and every one? Or shall differences be recognized; and if so, upon what principle?

The preceding analysis has directed attention to a working criterion for the sanctioner, namely, the capability of the participant to modify his conduct; in a word, his "educability." If he is educable, the sanctioner is acting according to the canons of a strategy of freedom if he regards the participant as an eligible target; otherwise he is not. To introduce a term of art that is conventionally employed in this context, though not always with our precise meaning, the educable participant is "responsible," and subject to sanction. If the participant is nonresponsible we speak of him as presenting a corrective, not a sanctioning, problem.[6]

The recommended principle, then, with which to clarify the goals of the sanctioner is: *only those should be deemed responsible who have standard opportunities to acquire the norms which are protected by the system of public order, and who have the capability of taking advantage of these opportunities.* They are "educated" (were "educable"); hence, we single them out as responsible members of the society in question.

Although our preference for human dignity means that in the long run we lean toward policies that eschew coercive measures, the public order systems of the contemporary world do in fact rely upon threatened (and applied) coercive sanctioning. From the earliest days of life infants and children learn to take these standard expectations of coercive deprivation into account when they choose among the conduct alternatives open to them. As a general rule, young and old are able to modify their conduct when expected deprivations are judged to be greater than expected gains. If the chances of detection for a violation are thought to be low, and if the possible advantages are judged to be considerable, it is standard to break the norms and to suffer the consequences if detected. Presumably the experience makes the individual a better estimator of the odds; it may increase the demand made by the individual upon the self to adopt a future pattern of more conformity, at least in the areas in question.[7]

Note that the preference for human dignity clearly forecloses us from resorting to educative sanctions when we are confronted by a "nonresponsible" person who has contributed to a destructive situation; that is, has been a factor in imposing a value deprivation of some consequence upon one or more individuals, the deprivations being contrary to established community prescription. Observe that a finding of nonresponsibility does not imply that if released the individual will constitute no menace to future public order. Quite the contrary: it may be rather obvious that, if turned free, he will contribute to future destructive situations.

What, then, are the appropriate alternatives? Plainly the protection of community values calls for *reconstruction* of the individual. To be reconstructed is to have the *predispositional system* altered in ways that eventually make it possible to influence the individual by educative sanctions. We speak of "corrective" measures as those aimed at reconstructing the nonresponsible; they comprehend whatever means are needed to prevent an unreconstructed person or group from damaging the community.

The foregoing considerations bear directly upon the clarification of our values in the management of sanction policy. A theory of responsibility should also provide a check list of the factors that need to be taken into account in concrete decision situations. The following is a list of potential targets of sanction.

Direct Targets

JUDGED OFFENDERS

In this category are all parties whom an authorized tribunal has currently judged to be offenders, or who have a record of having been so judged by other appropriate tribunals. In the ordinary work of adjudication, spokesmen of the community see themselves as most immediately confronted by the problem of how to proceed in dealing with those who have been officially designated as offenders.

Indirect Targets

UNDETECTED OFFENDERS

That a community's law enforcement machinery is bound to fall short of infallible detection of individuals who have deviated from community norms, and who, if apprehended, would be judged to be offenders, is widely recognized.[8] Yet, the sanctions currently applied to known offenders probably also affect the future conduct of those whose deviations have not been discovered.[9]

POTENTIAL OFFENDERS

For similar reasons, sanctions are often imposed with persons other than the immediate offender in mind. Society expects that individuals who as yet have performed no offense may be deterred from doing so in the future. The expectation relates not only to an offense of the same category as that sanctioned but also to those of different categories.[10] A generalized "law-abiding" response is believed to be cultivated by at least some sanctioning measures.

ERRONEOUSLY JUDGED OFFENDERS

Another apparently inevitable characteristic of law enforcement is that innocent parties are sometimes convicted.[11] Occasionally, officials discover their errors and admit them.[12] But a number of undetected or unredressed cases may be extant at any given time. The future conduct of these unfortunates will be affected by the deprivations inflicted upon them and, furthermore, they will in all probability respond attentively and sensitively to news of current sanctioning activities.

OTHER MEMBERS OF THE PUBLIC

This category refers to members of the community considered as active citizens rather than as individuals who are potential violators of the law. Judges are not always unaffected by the criticisms that they expect to receive from professional colleagues, friends, the mass media, and other elements of the public at large.[13] Presumably, too, judges are sometimes influenced by anticipated effects of a decision upon the stability of the community's political process.[14] They may believe that mobs are likely to form to protest against certain possible actions of the court in dealing with a defendant. Mob action may even be expected to turn into rebellion, secession, or social revolution. We place these contingencies here rather than in preceding categories, despite the fact that potential offenses are involved, because of the potential importance of considerations of public security in each case.

The first four categories might be reclassified as one type of role—the "offender" and the fifth category as another type of role—the "citizen." An advantage of doing this is that it emphasizes the point that one individual may perform more than one role relevant to the present analysis. Conceivably the same individual can play roles and subroles that fit into all the categories mentioned. An offender may be held responsible for an act that he did not commit, hence falling within categories 1 and 4. But he may have committed other offenses or the same offense on a different occasion and thus also fit into category 2. He may be among potential offenders (category 3); and he may exercise some influence as a member of the commenting or voting public (category 5).

THE CHOICE OF EDUCATIVE OR CORRECTIVE MEASURES

We have stated that decision makers in the sanctioning process are rational when they choose the policy alternatives most likely to maximize the goal values of the public order system. The future response of any target to an *environmental* factor—such as a change made for sanctioning purposes—depends upon the *predispositions* at the time changes are introduced. Our theory of sanction has emphasized the predispositional differences between targets who are eligible for educative sanctions and who are more appropriately subjected to corrective measures. The following distinctions can be employed by decision makers (and advisors) to remind them of the predispositions of the nonresponsible targets who are potentially available for "corrective" measures.[15]

The Immature

The immature are not expected to benefit from experience to the same extent as adult members of the community do. Children and young people must struggle continually to control impulses they have mastered insufficiently. Although the basic impulses of man continue through life, common observation reveals that young people are less likely than adults to have perfected a workable conscience—largely an automatic agency of internal control.[16] Indeed, maturity in our civilization consists of achieving a culturally standard level of internal responsibility for one's conduct.[17] The salient characteristic of a mature person is that he adapts his conduct to realistic estimates of its consequences. He learns rather quickly from successes and failures; particularly, he is able to learn by hearing about the experiences of others. The sanctioning provisions of a legal code are for the most part aimed at "standard learners," at "typically educable" members of the community. If enforcible deprivations are provided for deviational conduct, the mature members of the community are expected to take these possible deprivations into account as potential costs in assessing the balance of indulgence and deprivation attendant upon behavioral alternatives. Furthermore, if these calculated risks are taken and an individual "doesn't get away with it," the sanction is (or can be) loaded to such a level that the target will learn to give more weight to the cost side of future deviations.[18]

The Uninformed (Unassimilated)

Some individuals simply are unable to take advantage of the warnings of a legal code because they are psychically or physically removed from the cultural setting which is taken as a premise by the code makers. By the uninformed, we mean those who, though they may be mature and may have enough native talent to learn the patterns of culture, have had insufficient access to an environment that would instill them with a command of the basic norms and techniques of a given social setting. One obvious instance of the unassimilated is the newly arrived and wholly untutored immigrant from a sharply contrasting culture. But the class of the uninformed transcends that of the immigrant. Within the confines of any large-scale society exist subcommunities whose members lack access to the schooling and other opportunities needed to assimilate the dominant norms and techniques of the culture: isolated religious communities and remote and parochially centered villages in the hill country or in other habitats shut off from communication with the main centers.[19]

The Defective and Diseased

No one will deny that educability can be impaired by congenital or other organic defects, or by primarily functional diseases.[20] The mere existence of a defect or disease does not, of course, automatically consign the individual to the category of nonresponsibility. A determinative connection must be established between the pathological condition and ineducability.

Any theory of responsibility is severely tested by the deviational conduct of an individual who suffers from no discoverable organic pathology, but who is prevented from making a normal assessment of cost by seemingly unmanageable internal factors. In extreme cases, the individual may spend much of his waking life struggling against a desire to perform an act he abhors and recognizes as having costly consequences, only to be seized by an intense desire to complete such an act, a desire that overwhelms conscious barriers. Despite conscious perception of cost (save perhaps during a moment of "seizure"), the individual is unable to apply his self-appraisal effectively.[21] In the language of the redoubtable and preoccupied New England lady who walked into a tree, she "saw it," but she "did not realize it." Furthermore, the same internal factors may exert such complete control over his conduct that the individual is unaware of any deficiency in his judgment despite repeated clashes with the machinery of public order. From the point of view of personality development, these individuals remain chronically immature as the result of early regression and may regress to acutely rebellious, destructively aggressive, wildly suicidal, or related extremes of conduct.[22] The common element in functional disorders of educability should not be phrased in terms of irresistible impulse, in the legal sense, but as "compulsiveness" or "compulsivity," so as to emphasize the graduated nature of these motivational systems. Such "line drawing" calls for an examination of the whole personality context.[23]

The Dissenter

The reference here is to the individual whose violation of obligation is self-justified by rejecting the ideological system in the name of which primary and sanctioning norms are defined and applied. This rejection may, if extreme, manifest itself in service to the ideology of a foreign power (as in espionage). Such an ideology may affirm a world revolutionary conception against the "counter-revolutionary" ideas that prevail among local authorities.[24] Or, the counterideological system may be as yet invoked by no foreign power; indeed, its supporters may be numbered on the fingers of one hand. Or, the ideology may champion a religious rather than a secular system; the religion may or may not be strongly entrenched abroad, and it may claim millions of adherents or a handful.[25] The latter cases—taken in conjunction with isolated political prophets—often merge into one of the preceding categories (especially that of the diseased).[26]

The Provoked and the Tempted

We speak here of opposites. Both categories imply relationships to the environment, the former an exposure to deprivation, the latter to indulgence. Both are estimates of disproportionality, indicating that imposition or opportunity exceeded the range assumed to be determinative for classifying ordinary conduct.

This phenomenon highlights a point that applies to the classification of all conduct, namely, that the classification of any detail of behavior or attitude depends upon the total situation of which it is part. We often revise "snap judgments" about human conduct as more information about environmental and predisposing factors becomes available. The muscle movements that constitute an act are not decisive nor are the content and intensity of conscious and unconscious impulses, moods, and perceptions; such details must always be assessed in the light of the significance of the environment for value indulgence or deprivation.

If the provocations are extreme, such as an unprovoked attack upon one's self or a beloved one, conventional law speaks of justification and excuse.[27] Temptations, too, can be exceptionally inviting, as when a poorly paid cashier who handles great sums has an opportunity to make off with millions.[28] In everyday speech and in many legal codes, these circumstances are referred to as extenuating or mitigating the violation, but there is some reluctance to recognize them as completely exculpatory, presumably for fear of encouraging deviational conduct.[29]

The Deceived

Some participants in the sequence of activities that culminate in redressable injury are not informed of the object of the enterprise.[30] Or, the defendant may be actively misled.[31] If such "innocent" ones are made targets of condemnation, they are unlikely to feel pangs of conscience. More probably, some will consider the sanction a provocative act that justifies them in seeking to take advantage of their outlawed state by becoming professional criminals or revolutionaries.[32]

The Mistaken

A few offenders cause harm without desiring to do so. From their own perspective, at least, they are innocent insofar as they took "reasonable precautions." [33]

The Careless

In contrast are those who did not take precautions that were "reasonable" in the pertinent cultural situation.[34]

Labeling or, more productively, analyzing the character of the offender is not enough; when the community as a whole is considered, our conception of responsibility brings to mind the degree to which the community is involved in producing the chain of damaging events that are brought to the notice of the decision maker and also the responsiveness of the body politic to decisions. In some cases, it is obvious without further inquiry that failure to reach a specific decision will arouse public indignation, endanger institutional stability, and subvert the international integrity of democratic institutions. An enlightened decision maker may perceive that the community's past record has contributed mightily to the factors that culminated in a particular controversy or series of controversies and that in the future the community itself is likely to precipitate violation of its own norms.[35] Looking to the future, however, and weighing the probable response of the public and its leaders, a court, for instance, may conclude that the community cannot be educated by a court decision and that the decision will provoke some citizens to commit damaging acts against public officials.[36] In the face of such circumstances, a candid judge must admit that the community is nonresponsible in that it requires a correctional change beyond the potential of the court, in the particular case, to effect. The court must then bow to the lack of insight and understanding on the part of the community with the same logic that it bows to the unwelcome fact of lack of education on the part of an individual defendant. In some instances, the immediate outcome is the same for the whole community and for the individual defendant who is not responsible.

Both go free. In others, the results diverge. The defendant, though not responsible, is subject to correction and may be required to undergo hospitalization or isolation until he has been reconstructed. The whole community cannot be dealt with in this fashion by its own instruments, whether the decision structures are legislatures, courts, or administrative agencies.

The circumstances confronting a decision maker in most cases, however, are by no means so extreme. More commonly, an adverse storm of criticism, accompanied perhaps by sporadic acts of violence, is to be anticipated.[37] Recognition of the community's causal contribution can coexist with a prediction that the community can be reconstructed eventually by a stream of "innovative" decisions.[38]

THE CHOICE OF SANCTIONER

Decisions that involve sanctions or corrections include the selection of the sanctioner, the organ or the official who is to perform the tasks at hand. What qualifications will increase the probability that the sanctioner will act in optimum accord with the objectives of the system as a whole? What modes of selection will, in all likelihood, put the person possessing the proper qualifications in the right place at the right time? What scope of decision shall be given to what organs and officials? What procedures shall be employed by the decision maker and executor to bring relevant events to his focus of attention and therefore to provide the best attainable grounds of inference for his final response?

A strategic requirement of fundamental importance is *prior prescription.* Before a sanctioner is authorized to act in a given situation there must be some showing that the conduct complained of has been made subject to sanction by the sanctioner in question, and that the prescription was made by a properly constituted prescriber prior to the destructive situation referred to.

Thus the principle enshrined in the maxim *No law; No punishment.*[39] The affirmative side of the policy is that *severe deprivations shall only be provided by authoritative prescription.* This includes two demands, namely, that the legal system is to be complete enough to embrace certain facts of social process, and that remedies are to be available to all who suffer deprivations in contravention of a prescription. It is true, of course, that legal systems do not lay their decision makers open to formal claims for damages that result from failure of the decision makers to "pass a law." [40] However, legislatures have often recognized the validity of claims where remedies were unprovided.

A principle that has begun to be applied throughout our legal order emphasizes the advantages that follow from *separating the judgment of eligibility for sanction from the selection and administration of sanction.*[41] At the applying phase, for example, the courts separate the verdict or judgment from subsequent specification of sanction. The use of parole boards is the most striking new development of the kind. The social context which is highly pertinent to an initial judgment is less relevant to the second; a different team of specialists is required to furnish information and offer the estimates needed.

A further principle is that initial *decisions regarding eligibility to sanction should be left in social contexts where the destructive situation complained of is alleged to have occurred.*[42] A great many calculations enter into the endorsement of this proposition, which is deeply grounded in social experience. In general, those who have suffered what they perceive as constituting a norm-violating deprivation have an immediate claim upon the community decision process for relief. This is a matter of rectitude; also other values are likely to be heavily at stake. Political stability of the commonwealth, for example, depends to some extent upon the administration of justice. Enlightenment is also involved, since potential witnesses and other informants are presumably more available near the scene of the deprivation.

If, however, locally experienced deprivations come from a common, comprehensive source, community strategy calls for the consolidation of claims in a jurisdiction large enough to consider the entire social context. In arriving at a realistic assessment of a destructive situation it is relevant not only to examine local instances of deprivation but to consider the policies of the depriver. This is essential to a judgment of responsibility or nonresponsibility.

Judgments are to be subject to review by decision makers whose jurisdiction includes the social context in which alleged deprivers and sufferers from deprivation are included.[43] If matters are left entirely in the hands of those who are likely to feel identified with a "victim," it is to be expected that sanctions will be used that, when examined in a wider social setting, appear disproportionate. It often happens that those who are adjudged to be deprivers have removed themselves and their assets from local jurisdiction, and if sanctions are to be carried out, must be reached elsewhere. A local jurisdiction that includes the "target" does not necessarily have confidence in the competence or the impartiality of the decision maker in the local jurisdiction that contains the "victim." An inclusive jurisdiction with authority to review local decisions is called for.

A further principle is to *encourage local and relatively informal settlement of controversies* whenever the advantages of speed and local knowledge are not outweighed by other relevant consequences. Hence the support given to collective bargaining, commercial and other forms of arbitration, and the like.[44] The parties to a given controversy are typically well aware of many of the deprivations and indulgences at stake; and of the prescriptions, often unwritten, that are established in the perspectives of participants in the local or pluralistic situation. Abuses arise when local participants are not evenly matched in power (or when they cannot join coalitions that supply missing weight). Alongside the territorially organized institutions of government our society has many institutions specialized to wealth and other values that rise from local through State and metropolitan communities to the national or international level. Dispute settlement can be allowed to proceed in highly decentralized fashion up to the point where conflicts are joined that generalize upward (or downward) throughout the informal as well as the formal arenas involved. At the local level, for instance, mine owners and union officials are sometimes about evenly matched in applying a general contract to local mines. Both sides are under the impression that each party can enlist coalition aid from the higher echelons of business or union organization. However, when conflicts begin at the national or state level they generalize downward to the grass roots, since every context becomes pertinent to the power balancing process of crisis periods. For the duration of the more acute stages of the conflict, at least, local flexibility is lost.[45]

Any comprehensive analysis of the choice of sanctioner would include comparative principles adapted to bring out the significant features of the many institutional practices employed in defining and qualifying sanctioners, in prescribing their jurisdiction, and in detailing the proper practices by which arguments and factual statements are brought to the attention of these decision makers.[46] All this comes within the scope of sanction law; but in this sketch we cannot go into detail.

THE PLACE OF SANCTIONING WITHIN THE LEGAL SYSTEM

All the strategies connected with sanctioning are affected by the role that they play within the legal system as a whole. The primary prescriptions of a legal system can usefully be divided for comparative purposes into five principal groups, or codes.[47]

A fundamental question about any legal system is the role laid down for government. The scope of government may be such that the entire social process is swallowed up; society is governmentalized. It is more common, however, to give to the specialized institution of government a more modest part to play. Individuals acting separately or in groups are expected to make a great many choices on their own, and to invoke the decision makers of the community only when they are entangled in controversies which they are unable to settle privately. When a stranger examines the prescriptions that prevail in our legal system he quickly recognizes that much is left to the initiative of private parties. Where this assumption is made we speak of the *supervisory* code (a subcode) within the system as a whole. Other provisions explicitly prescribe the limits within which private initiative is permitted to operate. If the stream of private activity overflows the banks drawn by community policy the community itself is authorized to step in and restore the previous state of affairs. Prescriptions of this kind belong to the *regulative* code. The government itself is charged with carrying on some activities continuously, such as military and police protection, or the postal services. To cover these operations we speak of the *enterprisery* code. This leaves for special consideration the prescriptions that deal directly with the allocation of responsibilities within the decision process itself. The *constitutive* code establishes the body politic and specifies who is authorized to engage in the enactment of general prescriptions, or to perform the intelligence, recommending, invoking, applying, appraising and terminating functions.

We join with the late George Dession in rejecting the traditional and greatly confused distinction between "civil" and "criminal" sanctions. The valid core of what has been traditionally called criminal we retain: we call it the *corrective* code.[48]

Among the basic problems of a developing science of sanction law is the appropriateness of sanctioning devices to the specific requirements of each major code. What is the optimum balance among the values used and between positive and negative measures? What is the most favorable articulation of final sanctions with presanctions, sanction equivalents, remedies, and administrative patterns? What are the most promising provisions for the selection of specialized sanctioners, and for the delimiting of jurisdiction and procedure? In the immediately following pages we consider each of the five codes for the purpose of underlining questions of sanctioning strategy having special importance to each. The treatment is not fully systematic; it is designed to encourage studies which will eventually make a balanced theoretical and empirical treatment feasible. In connection with a code prominence is given to one or more hypotheses to serve as suggestive guides to inquiry.

Sanctioning Within the Constitutive Code

The constitutive code specializes upon the decision process itself; hence, sanctioning strategies are aimed at maintaining the freedom of the body politic from external dictation, and also the integrity of the authoritative decision process from internal interference. Since the arena of world politics is the scene of rival systems of public order, not of a universal system, sanctioning problems are of peculiar importance.[49]

Even though a body politic is committed to popular government it may be confronted at home by coercive attempts to defy and nullify the basic frame of government. Men of equal devotion to the long run aims of a free society differ in the concessions they judge to be required to cope with active or threatened violence and related modes of coercion. Looking at past revolutionary changes two major lines of analysis are usually followed. On the one hand we are told that sanctioning authorities met growing turbulence with too little, too late. It is argued that they should have responded more decisively and immediately before the situation got out of hand. The other line is that the members of the ruling class, with astonishing blindness to their valid interests, failed to adopt affirmative policies that would have enabled them to maintain a large part of their power by the tactic of admitting new and rising elements to a larger share. Instead, the authorities conceived of the problem in "police terms," thereby entertaining exaggerated expectations of what could be done by the use of negative sanctions.[50]

The key proposition, then, is that *systems of public order destroy themselves when they rely to an exaggerated degree upon one policy among the set of policies upon which the protection and fulfillment of the system depends.*

It is where conceptions of right and wrong are geographically segregated, rather than dispersed, that we face the most difficult problems relating to the use of negative, and especially, violent sanctions. The legislators and top policy appliers of the body politic are not infrequently caught between a constitutionally articulated policy and a relatively solid wall of sectional resistance. The Whiskey Rebellion was one of the earliest struggles between locally supported resistance and federal authority in the excise field. This conflict has gone on throughout the history of the Republic and detailed studies would prove especially rewarding in the present context. School segregation is the latest in a long series of struggles which have characterized the attempts of rising elements in the social structure of the United States to liquidate Negro-white castes.

In the towering crisis of the Civil War the history of the United States provides a storehouse of warning and guidance requiring proper evaluation in the perspective of sanction policy.

Can we formulate hypotheses that will guide the search for

strategies dealing with sectional differences toward sanctions? Possibly the most important proposition favors "*a policy of continuous moral pressure designed to divide the consciences of the local minority against itself.* The result can be furthered by offering *positive inducements in support of policies that hasten the social transformations that work against the older attitudes* (increased industrialization, further opportunities for experience elsewhere, etc.)." [51]

Problems of coercive sanction are prominent in the deliberations of those who are attempting to consolidate "a more perfect union" of previously independent bodies politic. The most challenging attempt of all is to overcome the separatist traditions of nation states and to provide by charter for an international order that curbs the independent use of coercion and places necessary coercion at the disposal of the whole. In this century the great historic attempts to expedite the formation of a universal system of public order occurred as aftermaths of two devastating wars. The League of Nations and the United Nations were drafted in the hope of strengthening the institutions of global-wide persuasion and weakening the factors that make for coerciveness.

It is noteworthy that even on these relatively auspicious occasions the draftsmen of the Covenant and the Charter were reluctant to challenge the traditional scope of the nation state's authority by placing too outspoken restrictions upon the war powers of each. The response to the League Covenant in the United States appeared to justify the utmost caution at Versailles. The question today and in the future is whether the Charter of the UN should be made more outspoken by amendment than left as it was at San Francisco.[52]

Although, as indicated above, the timing of such initiatives is an essential prerequisite of effectiveness, and depends upon comprehensive current appraisals, it is possible to draw attention to principles (or hypotheses) pertinent to the problem. *Indirect statement of the coercive authority of the central government favors consent during the early stages in the consolidation of a body politic which is voluntarily forming a more perfect union.* But there is indication that *when a great deal of acceptance has been achieved statements that unambiguously authorize the use of coercion by the inclusive arena contribute to the net decline of active or threatened coerciveness.*

Although the grounds upon which this general inference is based are fragmentary, they include some well-known facts about the realities of political life. During the early stages of confederation and federation potent groups are usually opposed to the growth of central authority. Hence, it is of great advantage to political leaders who support measures which call for the use of central government to disclaim any intention of undermining the integrity of local units. If the social process within the body politic grows until it sustains the expanded role of central authority, the tactical situation alters accordingly. Attempting to head off further centralization local elements precipitate crises of opposition to the center which may reach the pitch of rebellion and civil war partly because a monopoly of coercion on behalf of the larger whole is vaguely authorized or entirely omitted in the authoritative charter (Constitution). Pivotal power positions are open to leaders who organize coalitions of dissatisfied elements in each locality and obtain assistance from groups which though organized throughout the whole commonwealth support special interests by the strategy of maintaining an ambiguous state of crisis. Opposition leaders can argue that component units did not give up their authority to withdraw from the larger commonwealth; nor did they delegate any right to anyone to coerce them into perpetual membership. Only unequivocal language can cut the formal ground from under the feet of these contenders.[53]

The geographical mobility of population under modern conditions results in exaggerating an old threat to representative government. Representative governments try to safeguard majority rule by providing for the apportioning of representatives among constituencies according to population. However, population shifts often produce glaring caricatures of majority rule owing to the failure of reapportionment norms to be applied, and of sanctioning provisions to be made effective. If chances of distortion are to be reduced, *arrangements must be made to handle reapportionment as automatically as possible, including the application of whatever sanctions are provided.* The attrition of popular rule can come about so gradually by the cumulative pressure of limited yet strategically situated interests that preventive devices are of critical importance in preserving the margins of reserve that are wisely included within every effective plan for the sharing of power.[54]

Sanctions for the Regulative Code

We turn now for a glance at issues pertaining to the regulative code. The history of America provides a remarkable reserve of experience that has been only partially evaluated in the present perspective. The frame of reference of the regulative code assumes that the activities with which it deals occur chiefly in private channels. The code states or presupposes an aggregate pattern to which private activities are to conform. The aggregate pattern is part of the system of public order; and since in American society we try to keep as many activities as possible in private hands, the regulative code presumably comprises most of the American system. A regulative problem arises whenever the stream of private choice and operation shows (or threatens to show) a significant discrepancy with aggregate norms required by the public order. Public policy has the task of eliminating discrepancies.

A recurring question with special reference to the regulative field is: how important is it, if at all, that *individual targets* be singled out as objects of sanction? To a degree individuals are unavoidable targets of any regulative operation since human beings identify themselves in varying degree with any target "group" or "organization," and especially with the "officer" role. Shall the attempt be to "play it cool" and to treat regulative questions as organizational? Questions of these kinds are less questions of strategy under prevailing conditions of knowledge than guides to investigation; we shall deal with some of the available methods of inquiry in the concluding chapter.

By contrast some strategies of regulation are moderately clear. What of the choice of sanctioner as between administrators and courts? The broad trend, of course, has been to strengthen the former. Thus "the regulation of financial organizations, . . . security issuance, and the organized securities and commodities exchanges, all aim to obtain a degree of security for investors and buyers through limitation of fraud, dishonesty, misrepresentation or incompetency,"[55] predominantly under administrative auspices. It is noteworthy too that "government promotion and ownership"[56] has assumed a growing role as a regulatory device, significantly under federal auspices.

Sound policy in dealing with complex, continuing and specialized operations calls for the discovery of limits within which public controllers alert themselves to the occurrence of possible deprivations of the community. As the limits are clarified, and it becomes evident to all participants how the public order is conceived by public authority, we see evidence of a working accommodation of policies in which private activities stop short of providing a challenge to the regulative machinery. *These accommodations can be evolved most quickly and effectively, it now appears obvious, when administrative agencies are set up to supplement the traditional role of the courts in these matters.*

In brief, "from the standpoint of public policy, the subtleties of monopoly and restriction of competition are too great to be resolved satisfactorily in the courtroom. In modern industry practically every firm possesses some degree of monopoly. Whether or not it is in keeping with public interest must be decided in each particular instance, seemingly by a body charged with developing public policy."[57]

In Part I we stressed the vagueness of extant concepts of monopoly and restriction of competition as obstacles to effective enforcement of the antitrust laws. We now note further that judicial bodies have kept an erratic hand on the steering wheel of administration, sometimes intervening quickly and with a heavy hand, though at other times seemingly deaf and dumb. Under these circumstances neither the principles nor the procedures of sanction are clear in the field of public control.

In connection with regulative codes it is possible to assert with confidence that the *strategy of graduated sanctions* is sound. Sanctions must range between relative mildness and great severity. If a wide gap exists between sanctions a regulatory authority will be greatly handicapped. If it initiates a very severe sanction not only business opinion but the opinion of appellate tribunals are likely to turn against it as unjustifiably punitive. In this connection we have in mind the nominal authority of the Federal Communications Commission to terminate a license rather than to renew it. Since the license is a valuable asset which is typically assimilated to long-term capital assets it is evident that "expropriation" can be justified, if at all, by the most fantastic misconduct on the part of a radio or TV licensee. In a capitalistic society the informal factors making for the protection of investment effectively outweigh the authoritative language of statute. The Federal Communications Commission suffers from the limitation that the truly permissible deprivations at their disposal are weak and largely ineffectual. The Commission must use a penknife or a meat ax, but most situations are appropriate for neither.[58]

It is well understood that regulated interests are continually tempted to become their own regulators by capturing effective control of the administrative and legislative bodies charged with responsibility for defining and applying the key features of the public order system to be given protection and opportunity for fulfillment.[59] In the to and fro of social interaction every initiative of a regulatory nature elicits its own technique of seeming compliance and at least partial evasion. When there are strongly competitive elements, or when a few large-scale organizations are battling out the terms of trade among them, the controversy tends to universalize, that is, draw in many interests in the social context. As a rule, the marginal participants do not regard themselves as sufficiently advantaged or disadvantaged to bestir themselves for or against any specific administrative rule, regulation or order. Involvement is a sign of crisis expectation among the chief participants in the tussle; and when as usually happens a crisis dies down as new arrangements crystallize, marginal groupings return to orbit.

From the perspective of sanction law *crisis situations are welcome opportunities to define the public order with enough consensus among significant official and unofficial elements to produce a relatively durable framework.* The crisis evokes public attention, which often is a sufficiently strong coalition element to establish prescriptive codes, to obtain the devoted support of public spirited and competent regulators, and to procure facilities ample to perform the elaborate intelligence and appraisal functions without which a regulative agency is blind. The comparative study of regulation undoubtedly confirms the point that crisis opportunities must be anticipated and seized if long run results are to be satisfactory.[60]

A question of key importance to the regulative code in particular concerns the qualifications of sanctioners. The political drive required to subject a given sphere of interaction to official regulation has often been furnished by disgruntled elements which have lost out in the struggle against larger units. The "small business" and "ex-business" men in favor of regulation have been joined by "consumers" who, although widely scattered throughout the community, have experienced at first hand episodes of deprivation which they attribute to the irresponsible conduct of organizations that have widely ramifying impacts upon the values enjoyed in the community. The "little man" was conspicuous in compelling the regulation of railroads and other means of transportation; of water, gas, electricity, and related utilities; of banks and financial institutions deeply affecting wealth; of food, drugs and other matters strongly affecting health; of sex and gambling operations believed to affect the family and public morals; and so on through what would be an inventory touching every value-institution process in the American system of public order.[61]

These regulative activities have had a systematic, ideological basis provided by economists, political, and juristic thinkers. Academic economists early acquired a reputation for the policy preferences which they expressed in favor of the defense of an economy of private enterprise relatively free of governmental control. In expressing these policy preferences economists were not always careful to say whether they had made empirical studies of the degree to which the specific institutions which they appeared to be defending did in fact coincide with the assumptions of the theoretical model of free private enterprise. Hence despite the apparatus of intellectual analysis which gave them a respected position among university intellectuals, the insinuation was widespread that they were blindly dogmatic and unwilling to face many of the facts which pointed to the existence of socially disturbing results from the American business system.

Although some economists of established professional standing spoke out in favor of "reform," they were not the "tone-setters" of academic departments or, most obviously, of the economists who had gone into business as consultants. Among academic groups it was easier, though not easy, for historians or political scientists —and especially scholars with a southern agrarian or western smalltown bias—to act as critics of the actual as distinguished from the theoretical performance of the American system. Some of these scholars, too, were more in touch with Marxist ideology than their colleagues. Without necessarily or even typically becoming identified with world revolutionary radicalism, they sometimes found in "municipal socialism," or in "the socialism of the pulpit," a congenial program of limitation upon unbridled private enterprise.[62]

These developments provide another instance of a recurring feature of American civilization, namely, the tension between businessmen, on the one side, and clergymen, teachers, research workers, and related professional groups on the other. Although physicians and lawyers were conventionally regarded as constituting "professions" they were trained in ways that emphasized client service rather than direct service of the whole community. Hence it was simple for many if not most lawyers and doctors to come to terms with the private business components of the American system.[63]

We know that a frequently recurring characteristic of intellectual life is the lack of reality on the part of professional intellectuals. They pursue highly specialized forms of activity and frequently lack the motivation or even the capacity to concern themselves with the mastery of the economic or political opportunities of the immediate environment. It must also be recognized that the specialist has what appears to be a natural affinity for bureaucracy; that is, for a neatly graded arrangement of duties and rewards within which practical risks can be kept at a minimum while specialized talents are cultivated. Administrative structures of this type dominate schools and colleges; and they are increasingly accepted wherever organized activities are far flung, whether inside government, business, ecclesiastical or other spheres.

We live in a three-channel society—the channel of private profit, of nonprofit private activity, of nonprofit governmental activity. With the relative growth of bureaucracy, the most vigorous and ambitious seekers after power or profit find themselves curiously circumscribed by developments that they find singularly uncongenial, and which produce a world of clerks, professionals, scientists, scholars, and administrators. Thus do energetic beasts of prey or creatures of adventure find themselves hemmed in by hordes of the timid, the sensible, the cautious, the indifferent, the preoccupied; in a word, the meek. The machinery of regulative sanctioning, which, like the police, courts, and prisons, is organized on a nonprofit plan, and tends to gravitate into the hands of persons who are devoid of empathy with business unless business interests manage to put their own stoodges in office.

The attempts of business to control its regulators is not unique to business. Every skill group, or in fact every self-identified element, automatically or deliberately seeks to reduce its vulnerability to deprivation by having people of its own outlook among its regulators. Even the money or job corruption that is a common tool of businessmen can be matched by corruption in nonprofit fields, as when compliant administrators in health or education cultivate "offers" that advance their careers after they leave the public service.[64]

Is the inference that regulative activities which are genuinely in defense of the public order are chimeras, and that no strategy can contribute significantly to a sound outcome? We doubt this conclusion, partly because we believe that in the future modern methods of operating our society can be effectively extended to many regulative problems. *One indicated strategy is to build larger competitive professional interests in evaluating the results of regulation, interests which are recruited from academic circles and also from among those immediately responsible for policy.* The cultivation of sanction law, for instance, can create a new and large forum in which new knowledge can steadily influence judgment and policy.

Sanctions for the Enterprisery Code

The main question that arises in connection with sanctioning policy for the enterprisery code is what adjustments should be made in view of the fact that government has sole administrative responsibility. The enterprisery code lays down standards for all activities which the government administers within the framework provided by the constitutive code. Basic qualifications and modes of selection, jurisdiction and procedure are constitutive matters; there remain, however, many lesser administrative arrangements to be specified in enterprisery codes.

Typical sanctioning problems in this area are: if individuals are negligent or abuse their authority should the negative sanctions to which they are exposed be heavier or lighter than when similar acts are performed in a private organization? Also, if individuals live up to their obligations, or go beyond them, should they receive higher sanctioning rewards of a positive kind than if the organization were unofficial?

We suggest that one principle is that sanctions be adjusted to equalize and nullify the incentives for coerciveness on the part of those who perform comparable roles in governmental and private organizations. An examination of prevailing practice indicates that this standard has been tacitly or expressly used in many situations characteristic of government enterprise. Violations of a trust exercised on behalf of the whole community are more seriously regarded in most jurisdictions than violations of obligation to a smaller constituency.

In connection with the enterprisory code it is important to recognize that governmentalization is itself a policy that is often adopted with sanctioning objectives in view. The demand for government administration is in many instances provoked by allegations of persisting corruption, negligence, and oppression on the part of private organizations, typically of business corporations. Furthermore, once an operation is in official hands great reliance is put upon *reorganization* as a sanctioning strategy.

First, the enterprise may be retained at the same level of government (*e.g.*, federal) but it may be moved from one department to another, or reorganized as an authority outside the department structure.

Second, the enterprise may be shifted from one level of government to another (*i.e.*, federal to state).

Third, the enterprise may be moved from government to private channels.

Although reorganization measures have an important place in

the armory of sanctioners it is especially pertinent to insist upon the contextual study of such instruments. Preoccupation with preventing or deterring corruption, for instance, can lead to policies that do grave damage to other value goals, and that defeat themselves in the specific area of sanction law. Have we paid too much heed to sanctioning considerations in the sense that our structures of administration have been saddled with precautionary restrictions as a result of crises of public excitement touched off by scandal—scandal in private activities which brought about governmentalization; scandal in local and state government that culminated in federalization; scandal in department administration that led to independent commissions?

It is probably true that considerations of sanctioning policy have contributed to the trend toward governmentalization, centralization, and concentration; and further, toward building the present rather unwieldy machinery of bureaucratic administration in American government. In order to protect the personnel of government from temptation to depart from standards of integrity and impartiality the civil service system has been rigidified. Fearful of executive authority, and not unmindful of scandalous occurrences among the departments, Congress has denied to the Executive branch freedom to rearrange administrative structures. Cognizant of abuses in the field of procurement Congress has not infrequently laid down requirements that handicap initiative. Within these limitations often the only way to get satisfactory administrative results is to take advantage of labyrinthine channels which are known only to the most seasoned denizens of the Washington maze.[65]

The implication is that sanction law studies should be carried out by *investigative teams capable of assigning weight to positive as well as negative goals when reorganization is under appraisal as a sanctioning strategy*. Continuing administrative operations require a program of positive incentives to innovate, to accept risks, to court public cooperation and support, to perform efficiently. We suggested before that reorganization can defeat even the sanctioning objectives sought at times of public excitement. In many cases activities lose visibility when they are put in the hands of government; and with invisibility comes temptation not only to sloth but corruption. Systems of reward—not only in terms of dollars, but in no sense to the exclusion of dollars—are essential to distinguished performance; and positive as well as negative sanctions are bound to play a prominent part in sustaining the aims of public order.

Sanctions of the Supervisory Code

The typical policy considerations that figure in problems presented to community decision makers under the supervisory code are remedies rather than sanctions. The body politic plays the umpire role in controversies over contracts and torts. The community is involved only at the initiative of a party who alleges an unlawful deprivation arising under a contractual agreement or by violation of a community norm of conduct. Presumably this lack of initiative on the part of the community at large, despite the involvement of a pattern of approved public order, is justified by the preference for keeping disputes at a minimum unless they are especially important for the whole body politic—in which case the community does take an initiative—or unless they reach a threshold of protest strong enough to activate private initiative. We have already expressed disbelief in the consistency of application of the formal distinctions in our conventional legal order. But research on sanction law is well-advised to start with conventional distinctions since this is the most feasible way to locate the case studies which are required if functional comparisons are to be made.

Granted that the supervisory code is concerned with private controversies in which the decision maker of the body politic plays the invited role of umpire, are there any sanction issues involved? We suggest that investigation will demonstrate that considerations of deterrence and prevention do, in fact, enter into the decisions which take the nominal form of remedies for wrong or for breached contract. The deprivations alleged by the parties are often said to be in the immediate future rather than the past; and the remedy sought may be to halt the allegedly pending deprivation until, at least, a formal determination is reached of the claims of the parties.

Many remedies call for specific performance, or for monetary calculation of the magnitude of deprivation illegally suffered by the plaintiff.

Even a superficial list of claims arising under the supervisory code suggests the hypothesis that *decision makers give weight to the deterrence or prevention of future violations of norms of public order*. The purpose of exemplary or punitive damages, for example, is admittedly punishment rather than restitution. In a word, exemplary or punitive damages "are assessed for the avowed purpose of visiting a punishment upon the defendant and not as a measure of any loss or detriment of the plaintiff." [66] The award of such damages is conditioned upon a showing of "a positive element of conscious wrongdoing," *i.e.*, "it must be shown either that the defendant was actuated by ill will, malice, or evil motive (which may appear by direct evidence of such motive, or from the inherent characteristics of the tort itself, or from the oppressive character of his conduct, sometimes called 'circumstances of aggravation'), or by fraudulent purposes, or that he was so wanton and reckless as to evince a conscious disregard of the rights of others." [67] The contemporary rationale of this form of sanctioning, as put by a leading authority, is that "it does tend to bring to punishment a type of cases of oppressive conduct . . . which are theoretically criminally punishable, but which in actual practice go unnoticed by prosecutors occupied with more serious crimes. . . . The danger of the addition of punitive damages seems calculated to increase decidedly the deterrent value of the verdict." [68]

Enlightened judicial opinion has held a plaintiff in a personal injury action subject to cross-examination as to his involvement in similar accidents and similar lawsuits on the assumption that "fortuitous events of a given sort are less likely to happen repeatedly than once." [69] Apart from its immediate impact upon the affected lawsuit, it stands to reason that acceptance of this discrediting process is calculated to discourage a litigious person in the future. One may note in passing that it approaches the indirect though nonetheless effective penalization of "accident-proneness" as well.

A record of oppressive or unconscionable commercial dealing in the context of a given controversy may bar the claim to equitable enforcement of an otherwise valid transaction under the doctrine of "clean hands." [70] Part of the motivation, we hypothesize, is to inhibit resort to the tainted practices in the future.

The implication for sanctioning strategy in the supervisory field is that *regulative considerations are legitimately included* among the contextual factors taken into account by decision makers. Presumably these considerations are less immediate in questions under the supervisory than the regulative code. But if the distinction which we continually urge between conventional and functional categories is borne in mind, it is natural to regard enterprisery and regulative dimensions as present—in degree—in all problems. By formal nomenclature a controversy may be phrased as enterprisery; yet the value weight of the parties may be such that prices and quantities of production are at stake for an entire industry or region. The five-fold division into codes was not made for formalistic purposes but rather as an aid in bringing functional matters explicitly into the open.

The Strategy of Corrective Measures

The most important questions that arise in administering the corrective code are not the choice of measures to be applied once an eligible target is identified; rather, the key question relates to the making of the original judgment. Corrective measures are deeply affected by the state of knowledge in medicine, psychology and related sciences; and once the principle of openness to the results of science has been accepted corrective measures are immediately modified in the light of changing estimates founded upon empirical advances in the several disciplines concerned. The original identification, however, is a much more complex matter since it is the act in the total process which is critical for all that follows; and, though closely intertwined with scientific evidence, typically calls for decisions to be made by community authorities who are laymen so far as the pertinent sciences are concerned.

We have underlined the point that the corrective code is designed to clarify the task of identifying target individuals and organizations who, though they contribute to disturbing situations, are nonresponsible. Since responsibility is a matter of education and educability, the decision maker must make up his mind whether the potential target of official measures falls short of the freedom of choice which is the criterion of an educated participant.

Community decision makers are especially dependent upon the evidence made available to them by scientists who specialize in psychiatry and the social sciences. The role of the first is obvious since psychiatrists are highly specialized upon the identification and possible control of personality factors that limit freedom. The role of social scientists—or, more specifically, of sociologists, anthropologists, economists, political scientists, and other social scientists—is not as yet so well understood as that of the physician, uncertain though the image of the psychiatrist may be. Social scientists specialize upon methods which are capable of disclosing group norms; and knowledge of these norms is an indispensable prerequisite of well-founded estimates of the effects that can be expected to follow from varying degrees of exposure to group norms.[71] Sociologists and other social scientists have not applied their methods in sufficient detail to enough group contexts to have on file all the information required to cope with many types of cases.

The decision maker who determines whether he is confronted by an educative sanctioning problem or a corrective problem is rather baffled by psychiatric testimony, despite the significance of psychiatry in connection with judgments of freedom. Psychiatric knowledge is in some ways distinctive: [72] 1. We rely upon it for much of our current understanding of how some extremes of thought and behavior are immediately dependent upon organic factors. 2. We owe to psychiatric research our present awareness of the pervasive role of unconscious factors in shaping human response. 3. Psychiatry has devised methods for the study and treatment of extreme conditions, some of which can be transferred to the preventive strategy of everyday life. 4. Psychiatric science has profoundly affected the social and psychological sciences by calling attention to the subtler interplay of the growth of individual personality and the character of the social context to which each person is exposed. We have learned the finer structure of culture, class, interest, and personality at various levels of crisis as a side effect of modern psychiatry.

Psychiatric knowledge has had an especially strong impact in connection with conceptions of responsibility and with procedures by which deprivers are sorted out and dealt with.[73] Psychiatric knowledge shows that often, *though not invariably,* those who are psychiatrically ill or handicapped are among the deprivers *largely* as a consequence of psychiatric variables. To the degree that psychopathological variables dominate the individual is acting without freedom of choice and cannot be regarded as responsible from the standpoint of a public order of human dignity. To the extent that such individuals threaten to be deprivers of themselves or others, they are *corrective* problems and liable to appropriate measures. Corrective measures aim at restoring or bringing the individual's freedom of choice to at least the minimum level that enables one to participate in the culture of a body politic. There has been great confusion in the procedures whereby the decision makers have had brought to their attention the factual statements, predictions, and forecasts of qualified psychiatrists and other specialists. The chief confusion has arisen from *failure to understand the questions* that can be put to the psychiatrist without asking him to abandon his role as a physician and to infringe upon the role proper to the decision maker, whether judge or jury.

Part of this confusion regarding proper questions comes from failure to perceive that *the legalistic language to be applied by the community decision maker is best applied when it is not used to interrogate psychiatrists.* Legalistic terminology may employ such expressions as "insane," "of unsound mind," "knowledge of right and wrong." It is not the role of the psychiatrist to use this mode of thought or talk; and the judge who couches questions to a psychiatrist in these terms, or who allows such terms to be employed in addressing a psychiatrist, or in the testimony of psychiatrists, is both confused, and confounding confusion.

The psychiatrist can be helpful to the court if he seeks to make clear in his own language, or in the language common to the culture, whether an individual is psychiatrically ill or handicapped, or was at a specified time. He can be asked to explain how psychopathological variables typically affect the conduct of individuals under specified types of circumstances. The circumstances referred to can be suggested by past situations involving the defendant, or by situations in which he may possibly be thrown in the future. Psychiatric generalizations, like all scientific generalizations, take the form of "if, then" statements of probability. It is not appropriate to ask the psychiatrist to make a forecast of how the defendant will act under hypothetical conditions—whether, for example, he will attempt to kill himself or someone else. The task of estimating the future of specific individuals is properly within the sphere of the decision maker who has the benefit of several sources of information about past incidents and the current state of scientific predictions. On the last point—the current state of psychiatric generalization—*it is always useful to obtain from the psychiatrist an estimate of the degree to which, in his judgment, there is professional consensus, or a high degree of experimental (or other) confirmation.*

In the United States progress is being made in avoiding the confusions that arise when incorrect questions are asked or when the double language point is overlooked in the phraseology of questions. Progress is also occurring in another procedural matter. "Sentencing" is often separated from the initial determination of what we here call responsibility or, in the case of a nonresponsible defendant, of a threatening depriver. In the former case educative measures are indicated; in the latter, corrective measures. The decision makers, the types of relevant testimony, and procedures can wisely vary between the two sets of problems.[74]

The strategy of sanctioning as outlined in this chapter has the best chance of succeeding when it is future-oriented and contextual, when it is adapted to all factors that significantly condition the result, and when attention is given to the principle of dominant though interconnected objectives. The range of objectives is important as means of bringing to the notice of decision makers the wide ramifications of every problem. We recognize the objectives of prevention, deterrence, restoration, rehabilitation, and reconstruction; and, in particular, we reject as incompatible with the goal of realizing a commonwealth of free men the demand to impose suffering as an end in itself, as a scope value of the sanctioning system.

13. THE STUDY OF THE SANCTIONING SYSTEM

THE FUNDAMENTAL approach to sanctioning that we recommend seeks to connect every recurring detail of the process with significant features of the whole. If this is to be accomplished it will be necessary to encourage types of research that are largely lacking at present; or which, if carried out, are executed by unpromising methods. We are concerned with the multivalued impact of any act of sanction upon both the target of sanction and the sanctioner. The greater the degree of involvement by the entire community in the sanctioning process the greater the effect of sanctioning upon the community. The point regarding degree of involvement, which reflects the magnitude and inclusiveness of the values at stake, obviously applies to the targets as well as to the launchers of sanctioning measures.

A realistic examination of any interaction in a sanctioning sequence confirms the point that all values of all participants are to some extent affected. When the degree of involvement is slight the scientific observer as well as the responsible decision maker may choose to ignore it in order to concentrate upon the most important values at stake. The specialized group with the most direct knowledge of how sanctioning affects the social setting in concrete cases is social workers. In many cities the breadwinner who clashes with "the law" cuts off the family income and this results in a new or renewed demand upon public welfare authorities for assistance. Despite the large amount of information obtained by conscientious case investigators it cannot be truthfully said that a realistic picture of the social significance of sanctioning has been made available for either scientific or policy purposes. The data have been ineffectively guided by relevant theory.

At the other extreme from the routine report of hard driven welfare workers are the published accounts of sensational cases. In our civilization the mass media are expected to cover the human interest angle of every crime or litigation that sparks public attention; and this means probing into the nooks and crannies of the lives of families, friends, employers, judges, attorneys, witnesses, jurors, and of the whole community. Nothing exceeds the fascination of a Lindbergh kidnapping case, or the Hall-Mills murder mystery, or the trial of Al Capone for tax evasion; or even climactic moments in the governmental investigations, such as the classical Hughes inquiry into the life insurance companies, or the federal investigation of the great banking houses after the collapse of '29.

It is universally recognized that the processes of social life proceed through many channels and at remarkably different rhythms. Thousands and indeed millions of contacts between officials and citizens leave no more mark upon public consciousness than the individual drop of water in the Hudson River. Yet at times the whole social landscape is lit with giant flares as hundreds of newspaper and newsreel reporters, radio and TV commentators, and special writers steam into a hitherto quiet and obscure New England town; or the privacy of a once sacrosanct Wall Street investment house.

Historians, social scientists, psychiatrists, and novelists are at one in suspecting the existence of the first invisible ties that bind the climactic intensity of the traumatizing episode with the monotonies of everyday living. When one pushes behind the drama to the context a remarkable realignment of vision occurs. The pre-drama grows more intensely absorbing as the details of the final upsurge recede in significance. Behind the ax murder lies the cumulative tension of a sad marriage, a disappointing child, a blasted career, a pre-psychotic friend, a declining social position, a disintegrating residential district. Looking beyond the kleig lights we find evidence of a slow and massive realignment of strength among organized labor, organized ownership and management, and organized politics and government.

It is not to be denied, however, that the sensational incident exercises weight of its own in the still partially mysterious march of history. Old social images are reaffirmed with a new cast of characters. But in a rapidly changing society there are new characters who create new images of social reality and redefine the myth of power, wealth, and other value distributions and tendencies as they are perceived by the community. Public exposure in a context of excitement crystallizes the image in the same way that a photograph captures a moment of realization and thereafter lives a life of its own, when it repeatedly comes to the focus of attention of the subject of the photograph, and fixes the dimensions of personality and culture.[1] The heroic image is a challenge to emulation; the ludicrous image a provocation to remould the persona.

If we are to improve our scanty understanding of the precise significance of events-in-context, it will be imperative to view every eligible detail in a multi-valued perspective that examines as many participants as can be identified, and shows how they perceive themselves as indulged or deprived, and how they are perceived by others, including the scientific observer who brings together a methodical picture of the whole.

What manner of man performs the sanctioning function at various stages of the total process? What expectations led him into sanctioning activity? Why does he stay in it? What does it do to transform his personality through the years and to modify his impact upon others in the official and nonofficial situations where he lives? [2]

It is more conventional, of course, to direct these questions to the targets of sanctioning rather than the sanctioner. But it is not to be overlooked that an equilibrium relationship appears to connect sanctioner and sanctioned. Society has a vast apparatus in being to handle a given volume of sanctioning. When the stream of targets begins to dry up at a given place, what happens? Is there a search for targets to keep the "investment" justified? Does the sanctioning machinery create a structure of interests that demands bigger and better prisons, bigger and better police forces, bigger and better statutory regulations? Is the effect to maintain a volume of activity that protects the public order; or is the cumulative impact to add to the rigidity of the legal and political process, and hence to hobble the effectiveness of the system which it is nominally engaged in defending?

Such questions are far from idle or merely whimsical speculations if we consider the self-perpetuating character of many of the traditional varieties of sanction, and especially the practice of incarceration. This time-honored device seeks to segregate targets from the community and—at its best—to create a special environment that motivates and equips these targets to return as useful members of society. Previously we have pointed to the evidence of recidivism as casting doubt upon the efficacy of incarceration as now applied.

Any program in the sanctioning field that aims seriously to accomplish corrective aims depends largely upon the caliber of the personnel. In part reconstruction depends upon models whom the subject can copy on the unconscious and conscious level. To what extent is the sanction target inspired to remodel himself as a result of the impressive characters whom he meets among policemen, judges, prison guards, and other sanctioning personnel? With no undue cynicism one may doubt that our society has fully grasped the challenge of sanctioning policy to seize the opportunity to correct past errors of the socialization process.

THE CORRECTIVE COMMUNITY

Modern therapeutic research is learning to proceed on the principles of *minimum segregation* and *minimum deprivation;* and to use the therapeutic community to create a series of *successive approximations* of full participation in society. As we understand the corrective problem it is similar in scope, since the targets of corrective action are those who are substandard in education, and require intensive help to acquire a requisite minimum level of motivation and capability.

The task of the *corrective community* is substantially identical with the problem of the *therapeutic community* as now understood.[3] In both cases the task is to handle the internal and external relations of the *special community* in such a way that the *transition back* to full participation is handled as economically as possible. In many cases this means choosing *new points of reentry* for the individual, especially if the older context was such that it provoked or rewarded perspectives and operations in violation of pertinent norms.[4] To some extent the *corrective community* can assist the individual to remodel himself to a degree that provides him with predispositions to meet future responsibility; but these predispositions need to be sustained by entry into a social context that puts minimum strain upon the remodeled personality system.

Undoubtedly we need more experimental programs designed to discover the most efficient modes of composing and conducting a corrective community. Our sanctioning activities will undoubtedly benefit by case studies that show the multi-value significance of situations at every phase of the sanctioning process in any jurisdiction. In every life situation the research task is to see the world from the viewpoint of every participant, which means that it is necessary to explore expectations, value demands and identifications of all concerned. To take these into account does not necessarily exercise much effect upon the immediate outcome of a decision process. Long-range effects, however, are probable since a society in which persuasion occupies an important place seeks to bring about conforming conduct, if possible, by voluntary changes in perspective. The actual state of relevant perspective must provide the point of impact for all strategies of prevention and rehabilitation.

THE MULTI-VALUED IMPACT OF INCARCERATION AND PAROLE

As an exemplification of the research that can contribute to the appraisal of sanctioning activity we refer to the proposal for the study of parole put forward by Jerome Skolnick. Some of the following paragraphs are adapted from his exposition.[5]

Conventional parole prediction studies assume that the individual's former place in the community is the major determinant of his behavior on parole. However, they do not evaluate the parolee's position in his most recently occupied social system, the prison society.[6] Likewise, studies of prison society do not consider the impact of the prison social system upon parole behavior.[7] Whether a convict lives for months, even years, as a *rat, center man, merchant, tough, gorilla, wolf, punk, hipster,* or *real man* is bound to leave an impression on his perspectives and evaluations of the facts of community life, where wives may replace *punks,* and *screws* are not met with except perhaps in the guise of parole officers.

An additional factor is the influence of the validity of the information that the convict has received concerning life on parole. A convict learns, and through learning develops a set of expectations regarding parole which may be unrealistically high or low, or fairly accurate. In any case the expectations with which he begins parole are likely to influence conduct. The social environment encountered by the parolee validates some expectations and undermines others. The result is to modify some motivations either in the direction of conforming to community norms or of rejecting them.

When we consider the factors in the prison setting that bear most directly upon the subsequent success or failure of the parolee we must weigh the significance of the communications regarding parole that are disseminated in prison society. What is said about the situation in which the prisoner will find himself when he steps into the world outside? Is the parolee's environment depicted as hostile and full of value deprivation? Or, on the contrary, is the environment described in terms that suggest an exceedingly indulgent reception? Who are the communicators who initiate the references made to parole? What members of the prison audience are disposed to accept or reject messages originated by these communicators? How realistic or unrealistic are the resulting expectations, and how does subsequent exposure to actual parole environments, by affecting such expectations, influence the success or failure of the parolee?

Probably the most important factor in the total flow of references to the parole environment is this: *the principal sources of information are parole violators.* Prisoners who succeed on parole do not come back, and they maintain little if any contact with those who fail and rejoin prison society.

At any given time three categories of prisoners have had parole experience: those who committed another criminal act (whether before or after the expiration of parole), technical violators returned by parole officers, and technical violators who turned themselves in. These men and women are acknowledged experts; they have been through the mill.

What is said, however, is not necessarily taken at face value. This depends, as in all communication processes, upon the predispositions of the audience toward the communicators. In prison society—as in any society—human relations display regular features; these constitute the social structure. Such structures depend upon value shaping and sharing, and the specific practices by which these activities are carried on. Part of the pattern includes the images with the aid of which participants perceive one another. These images—reflected in the argot terms of *rat, real man,* and the like—reflect the actual division of activity within the prison and in turn affect what goes on. To be perceived as a *real man* is to receive high respect; to be regarded as a *rat* is at the other end of the scale. Actually what a *rat* says about the parole environment may be more realistic than what the *real man* says. But the perhaps blatantly distorted messages originating with the latter are recalled, believed, and firmly incorporated into the system of expectations held by candidates for parole.

From the standpoint of the larger community it is obvious that prisoners occupy a relatively disadvantaged position in terms of all values. Reviewing the situation systematically, we note that the convict is deprived of: (a) autonomy (power); (b) opportunities to exercise skill (skill); (c) opportunities to earn a living (wealth); (d) status in the legitimate world (respect); (e) moral standing (rectitude); (f) access to information (enlightenment); (g) contact with friends and family (affection).

It is inaccurate to conclude, however, that every member of the prison population views the prison as equally deprivational, or that every convict has the same intensity of motivation to obtain freedom; and it is apparent that among those who want to get outside prison walls there are great differences in motivation to conform to the norms of the larger society. All these differences affect the approach of a prisoner who is technically eligible for parole, and his subsequent record.

That prison society holds many attractions is suggested by the observation, so surprising to many newspaper readers, that old convicts often go to extreme lengths to prevent their permanent release. Evidently they have developed a way of life that provides an alternative to life as a regular member of the larger community. The subculture of the prison, so far as they are concerned, has become a source of net indulgence when compared with return to civic participation.

Less drastic examples are well known to parole officers and prison officials. And it is highly probable that parolees or ex-convicts who themselves think that they want to be free, or stay free, are driven by other motivations which they do not fully understand to rejoin prison society. Some provocative behavior is so offensive and so clumsy that its chief function is to bring the perpetrator back to his special world.

Several factors are at work in human personality to produce what at first sight appears to be an anomalous result. By what mechanisms do people continue to prefer to live rather than to commit suicide? Under what circumstances does the mechanism break down, and plunge the individual into listless despair or active invitation to death? [8]

We may summarize the miscellany of insights now current regarding the phenomenon of adaptation by speaking of the *mechanism of tolerable perspectives.* What this means can be illustrated in a number of familiar cases. We notice that some prisoners appear to focus their attention upon the here and now, and to explore the opportunities of the restricted environment for obtaining such gratifications as they can find. They preoccupy themselves with the immediate, dismissing either the rehearsal of the past or the elaboration of the future.[9] Such prisoners specialize in prison politics; or they become "inside dopesters" about what has just happened and what is pending; or they move into other active roles. These patterns of specialized activity corroborate or inspire additions to the argot terms available for identification at any given time.

Another adjustment to prison takes the form of ignoring or minimizing the present. This can be most effectively done by individuals who rely upon "defense by detachment," which enables them to survive without allowing themselves to experience the emotions of rage, love, or any vivid affect whatever. Presumably these prisoners have a history of early exposure to an unsatisfactory family environment in which they learned to meet the present by passive endurance and to live in a psychological equivalent of suspended animation. Such persons may not allow themselves to plan or to anticipate the future in detail.

Another solution is closely related to detachment since it minimizes participation in the present. The prisoner allows his focus of attention to be absorbed in fantasies of the past or future; or in the pursuit of knowledge or the elaboration of ideological systems. Fantasies may be externalized as talk, in this way providing a means of obtaining empathic indulgence and respect from persons in the immediate environment. The pursuit of knowledge by reading and reflection provides skill and enlightenment, which is more than simple "escape" from recognition of the disagreeable present.

It is probable that by means of proper interviewing and participant observation we can discover the full range and frequency of the uses made by prisoners of the mechanism of tolerable perspectives; and, further, that we can connect various patterns of use with predispositions at the time of entry into prison society, and with behavior during and after prison. The expectations which an individual permits himself to entertain regarding the parole environment will be in part determined by the mechanism referred to here, since perceived value deprivations or indulgences in a prison or postprison situation depends upon the degree to which current, past, and future events are inflated or deflated in the perspectives of the prisoner.

A basic hypothesis put forward for the study of parole [10] is that *expectations among current prisoners regarding value indulgences or deprivations on parole are more like the expectations of parole violators than of parole successes.*

Furthermore, it is possible to outline hypotheses regarding the realism or unrealism of expectations and the significance of this factor for success or failure. The most important distinction is between parole candidates who expect to enjoy *moderate indulgence* and those whose anticipations are that they will experience *extreme indulgences* or *extreme deprivations.*

Studies of how patients meet such deprivational situations as surgery point to the importance of distinguishing between extreme and moderate anticipation. The most original discovery has been that when patients expect to suffer horribly, and in fact do not, they do not respond with joy and relief; rather, their inner state has become chronically anxious, and anxiety interferes with realistic perception of the relative indulgence they are receiving from the environment. The acute dysphoria of anxiety is nourished by unconscious conflicts which are not eliminated by the events in the individual's real environment.[11]

Hence, it is predicted by Skolnick that parole candidates who anticipate extremely low value indulgence are most likely to display guilt, lassitude, and apathy in attempting to work out problems that arise during the parole period. Candidates with extremely sanguine expectations are especially likely to display anger and resentment toward parole authorities during critical parole periods.

What characteristics of the parolee's environment significantly affect success or failure? The following hypotheses deal with this question:

Parolees who return to an environment that is moderately accepting of prison norms will be more likely to achieve success on parole than those who return to an environment which either completely accepts or completely rejects prisoner norms.

Parolees who return to an environment which completely rejects prisoner norms are more likely than others to bear a heavy burden of guilt for having left their fellow prisoners behind, plus concomitant hostility toward individuals in the nonprison environment regardless of, and perhaps because of, attempts by these persons to appear friendly and helpful.

Parolees who return to an environment which completely accepts prisoner norms are more likely than others to make no attempt whatsoever to assimilate the legal and communal norms of the legitimate world, since rewards are associated with defying this world, including its symbols of authority.[12]

THE NEED FOR CONTEXTUAL PRESENTATION

The multi-valued study of the sanctioning system is handicapped at present by inappropriate instruments to serve the needs of teaching, research, advice, and final decision. The contextual character of the decision process calls for the translation of the relevant manifold of events into workable terms suitable to the many roles that must be played in the process.

We suggest that advances which have been made in the theory of problem solving and in devices for contextual presentation provide students of sanctioning, as of every significant feature of law in the social process, with methods much more pertinent to the intellectual tasks confronting the student, investigator, policy advisor or final decision maker than anything hitherto available. We shall refer to the emerging technique as the decision seminar, and outline some of the principles and procedures by which the fundamental conception can be adapted to the problems which concern us here.

RECENT ADVANCES IN TECHNIQUE

One mark of the accelerating rate of development in political and legal studies, as in all branches of knowledge, is the appearance of new patterns of university instruction and inquiry. The RAND Corporation took the initiative in adapting the technique of war gaming to the consideration of diplomatic questions, and this has led to a crop of promising extensions into education and business as well as government.[13] As originally conceived the games method was not primarily aimed at the in-service training of diplomats or the preservice preparation of students of national government or international politics. It was intended to yield immediately important policy results by modifying the perspectives of key policy advisors and decision makers. However, the pedagogical significance of the technique was so obvious that diffusion began at once into the university world.[14]

Another recent device has had less immediate impact upon thoughtful teachers, although it is now a favorite instrument among some executives in business and other big-scale organizations. The reference is to "brain-storming," an adaptation to group action of the free association technique originally employed by Freud for therapeutic purposes. The idea is to create a permissive social environment in which individuals have the courage to break out of conventional stereotypes of thought.[15] Brain-storming has something in common with "buzz sessions" in which, for instance, large gatherings may be broken up for private, small-group consideration of a subject, free of the intimidating necessity of addressing a large audience every time anyone opens his mouth.[16]

Another suggestive set of models has come from the theory and practice of role playing. In fact, role playing devices have been well established for years in professional education.[17] Law schools arrange moot courts to give students a foretaste of the realities of litigation.

War or diplomatic gaming technique has several advantages over older types of seminar method. For one thing, the participants are always active; it is less easy to become passive and torpid than in conventional seminars. For another, the habit of acting with tentative decisiveness is cultivated, since participants must provisionally commit themselves about the future. The rules of the game are applied by umpires who play the future role of "Nature" or "Destiny"; and the rules require definiteness in place of the vagueness so often confused with "good judgment." Creativity is encouraged by the premium put upon successful invention. Motivations to study past events are kept high since the uses of history are demonstrated by the search for suggestive likenesses and differences. Furthermore, new scientific hypotheses are germinated in the light of new factor combinations; and scientific procedures are adapted to the task of improving the inflow of information *about* the future *through* the future.

Stimulating as the technique of gaming is, it is not without limitations. Players are tempted to develop "umpire consciousness" and to adapt their solutions accordingly. But the care and feeding of umpires is not among the distinctive skills of responsible advisors, since presumably an advisor's role in actual policy processes is to substitute for the umpires who are nonexistent in reality. Hence gaming technique needs to be supplemented by methods that give no one the last word—since the last word is only spoken as future events unfold.

Among the promising lines of development that have begun to modify education we cannot fail to mention film, radio, TV, and other "audio-visual" aids. Medical education in particular has benefitted from devices which make it possible to magnify delicate surgical interventions. Similarly, techniques of visual magnification (or reduction) have contributed to the regular training of physicists, chemists, biologists, geologists, and astronomers.

Complex audio-visual-print images (AVP images) have important advantages for the study of the decision process itself, as well as for the technique of decision making. AVP images lend themselves to *continuing awareness of space-time dimensions;* and these, as we know in the historical and social sciences—and increasingly in all science—are crucial. AVP images have the further advantage of permitting an abstraction to be closely related to empirical observation. In any context pertinent to community policy it is perilous to lose sight of the connection between the *observer-as-generalizer* and the *observer-as-primary-recorder*. In practice primary records are less distinctive than "concept" terms imply.

Because AVP images condense information without losing context they are important storage and recovery devices which serve the purposes of memory and recall. The contextual point applies to the connection between descriptive knowledge of any kind and society as a whole. AVP images increase the potential speed of operations by which the decision makers of society can have pertinent information brought to their notice at the moment when motivations are highest to give it consideration.

Many scholars and scientists are busily engaged in adapting new theories and new engineering know-how to information storage and retrieval with the aid of machines.[18] This is the most recent and impressive indication that the "industrial revolution" has not only transformed the power plant, the factory, and the kitchen, but has at last reached into the ivory tower (and touched the ivory domes). The same questions arise in regard to machines as were raised in reference to sophisticated modes of summarizing and generalizing mathematical and statistical relationships. For instance: What are the empirical contexts? What is the relationship between the events at the focus of attention of the initial observer and the records transmitted from stage to stage as data and interpretation? How are the empirical references at the terminal stage related to the starting point? AVP images are as much needed here as elsewhere in decisions.

Besides performing storage and retrieval functions, AVP images aid *imagination*. Since policy is a choice among future events, the role of imagination in the decision process is large. AVP images provide enough contextuality of reference to keep policy makers and executives in closer touch with reality than when images of the kind are missing.

Educational methods are also influenced by the use of *simulation models*. For years it has been necessary for engineers to use models in the shape of wind tunnels, bridges, dams, electric generators, and transmission towers. For a moment, at least, a model is a "frozen policy," a potential arrangement of mass and energy which is open to critical evaluation. In social policy only operations closely linked with engineering—like city or regional planning—are accustomed to regard the preparation of models as an indispensable part of the decision process.

The advances that have been made in audio-visual technique, machine computation and model building permit a new, direct approach to the presentation of past, present, and future events. Not the individual device but the coordinated application of all available instruments is the indicated strategy. How can these developments be effectively employed in connection with the study of sanctioning?

THE POTENTIALITIES OF THE DECISION SEMINAR

Our answer is that seminars can be adapted to the opportunities now at our disposal for contextual presentation of the multi-valued approach. What principles shall guide us in perfecting a program of key decision seminars?

For one thing decision seminars can be designed to *parallel the problems of a whole community context or of a specific participant.* We might set up seminars to parallel the sanctioning process in a locality, a region, a nation, or the international arena. Or seminars might focus upon the office of the prosecutor, the chief of police, a court, a correctional agency, a parole board.

In any case it is essential to conceive of a decision seminar as a continuing enterprise that extends beyond the period of membership of any group of participants. The criterion of continuity emphasizes the possibilities for cumulative research and learning that such an operation affords.

Another point is to make sure that the seminar provides *an environment in which the decision process under study is presented as a whole and as continuous in time.* This principle refers to the continuity of the object of study, not the act of study. It emphasizes the importance of providing seminar members with highly selective focus of attention. A *recall* function is to be performed; that is to say, fundamental categories are used to remind participants of the salient features of the context.

The meaning of this requirement may be more apparent if we describe a highly provisional application of the technique that was made in reference to Vicos, the Peruvian hacienda administered for several years as a project of Cornell's Department of Anthropology. In 1954–55 four members of the Center for the Behavioral Sciences at Stanford, California, organized a seminar to analyze and advise on policy regarding the future of Vicos. One member of the seminar provided most of the information relating to the community. He welcomed the seminar as an opportunity to think through the policy alternatives open to him on the hacienda.[19]

The seminar always used the same room for its deliberations and divided up the wall space into sections which were used to refer to various sectors of the social process in and around Vicos. For instance, one space was assigned economics; another politics; a third family and intimate affairs; a fourth safety, health, and comfort; and so on until the entire social process was allocated. A line was drawn around the room at eye level ("1954"). Other lines were drawn below this to indicate the year when the Cornell intervention began, and to allow for pre-Cornellian events to be entered. Above the midline was the future. As information was gathered about any given sequence of events a slip was tacked to the beaver board covering of the wall to serve as a continuing reminder of what had taken place. Maps, abstracts, and guides to notes and bibliography were included. The space above the midline was used to record estimates of the future, assuming no change of policy, and estimated developments, assuming policy changes. The future was also characterized at selected cross sections according to preferred value patterns (and specific institutional objectives). Each cross section served as a rough model of the community.

For purposes of ready reference we speak of the foregoing devices as *chart-room technique*. The fact that audio-visual devices are employed is not the vital point, but *the contextual use of audio-visual instrumentalities, as continuing aids to storage, recall, and imagination.*

The fundamental intellectual tasks to be performed in problem solving are furthered in seminar settings of this kind.

Trend Reports

A trend report describes a selected sequence of past events and raises questions relating to the weighing of sources, the fullness of available data, and the like. If the report is quantitative it poses such statistical issues as sampling and time series.[20]

Scientific Reports

We use the term "scientific" to designate reports that undertake to explain a given result in the light of theory and data. The task may be approached by case studies, correlational analysis, or experimentation. In practice few reports concerning trend are entirely devoid of scientific generalization or of attempted correlations. However, the methodological contrast between a chronology, on the one hand, and a time series analysis of votes and business cycles, on the other, is evident. The discussion of a scientific report deals with the clarity of the generalizations offered, and with the degree of confirmation produced by the methods employed and the findings obtained.[21]

Projection Reports

The reference is to estimates of the future on the assumption that the seminar has no influence upon events. Discussion relates to the methods of extrapolation used, and the probability that an estimate of a given magnitude is high or low.[22]

Goal Reports

The function of such a report is to offer a clarification of overriding policy objectives. Discussion can move in two directions: toward a consideration of the grounds of the goals put forward; toward explicit specification of goals in institutional terms.[23]

Policy (Alternative) Reports

A policy report invents or selects a policy, or a set of policy alternatives by which postulated goals can be achieved, and offers an evaluation of costs, gains and probabilities. Discussion may elicit new policy inventions or focus entirely upon criticizing proposed evaluations.[24]

The seminar *agenda* is designed to harmonize the procedures open to the group during a given period which best enables the aims of the seminar to be accomplished. In general, the instructional purpose is to provide skill in the use of all available aids to problem solving.

The Filing of Independent Estimates

Since one objective of decision seminars is to orient the participant toward the future an important place on the agenda is properly assigned to the obtaining of independent estimates by seminar members of future decisions. Assume that the seminar is paralleling the decision process of an entire body politic, such as the local municipality, the state, or the entire metropolitan area. Attention would be focused at regular intervals upon the future of each phase of the decision process. What bills are likely to be approved by the legislative bodies in question during the next session? What sanctioning arrangements will probably be included? What are the probable changes in the curves of arrest for various alleged offenses? In convictions? Paroles? What changes in sanctioning news are likely to occur? What changes in sanctioning statutes (or in other features of the process) will be promoted? By whom? With what outlay? What reports upon sanctioning policies and results are likely to be made? By whom?

In order to facilitate independent judgment the individual can be asked to file his estimates with the clerk of the seminar, who keeps identities secret until authorized to divulge the information.

The Consideration of Estimates

Individual estimates can be consolidated into a report by the clerk who—if the material is available in advance—may also prepare visual summaries. In this way contrasting expectations can be precisely set forth within the setting provided by the accumulated information already at the attention of the seminar. The ensuing discussion—in which the participants acknowledge their estimates or not, as they see fit—provides an important test of everyone's expectations. At the end of the seminar each individual is requested to submit a revised estimate, if he so desires, which is kept confidential as part of the member's permanent file.

The Reconsideration of Estimates

When a seminar has met long enough for some events which were once in the future to recede into the past of the members of the seminar, an opportunity exists for each individual to consider why he made accurate or inaccurate forecasts. What bases of inference were used? What possible sources were overlooked, deemphasized, overemphasized? Why? A place is to be found on the agenda for "autopsies" of this kind. Here again the individual is permitted to act as judge of the disclosures that he is willing to make. Insight can also be fostered by an occasional scientific report of past forecasts and the factors that appear to account for them. For example, a significant relationship may exist between estimates which play up or down various categories of events, and age, sex, training, experience, personality traits, and other such factors. The scientific report of the proceedings provides data of importance regarding decision processes in general, and also contributes to the insight of present seminar members. In some instances it will be practicable to follow the response of members to the reports of past performance, which contributes another body of data to our presently insufficient knowledge of who is capable of improved predictive skill on the basis of information about his past performance.

The Examining of New Information

Places on the agenda are needed for reports of trend, projections, and scientific factors. New information is also introduced as a by-product of other reports.

The Clarification of Goals, Evaluation of Alternatives

Alternative definitions can be compared with one another; and policy alternatives can be examined according to costs and gains in value terms.

The items that appear on the agenda are adaptable to many special purposes. For instance, the forecasting of relatively immediate events may be an important feature of some seminars, though of very little significance for others. A seminar may deliberately limit its scope to long-range contingencies. During many sessions a given seminar may deal with historical trends or case studies, and put little emphasis upon the detailed projection of the future, or upon tightly formulated scientific or policy models. It often happens that no attempt is made to present a well-rounded configurative approach during a given year, since new tools may need to be devised to provide a body of basic material.

Many *special procedures* can usefully be adapted to the total agenda of a seminar.

Seminars have traditionally been conducted in splendid isolation from one another presumably out of deference to the Robinson Crusoe mentality of scholars. It will be a step forward when a great many seminars dealing with similar subject matter or using the same methods are linked together. This is not togetherness for its own sake nor is it a proposal to weaken the quality of advanced education. On the contrary the chances are good that students and teachers will find themselves seized by new motivations since they can recognize the fact that they are part of a common undertaking whose payoffs are immediate and intermediate as well as remote. Undoubtedly many seminars will continue to operate as relatively isolated units. Certainly there need be no disposition to induce teachers to enter into cooperative arrangements unless they are convinced of the net advantage of the step.

THE INTELLIGENCE AND APPRAISALS OF THE COMMUNITY

The decision seminar in the field of sanction law can parallel and even guide the agencies of decision in every jurisdiction. When we review the data requirements appropriate to sanctioning intelligence and appraisal, it is obvious that the magnitude of the task is such that selective principles must be applied. A division of labor is indicated among individuals and organizations, public or private, within the body politic. The data can be divided for convenience of discussion and assignment as follows: (1) Census information; (2) Case studies; (3) Correlation, experiment, and pretest.

By census information we mean data which are gathered and published at regular intervals regarding the sanctioning system as a whole. Information of this type is appropriately assigned to governmental agencies since the official machinery is well adapted to routine coverage. While much remains to be done, existing reports issued by agencies involved in sanctioning have improved greatly within recent years. For details we refer to the reports themselves and to the standard discussions of statistics in this field.[25]

The case study method is peculiarly important in the prospective development of sanction law. A properly executed case investigation provides the depth perspective without which census data cannot be understood. It is perhaps redundant to explain that when we refer to a "case study" something more is meant than the examination of Appellate Court opinions, which has been a distinctive mark of American legal education since Langdell at Harvard. Even in the law schools a quiet revolution has been transforming the "case book" of Appellate Court opinions into something closer to the specifications of a book of case studies which put the language of opinion into relevant social context.[26]

The case study method at its best seeks to view a situation from the inside as well as the outside. Hence the aim is to discover the perspectives of every significant participant, including his perspectives of other participants; and to connect these perspectives in an orderly way with the context of the social process. To return to the fundamental question about all interaction situations: what participants with what perspectives and base values employ what strategies to affect what outcomes how and with what effect? In the sanctioning process the sequence of interaction, in common with every legal process, moves from pre-arena through arena and post-arena stages. At every stage and in every community setting it is enlightening for policy and science to concentrate from time to time upon the understanding of individual cases, since the results contribute to the interpretation of the numerical map provided by census methods.

Indispensable as case studies are they rapidly lose their usefulness in any given context. It is easy for an investigator to get bogged down in anecdote as he learns more about "specific murderers," "prison wardens," "prosecuting attorneys," "criminal lawyers," "judges," "jurors," "parole board members," "police court reporters," etc. Instead of piling up more case histories the investigator is well advised to move as quickly as possible to correlational and experimental methods.[27]

The correlational, experimental, or pre-test approach makes it necessary to identify the key variables which are interacting with one another to produce the results which are under study, and to select the "operational indices" of each variable.[28] The privisional choice of variable implies an hypothesis, as when we make up our minds to examine the sanctioner's characteristics in terms of community, class, interest, personality, or crisis exposure.[29]

The methods of social intelligence and appraisal contribute most to knowledge when they are employed as part of a comprehensive continuing program. For example, census data may call attention to neighborhoods where norm violations are high. Case studies of neighborhoods may indicate, among other factors, that the neighborhood's low respect position profoundly affects its record of nonconformity. Correlational procedures may narrow the identity of the most active group of offenders to second generation immigrants whose parents have not improved their class position in several years, and who find in the "rackets" a number of accessible interest groups willing to provide money, respect, and the prospect of effective power. Such findings may suggest that census data should be obtained in the future that summarize the location of counter-mores business establishments. The results may also stimulate inventors of social policy to consider how to intervene in problem neighborhoods in order to change the configuration of variables that strengthen pro rather than anticonformity motivations and activities. For example, it may be decided to pre-test an employment service that brings young people in contact with good job opportunities which are outside the network of shady operations.

When the approach to the sanctioning system is truly contextual every intellectual task is performed in relation to it: clarification of goal, description of trend, discovery of conditions, projection of the future, invention and evaluation of alternatives. The contextual conception is a built-in check upon the exaggeration or neglect of each component of the total task.[30]

In concise summary of the present proposal to develop the field of sanction law: An examination of trends in the use of "criminal" and "civil" sanctions in the legal system of the United States sustains two main conclusions: many of the measures employed are in obvious contradiction of the basic goals of the commonwealth; many of the consequences undermine rather than protect and fulfill the institutions and values of the system of public order.

As a means of improving the effectiveness of sanctioning it is imperative to conceive of the process of sanctioning as a unified whole. The principles of sanctioning strategy are principles of content and of procedure. Principles of content clarify the objectives of sanction, or deterrence, restoration, prevention, rehabilitation, reconstruction. Principles of procedure specify who, selected how and with what base values, can best accomplish the objectives of sanctioning by what combination of positive and negative measures adapted to the requirements of the supervisory, regulative, enterprisory, constitutive, and corrective codes of the legal system.

The intellectual and procedural tools now at the disposal of the social and behavioral sciences, properly adapted and applied, are capable of providing a continuing flow of intelligence and appraisal information concerning the impact of any detail of the social process upon the context of values and institutions in which the detail is located. If the relevant context within which decisions are to be made is to be brought to the focus of the decision maker's attention, special methods are needed. As a step in this direction we outline the technique of the decision seminar which can be adapted to the problems of scholars, advisors, and decision makers.

It is within our capability to narrow the gap between aspiration and performance in the functioning of the sanctioning system. This is the proper scope of sanction law.

NOTES

INTRODUCTION

1. McDougal & Lasswell, *The Identification and Appraisal of Diverse Systems of Public Order,* 53 AM. J. INT'L L. 1–29 (1959).
2. See *e.g.,* NORTHROP, THE COMPLEXITY OF LEGAL AND ETHICAL EXPERIENCE (1959); POUND, JURISPRUDENCE (1959); SAYRE (ED.) INTERPRETATIONS OF MODERN LEGAL PHILOSOPHIES (1947).
3. See *e.g.,* LASSWELL, POWER AND PERSONALITY (1948).
4. See Dession and Lasswell, *Public Order Under Law,* 65 YALE L.J., 174, 184 (1955).
5. For much detail consult MCDOUGAL AND ASSOCIATES, STUDIES IN WORLD PUBLIC ORDER (1960).
6. See Dession and Lasswell, *supra* note 4, passim.
7. *Ibid.*

1: THE FUNCTION OF SANCTIONS IN OUR SYSTEM OF PUBLIC ORDER

1. Naturalization is expressly conditioned on "good moral character," Immigration and Nationality Act, § 316, 66 Stat. 242 (1952), 8 U.S.C. § 1427 (1958). Admission to jury service is barred by conviction of a crime punishable by imprisonment for more than one year. 28 U.S.C. § 1861 (1958).
2. 66 Stat. 267 (1952), 8 U.S.C. § 1481 (1958).

3. See *e.g.*, U.S. CONST. art. I, § 3. 4. U.S. CONST. amend. XIV, § 2.
5. DAUGHERTY & PARRISH, THE LABOR PROBLEMS OF AMERICAN SOCIETY 623–24 (1952).
6. Marvin v. Trout, 199 U.S. 212, 225 (1905).
7. See generally GELLHORN, INDIVIDUAL FREEDOM & GOVERNMENTAL RESTRAINTS 105–51 (1956).
8. Alcorn v. Alexandrovicz, 112 Conn. 618, 153 Atl. 786 (1931).
9. Dobbins Distillery v. United States, 96 U.S. 395 (1877).
10. 26 Stat. 209–10 (1890), 15 U.S.C. § 6 (1958).
11. National Ass'n For the Advancement of Colored People v. Alabama, 357 U.S. 449 (1958); People v. Pieri, 269 N.Y. 315, 199 N.E. (1936).
12. See generally MADDEN, PERSONS AND DOMESTIC RELATIONS 256–335, 369–82 (1931).
13. See generally Arens, *Conspiracy Revisited,* 3 BUFFALO L. REV. 242 (1954).
14. BLODGETT, PRINCIPLES OF ECONOMICS 40 (1948).
15. U.S. CONST. art. I, § 8. 16. STAFFORD, EQUITY 291 (1934).
17. GELLHORN, *op. cit. supra* note 7, at 106.
18. Barsky v. Board of Regents, 347 U.S. 442, 472 (1953) (Douglas, J., dissenting).
19. See generally GELLHORN, SECURITY, LOYALTY, AND SCIENCE (1950).
20. 20 Stat. 359 (1879), as amended, 39 U.S.C. § 226 (1958).
21. See generally GELLHORN, *op. cit. supra* note 19.
22. 18 U.S.C. §§ 1461, 1463 (1958). 23. 18 U.S.C. § 1341 (1958).
24. 18 U.S.C. § 1717 (1958). 25. 18 U.S.C. § 1461 (1958).
26. 18 U.S.C. §§ 1461, 1463. See also 64 Stat. 451 (1950), 39 U.S.C. 259 a–b (1958).
27. See EMERSON & HABER, POLITICAL AND CIVIL RIGHTS 714–15 (1st ed. 1952).
28. See *e.g.*, DEL. CODE ANN. tit. 11, § 701 (1953); it is noteworthy in this connection that Delaware has penalized the use of cameras at whipping posts. DEL. CODE ANN. tit. 11, § 411 (1953).
29. Radin, *The Goal of Law,* 1951 WASH. U.L.Q. 1, 19. 30. *Ibid.*
31. DESSION, CRIMINAL LAW, ADMINISTRATION AND PUBLIC ORDER 590 (1948).

2: SANCTIONING MEASURES AND THE SHARING OF RESPECT

1. For a concise summary of what is by now traditional state law on this subject see BARNES & TEETERS, NEW HORIZONS IN CRIMINOLOGY 749–750 (2d ed. 1951). See also *Note, Suspension of Civil Rights Upon Conviction for Felony,* 21 ST. JOHN'S L. REV. 117 (1946); *Note, The Legal Status of Convicts During and After Incarceration,* 37 VA. L. REV. 105 (1951). Some progress through the executive grant of pardons, designed to effect restoration of Civil Rights, is exemplified by Wisconsin; see Note, 1951 WIS. L. REV. 378.
2. See *Note,* 103, U. PA. L. REV. 60 (1954) for a survey of registration laws.
3. See *e.g.*, Hawker v. New York, 170 U.S. 189 (1898), sustaining constitutionality of legislative enactment barring the person convicted of crime from the practice of medicine as one not of good character.
4. Wolf v. Colorado, 338 U.S. 25, 27 (1949).

5. N.Y. Code Crim. Proc. § 514 (Emphasis added).
6. Barnes & Teeters, *op. cit. supra* note 1, at 750.
7. Goransson, *The Treatment of Offenders In Sweden* 3 (London, Howard League Pamphlet 1949).
8. State v. Jones, 50 N.H. 369 (1871).
9. Durham v. United States, 214 F.2d 862, 876 (D.C. Cir. 1954).
10. Williams v. United States, 250 F.2d 19, 25–26 (D.C. Cir. 1957).
11. Some of the cases in which the Durham Rule has been considered, but not accepted, include: Voss v. United States, 259 F.2d 699 (8th Cir. 1958); Sauer v. United States, 241 F.2d 640 (9th Cir.), *cert. den.*, 354 U.S. 940 (1957); Andersen v. United States, 237 F.2d 118 (9th Cir. 1956); United States v. Hopkins, 169 F. Supp. 187 (D. Md. 1958); Harrison v. Settle, 151 F. Supp. 372 (W.D. Mo. 1957); Massey v. Moore, 133 F. Supp. 31 (S.D. Tex. 1955); United States v. Kunak, 5 U.S.C.M.A. 346 17 C.M.R. 346 (1954); United States v. Smith, 5 U.S.C.M.A. 314, 17 C.M.R. 314 (1954); People v. Webb, 143 Cal. App. 2d 402, 300 P.2d 130 (Dist. Ct. App. 1956); People v. Ryan, 140 Cal. App. 2d 412, 295 P.2d 496 (Dist. Ct. App. 1956); State v. Davies, 146 Conn. 137, 148 A.2d 251 (1959); People v. Carpenter, 11 Ill. 2d 60, 142 N.E.2d 11 (1957); Flowers v. State, 236 Ind. 151, 139 N.E.2d 185 (1956); Saldiveri v. State, 217 Md. 412, 143 A.2d 70 (1958); Cole v. State, 212 Md. 55, 128 A.2d 437 (1957); Bryant v. State, 207 Md. 565, 115 A.2d 502 (1955); Thomas v. State, 206 Md. 575, 112 A.2d 913 (1955); Commonwealth v. Chester, 337 Mass. 702, 150 N.E.2d 914 (1958); Anderson v. Grasberg, 247 Minn. 538, 78 N.W.2d 450 (1956); State v. Kitchens, 129 Mont. 331, 286 P.2d 1079 (1955); Sollars v. State, 73 Nev. 248, 316 P.2d 917, *rehearing denied,* 73 Nev. 343, 319 P.2d 139 (1957); State v. Lucas, 30 N.J. 37, 152 A.2d 50 (1959); State v. White, 27 N.J. 158, 142 A.2d. 65 (1958); State v. Collins, 50 Wash. 2d 740, 314 P.2d 660 (1957).
12. See *e.g.*, Anderson v. United States, 237 F.2d 118, 127 (9th Cir. 1956).
13. Weihofen, Mental Disorder as a Criminal Defense 51 (1954); for digest of tests of responsibility in the various jurisdictions up to 1954 see *id.* at 129–173.
14. Hart v. Commonwealth, 131 Va. 726, 109 S.E. 582 (1921).
15. D.C. Code Ann. tit. 22, 2801.
16. N.Y. Pen. Law 261.
17. Wis. Stat. Ann. § 943.32 (1957).
18. Ala. Code tit. 14, § 415 (1940).
19. N.Y. Times, Aug. 17, 1958, p. 13, col. 4.
20. See table on variations in order of severity in Drummond, The Sex Paradox 350–51 (1953).
21. Skinner v. Oklahoma *ex rel.* Williamson, 316 U.S. 535, 541 (1942) (Douglas, J.).
22. See Miller, Criminal Law 371 (1934). *Cf.* N.Y. Pen. Code, §§ 1294, 1296, 1298.
23. Mannheim, Criminal Justice and Social Reconstruction 90–91 (1946).
24. See *e.g.*, Wildeblood v. United States, 273 F.2d 73 (D.C. Cir. 1959) for a fairly characteristic example of such sanctioning.
25. The order of the United States Court of Appeals for the District of Columbia Circuit, granting the petition for leave to proceed on appeal with-

out prepayment of costs in Conway Ellis Clarke v. United States, Appeals No. 14430, 14431, in the United States Court of Appeals for the District of Columbia Circuit dated September 29, 1958, contains advice, neglected to this day by Bench and Bar: "Circuit Judge Bazelon states that if he should be a member of the division of this Court which hears this appeal, he would wish the parties to brief and the Court to consider the . . . question whether an alternative sentence of fine or imprisonment is an invalid discrimination between those who are able to pay and those who are not."

26. New York, for example, explicitly exacts compliance with the requirement of an underlying felony, *independent* of the homicide, *i.e.*, one not involving the fatal assault. See *e.g.*, People v. Wagner, 245 N.Y. 143, 156 N.E. 644 (1927). While, of course, the felony may be only an independent assault, people v. Luscomb, 292 N.Y. 390, 55 N.E.2d 469 (1944), it will, as a practical matter, often involve the violation of property rights. See *e.g.*, People v. Meyer, 162 N.Y. 357, 56 N.E. 758 (1900); People v. Deacons, 109 N.Y. 374 16 N.E. 676 (1888). "The overwhelming number of American jurisdictions," moreover, "limit the felony murder doctrine to the underlying felonies of arson, burglary, rape and robbery." Ludwig, *Foreseeable Death in Felony Murder*, 18 U. PITT. L. REV. 51, 53 (1956). See *id.* materials cited therein.

27. FOSTER, CROWN LAW 258 (1809 ed.).

28. HOLMES, THE COMMON LAW 58 (1881).

29. N.Y. PEN. LAW § 240 (Emphasis added).

30. N.Y. PEN. LAW § 241 (Emphasis added).

31. N.Y. PEN. LAW § 2120 (Emphasis added).

32. N.Y. PEN. LAW § 2124. Other circumstances of aggravation in this section include being armed with a dangerous weapon or inflicting "grievous bodily harm or injury upon the person from whose possession . . . the property is taken."

33. N.Y. PEN LAW § 2125 (Emphasis added).

34. N.Y. PEN. LAW § 241 (Emphasis added).

35. N.Y. PEN. LAW § 240 (Emphasis added).

36. N.Y. PEN. LAW § 1420 (Emphasis added).

37. N.Y. PEN. LAW § 1420 (Emphasis added).

38. The Nation, Feb. 2, 1957, p. 89.

39. 103 Wash. 409, 174 Pac. 973 (1918).

40. *Id.* at 413, 174 Pac. at 974. 41. *Id.* at 411, 174 Pac. at 974.

42. *Id.* at 427, 173 Pac. at 979 (Emphasis added).

43. *Id.* at 428, 173 Pac. at 979. See also *In re* Remus, 119 Ohio St. 166, 162 N.E. 740 (1928).

44. For a survey of the national scene see Weihofen & Overholser, *Commitment of the Mentally Ill*, 24 TEXAS L. REV. 307 (1946).

45. See *supra* note 44. For a relatively recent case on "notice" in commitment proceedings see Kleinschmidt v. Hoctor, 361, Mo. 29, 233 S.W.2d 649 (1950).

46. N.Y. MENTAL HYGIENE LAW § 75.

47. N.Y. MENTAL HYGIENE LAW § 74 (3). A similar enactment is MASS. GEN. LAWS ch. 123, §§ 50, 51 (1957). For world trends see WORLD HEALTH ORGANIZATION, HOSPITALIZATION OF MENTAL PATIENTS, A SURVEY OF EXISTING LEGISLATION (Geneva, 1955).

48. See *e.g.*, People v. Lewis, 260 N.Y. 171, 183 N.E. 353, *cert. denied*, 289 U.S. 709 (1932); Holmes's Appeal, 379 Pa. 599, 109 A.2d 523 (1954); see generally Diana, *The Rights of Juvenile Delinquents; An Appraisal of Juvenile Court Procedures*, 47 J. CRIM. L., C. & P.S. 561 (1957).

49. 379 Pa. 599, 612, 616, 109 A.2d 523, 529, 530 (1954).

50. 260 N.Y. 171, 182, 183 N.E. 353, 357. (1932).

51. See *e.g.*, United States *ex rel.* Potts v. Rabb, 141 F.2d 45 (3rd Cir.), *cert. denied*, 322 U.S. 727 (1944); Cox v. Vaught, 52 F.2d 562 (10th Cir. 1931); see also collection of case law in Annot., 59 A.L.R. 567 (1929) and Annot., 24 A.L.R. 1432 (1923); *cf.* the dictum in State v. Lawler, 221 Wis. 423, 428, 267 N.W. 65, 68 (1936): "If it be made to appear that there was no evidence before the grand jury or the sole evidence upon which it acted was illegal, the indictment may be quashed."

52. See Annot. in 59 A.L.R. 567 (1923) for representative collection of case law on this subject before Costello v. United States, 350 U.S. 359 (1956). For the successful use of habeas corpus to challenge the evidentiary foundation of the grand jury see Deaver v. State, 24 Ala. App. 377, 135 So. 604 (1931).

53. 350 U.S. 359 (1956).

54. *In re* Fried, 161 F.2d 453, 458 (2d Cir. 1947).

55. See *e.g.*, Elliff, *Notes on the Abolition of the English Grand Jury*, 29 J. CRIM. L. & CRIMINOL. 3 (1938).

56. Knauff v. Shaughnessy, 338 U.S. 537 (1950).

57. *Id.* at 550 (Jackson, J. dissenting). 58. *Id.* at 550–551.

59. Immigration and Nationality Act §§ 201, 202, 66 Stat. 175–76 (1952), 8 U.S.C. §§ 1151–52 (1958).

60. See *e.g.*, Harisiades v. Shaughnessy, 342 U.S. 580 (1952).

61. TAYLOR, GRAND INQUEST 280 (1955).

62. *Ibid.* See also BARTH, THE LOYALTY OF FREE MEN 49–73 (1951); GOVERNMENT BY INVESTIGATION (1955); OXNAM, I PROTEST (1954).

63. Watkins v. United States, 354 U.S. 178, 185 (1957) (Warren, Ch.J.) (quoting from testimony of John T. Watkins before House of Representatives Committee on Un-American Activities.

64. *Id.* at 187. 65. *Id.* at 200.

66. *Id.* at 197; See generally Carr, *The Un-American Activities Committee and the Courts*, 11 LA. L. REV. 282 (1951).

67. Our scepticism in this regard appears to have been vindicated by the majority opinion of the Supreme Court in Barenblatt v. United States, 360 U.S. 109 (1959).

68. Boudin, *The Constitutional Right to Travel*, 56 COLUM. L. REV. 47 (1956).

69. *Id.* at 74.

70. See generally Boudin, *supra* note 68, and cases cited therein; see also Fanelli, *Passport—Right or Privilege?* 300 ANNALS 36 (1955).

71. See Kent v. Dulles, 357 U.S. 116 (1958); Dayton v. Dulles, 357 U.S. 144 (1958).

72. For a brief survey of the development of this field and succinct analysis of its problems see Biddle, *Subversives in Government*, 300 ANNALS 51 (1955).

73. BIDDLE, THE FEAR OF FREEDOM 209 (1951); see generally ANDREWS, WASHINGTON WITCH HUNT (1948); Emerson & Helfeld, *Loyalty Among Govern-*

ment Employees, 58 YALE L.J. 1 (1948); Fraenkel, *Law and Loyalty,* 37 IOWA L. REV. 153 (1952).

74. Bailey v. Richardson, 182 F.2d 46, 66 (D.C. Cir. 1950) (Edgerton, J. dissenting) *aff'd per curiam* 341 U.S. 918 (1951) (equally divided court). This case validated the loyalty program for federal government employees. See also Peters v. Hobby, 349 U.S. 331, 350–52 (1955); *cf.* Joint Anti-Fascist Refugee Committee v. McGrath, 341 U.S. 123 (1951).

75. Wood v. Wood, L. R. 9 Ex. 190, 196 (1874) (Kelly, C. B.).

76. MASS. CONST. art. XXIX. "Where a person acts as both prosecutor and judge in the same case, it is clear that there is a reasonable apprehension of bias. To say that such a person would not be interested in securing a conviction would be to hold too high an opinion of the integrity of mankind." Sedgewick, *Disqualification on the Ground of Bias as Applied to Administrative Tribunals* 23 CAN. BAR REV. 453, 456 (1945).

77. Mr. Justice Frankfurter, concurring, in Joint Anti-Fascist Refugee Committee v. McGrath, 341 U.S. 123, 170–71 (1951).

78. McKinley's Case (1817) 33 How. St. Tr. 275, 506. See generally O'BRIAN, NATIONAL SECURITY AND INDIVIDUAL FREEDOM (1955).

79. NASH, YOU CAN'T GET THERE FROM HERE 123 (1957).

80. Mostyn v. Fabrigas, 1 Cowp. 161, 175 (1744) (Emphasis added).

81. Gregoire v. Biddle, 177 F.2d 579 (2d Cir. 1949); *cert. denied* 339 U.S. 949 (1950).

82. *Id.* at 581.

83. See *e.g.*, Orfield, *New Trial,* 2 VILL. L. REV. 293 (1957).

84. See generally Donnelly, *Unconvicting the Innocent,* 6 VAND. L. REV. 20 (1952); Borchard, *State Indemnity for Errors of Criminal Justice,* 21 B.U.L. REV. 201 (1941).

85. See Donnelly, *supra* note 84, at 33–35 and materials cited therein.

86. See *e.g.*, limitation of damages to $5000 under the FEDERAL ERRONEOUS CONVICTIONS ACT, 62 Stat. 978 (1948), 28 U.S.C. § 2513 (1958).

87. See BORCHARD, CONVICTING THE INNOCENT (1932); FRANK & FRANK, NOT GUILTY (1957).

88. See Manager S. v. Odessa Bakery, as presented in KONSTANTINOVSKY, SOVIET LAW IN ACTION, THE RECOLLECTED CASES OF A SOVIET LAWYER 51–52 (Berman ed. 1953).

89. See discussion, *infra.*

90. See note 53, *supra.*

91. See *e.g.*, Bridges v. Wixon, 326 U.S. 135, 157 (1945) (concurring opinion of Murphy, J.).

92. See *e.g.*, general language of N.Y. PEN. LAW § 512a. For an example of extant judicial recognition of corporal punishment as valid discipline see State v. Mincher, 172 N.C. 895, 90 S.E. 429 (1916).

93. See PRESIDENT'S COMMITTEE ON CIVIL RIGHTS, TO SECURE THESE RIGHTS 25 (1947).

94. Wolf v. Colorado, 338 U.S. 25, 27 (1949) (Frankfurter, J.). See generally Allen, *The Wolf Case: Search and Seizure, Federalism and Civil Liberties,* 45 ILL. L. REV. 1 (1950).

95. Olmstead v. United States 277 U.S. 438 (1928) (wire tapping held not subject to the ban of the Fourth Amendment). Interception and/or divulgence of messages sent by wire has been subsequently subjected to federal

statutory ban. See § 605 of FEDERAL COMMUNICATIONS ACT, 48 Stat. 1064, 1103 (1934), 47 U.S.C. 605 (1958). Data, directly or indirectly procured in violation of this ban, have been held inadmissible in federal courts: Nardone v. United States, 308 U.S. 338 (1939); Nardone v. United States, 302 U.S. 379 (1937). See also Goldman v. United States, 316 U.S. 129 (1942) (attachment of dictaphone to outer wall of defendant's room and consequent electronic surveillance held not subject to either statutory or constitutional prohibition). On Lee v. United States, 343 U.S. 747 (1952) held procurement of incriminating statements through auditory detecting device concealed in investigator's pocket in private conversation with the suspect not subject to either statutory or constitutional prohibition.

Legitimization of wire tapping by state officers on the basis of court orders, obtained *ex parte*, is purported to be affected by state legislation in numerous instances on the assumption that the federal ban is restricted to federal law enforcement. See *e.g.*, N.Y. CODE CRIM. PROC. § 813a which is characteristic of such practices. For a concise survey of state law on the dominant form of electronic surveillance see Rosenzweig, *The Law of Wire Tapping*, 32 CORNELL L.Q. 514 (1947). This assumption seems to have been rendered untenable by the holding of the Supreme Court in Benanti v. United States, 355 U.S. 96 (1957), that wire tapping by state officers pursuant to state law is also violative of Sec. 605 of the FEDERAL COMMUNICATIONS ACT *supra*. To this day, however, the states have been left free to admit communications, intercepted in violation of the federal statutory standard, in evidence in state courts. Schwartz v. Texas, 344 U.S. 199 (1952). See generally Westin, *The Wire Tapping Problem*, 52 COLUM. L. REV. 165 (1952).

96. *Supra* note 95.

97. *Id.* at 473–474. See Irvine v. California, 347 U.S. 128 (1954); Leyra v. Denno, 347 U.S. 556 (1954).

98. Wolf v. Colorado, 338 U.S. 25, 28 (1949).

99. *Id.* at 27.

100. Weeks v. United States, 232 U.S. 383 (1914); Silverthorne Lumber Co. v. United States, 251 U.S. 385 (1920). See also Rule 41e, F.R. Cr. P., 18 U.S.C. (1951).

101. Wolf v. Colorado, *supra* note 98, at 28; *cf.* Rea v. United States, 350 U.S. 214 (1956).

102. Wolf v. Colorado, *supra* note 98, at 31.

103. At the time of the Wolf case, the number of states rejecting the federal example was listed at thirty-one. *Id.* at 38. It is smaller today. Significantly, several states have adopted the equivalent of the federal exclusionary rule since the Wolf case. See *e.g.*, Rickards v. State, 45 Del. 573, 77 A.2d 199 (1950), and People v. Cahan, 44 Cal. 2d 434, 282 P.2d 905 (1955) for the changes respectively effected by Delaware and California in emulation of the federal example in recent years. For the most recent tabulation of states accepting and rejecting the exclusionary rule see Elkins v. United States, 364 U.S. 206 (1960).

104. *Supra* note 98, at 41.

105. *Id.* at 42–44; see also to the same effect, United States v. Pugliese, 153 F.2d 497, 499 (2d Cir. 1945) (L. Hand, J.) *cf.* Irvine v. California, 347 U.S. 128 (1954); California has, as previously noted, since adopted the equivalent of the Federal exclusionary rule. People v. Cahan, 44 Cal. 2d 434, 282

P.2d 905 (1955); see also generally Rudd, *Present Significance of Constitutional Guarantees Against Unreasonable Searches and Seizures,* 18 U. CINC L. REV. 387 (1949).

106. People v. Cahan, *supra* note 105, at 445, 282 P.2d at 911–12.

107. *Id.* at 447, 282 P.2d at 913.

108. U.S. v. Pugliese, 153 F.2d 497, 499 (2d Cir. 1945) (L. Hand, J.).

109. That is, every subdivision with police functions.

110. See generally KONVITZ, THE CONSTITUTION AND CIVIL RIGHTS 74–77 (1947); as to the use of the legislative weapon against existing patterns of racial and religious discrimination see EMERSON & HABER, POLITICAL AND CIVIL RIGHTS 43–102 (1st ed. 1952); Konvitz, *supra* at 47–63.

111. FRANK, COURTS ON TRIAL 94 (1949).

112. See *e.g.,* VANDERBILT, THE CHALLENGE OF LAW REFORM 76–133 (1955); CALLISON, COURTS OF INJUSTICE 189–90 (1956).

113. See Williams v. Overholser 259 F.2d 175 (D.C. Cir. 1958), in which the U.S. Court of Appeals for the District of Columbia held that statutory lunacy proceedings, providing for civil commitment, could not be arbitrarily by-passed and therefore the criminal court was without power to order the commitment of the mentally ill in any case except one involving incompetency to stand trial. It is to be noted that the mental commitment proceedings often occur under statutes of vague and uncertain verbiage and dubious constitutionality.

114. The phrase "Bad Man, Sick Man" was used in the perceptive editorial comment of the Washington Post, May 30, 1958, p. A18, col. 1.

115. In the phrase of a recent legal publicist, we see the increasing infliction of "medicine . . . [as] punishment *sans* due process of law." See DeGrazia, *The Distinction of Being Mad,* 22 U. CHI. L. REV. 339, 355 (1955).

116. See *e.g.,* D.C. CODE ANN. § 24–301 (Supp. 1957).

117. Baker & DeLong, *The Prosecuting Attorney,* 24 J. CRIM. L. & CRIMINOL. 1025, 1061 (1934). See DESSION, CRIMINAL LAW, ADMINISTRATION AND PUBLIC ORDER 373–74, note 10 (1948).

118. See DESSION, *op. cit. supra* note 117 at 374.

119. *Ibid.* See also CALLISON, *op. cit. supra* note 112 at 369: "The surveys indicate that the average [of cases disposed of by plea-bargaining in the nation] is around eighty per cent."

120. BARNES & TEETERS, NEW HORIZONS IN CRIMINOLOGY 274 (2d ed. 1951). See also generally SMITH, THE CRIMINAL COURTS (1921); MOLEY, POLITICS AND CRIMINAL PROSECUTION (1929).

121. Illustrative of typical dragnet laws is N.Y. PEN. LAW §§ 43, 722. See generally Note, 59 YALE L.J. 1351 (1950).

122. Alcorta v. Texas, 355 U.S. 28 (1957).

123. Griffin v. Illinois, 351 U.S. 12, 19 (1956).

124. See *e.g.,* Betts v. Brady, 316 U.S. 455 (1942); consider the relatively privileged position of the federal defendant, Johnson v. Zerbst, 304 U.S. 458 (1938). See generally BEANEY, THE RIGHT TO COUNSEL IN AMERICAN COURTS (1955); *Comment,* 17 U. CHI. L. REV. 718 (1950) and cases cited therein. The opposing views within the Supreme Court, as of 1948, appear to have been well summarized by Mr. Justice Reed in Uveges v. Pennsylvania, 335 U.S. 437, 440–41 (1948): "Some members of the Court think that where serious offenses are charged, failure of a court to offer counsel in state criminal trials

deprives an accused of rights under the Fourteenth Amendment. They are convinced that the services of counsel to protect the accused are guaranteed by the Constitution in every such instance. . . . Others of us think that when a crime subject to capital punishment is not involved, each case depends on its own facts. . . . Where the gravity of the crime and other factors—such as the age and education of the defendant, the conduct of the court or the prosecuting officials, and the complicated nature of the offense charged and the possible defenses thereto—render criminal proceedings without counsel so apt to result in injustice as to be fundamentally unfair, the latter group holds that the accused must have legal assistance . . . whether he pleads guilty or elects to stand trial, whether he requests counsel or not."

125. United States *ex. rel.* Smith v. Baldi, 344 U.S. 561 (1953).

126. Brownell, Legal Aid In The United States 86 (1951). See also Donnelly, Book Review, 64 Yale L.J. 1089 (1955).

127. See *e.g.*, Elliff, *Notes on the Abolition of the English Grand Jury,* 29 J. Crim. L. & Criminol. 3 (1938); Lieck, *Abolition of The Grand Jury in England,* 25 J. Crim. L. & Criminol. 623 (1934).

128. For a particularly flagrant example see United States v. Shipp, 214 U.S. 386, 407–408 (1909), in which court-appointed counsel decided that the defendant even if unjustly convicted should not prosecute an appeal in the face of an inflamed public opinion.

129. Dession, *The New Federal Rules of Criminal Procedure II,* 56 Yale L.J. 197, 247 (1947).

130. See generally Brownell, *op. cit. supra* note 126.

131. Griffin v. Illinois, 351 U.S. 12 (1956).

132. *Id.* at 19.

133. See generally Potts, *Rights to Counsel in Criminal Cases,* 28 Texas L. Rev. 491 (1950).

134. See *e.g.*, Darr v. Burford, 339 U.S. 200 (1950).

135. Freund, Sutherland, Howe & Brown, Constitutional Law, 1089 (1st ed. 1952).

136. Frank, Courts on Trial 33 (1949); See generally Smith, The Criminal Courts 90 (1921); Clark & Shulman, A Study of Law Administration in Connecticut 47 (1937). Perhaps the most succinct and persuasive presentation of the plight of the poor defendant is Miller, The Difficulties of the Poor Man Accused of Crime, 124 Annals 63 (1926).

137. See *e.g.*, Offutt v. United States, 348 U.S. 11 (1954); Billecci v. United States, 184 F.2d 394 (D.C.Cir 1950); People v. Mulvey, 1 App. Div. 2d 541, 151 N.Y.S.2d 587 (4th Dep't 1956).

138. See *e.g.*, Lasswell, Power and Personality (1948); see also Adorno, The Authoritarian Personality (1950).

139. Frank, Law and the Modern Mind 112 (1949).

140. Kinsey, Sexual Behavior in the Human Male 391 (1948); see also Aristotle, Rhetoric, Bk. II, ch. 1.

141. An experiment in a high school class in Buffalo, N.Y., conducted under the joint auspices of the University of Buffalo Psychology Department and Law School, involving the matching of the results of the Adorno "F Scale," designed to measure "authoritarian" personality, with a specially constructed test, eliciting responses to hypothetical situations, designed to measure proneness to attach blame, established .351 as the correlation between "authoritarian" personality and proneness toward the attachment of blame through

"guilt" findings. The technique can be extended to make possible an estimate of the weight of this factor in many group contexts.

142. Gaudet, Harris, & St. John, *Individual Differences in the Sentencing Tendencies of Judges,* 23 J. CRIM. L. & CRIMINOL. 811, 813–14 (1933).

143. Comment, *The Influence of the Defendant's Plea on Judicial Determination of Sentence,* 66 YALE L.J. 204, 206–07 (1956).

144. 2 RABELAIS, GARANTUA AND PANTAGRUEL 37 (London, Dent & Co., Everyman's Library ed. 1946).

145. *Id.* at 40 (Emphasis added).

146. See Sobeloff, *A Recommendation for Appellate Review of Sentences,* 21 BROOKLYN L. REV. 2 (1954).

147. Griffin v. Illinois, 351 U.S. 12, 19 (1956) (Black, J.).

148. WEIHOFEN, THE URGE TO PUNISH 164 (1956).

149. See *e.g.*, the views of Romilly on the disparities in the application of the death penalty in an earlier age: "Drawing upon the rich experience he had acquired at the bar, Romilly . . . states that circumstances which might influence a judge in deciding which offenders ought to suffer death, are both variable and unpredictable. 'It has often happened, it necessarily must have happened, that the very same circumstance which is considered by one judge as matter of extenuation, is deemed by another a high aggravation of the crime . . . and it is not merely the particular circumstances attending the crime, it is the crime itself, which different judges sometime consider in quite different points of view." I RADZINOWICZ, A HISTORY OF ENGLISH CRIMINAL LAW 326–27 (1948).

150. MOLEY, OUR CRIMINAL COURTS 47 (1930).

151. See generally Dayton, *Costs, Fees and Expenses in Litigation,* 167 ANNALS 32 (1933) as suggestive of the problem.

152. RODELL, WOE UNTO YOU, LAWYERS 226 (1939).

153. II PIKE, A HISTORY OF CRIME IN ENGLAND 78 (London 1873).

154. Sir William Meredith in House of Commons, as quoted in I RADZINOWICZ, *op. cit. supra* note 149, at 427.

155. WALSH, A HISTORY OF ANGLO-AMERICAN LAW 303 (1950). See also 1 HOLDSWORTH, THE HISTORY OF ENGLISH LAW 325–26 (7th ed. rev. 1956).

156. See *e.g.*, Powell v. Alabama, 287 U.S. 45 (1932); People *ex. rel.* Burgess v. Risley, 66 How. Pr. 67 (N.Y. 1883).

157. INTERNATIONAL MILITARY TRIBUNAL, NAZI CONSPIRACY AND AGGRESSION, OPINION AND JUDGMENT 53 (1947).

158. Boiling to death was the prescribed penalty for poisoning under Henry VIII. See I STEPHEN, A HISTORY OF THE CRIMINAL LAW OF ENGLAND 476 (1883).

159. See *e.g.*, DEL. CODE ANN. tit. 11, § 701 (1953).

160. 1 Radzinowicz, *op. cit. supra* note 149, at 143.

161. See *e.g.*, change from doctrine of Plessy v. Ferguson, 163 U.S. 537 (1896), to that of Brown v. Bd. of Education, 347 U.S. 483 (1954).

3: SANCTIONING MEASURES AND THE SHARING OF ENLIGHTENMENT

1. Von Hentig, *Punishment,* 12 ENCYC. SOC. SC. 712, 713 (1937). See also ELLIOTT, CONFLICTING PENAL THEORIES IN STATUTORY CRIMINAL LAW (1931).

2. See *e.g.*, *In re* Oliver, 333 U.S. 257 (1948).

3. MASS. CONST. art. XXIX.

4. See generally DRUMMOND, THE SEX PARADOX 82 (1953); WORLD HEALTH ORGANIZATION, HOSPITALIZATION OF MENTAL PATIENTS, A SURVEY OF EXISTING LEGISLATION 77–78 (Geneva, 1955) (summary of official protection against improper treatment); Arens, Book Review, 4 BUFFALO L. REV. 144 (1954).

5. Wong Wing v. United States, 163 U.S. 228, 235 (1896).

6. Bridges v. Wixon, 326 U.S. 135, 154 (1945).

7. *Ibid. cf.* Harisiades v. Shaughnessy, 342 U.S. 580 (1952).

8. A similar contrast is highlighted by a study of comparable deprivations (including capital punishment) when attributable to "political" and "judicial" action. See Hirota v. MacArthur, 338 U.S. 197, 199 (1948) (concurring opinion of Douglas, J.).

9. Watkins v. United States, 354 U.S. 178 (1957), a welcome curb upon grosser forms of legislative irresponsibility, is, as previously observed, unlikely to effect a change in the present picture.

10. United States v. Lovett, 328 U.S. 303 (1946).

11. *Id.* at 314; see also Watkins v. United States, 354 U.S. 178 (1957).

12. Bailey v. Richardson, 185 F.2d 46, 70–71 (1950) (Edgerton, J. dissenting) *aff'd per curiam* 341 U.S. 918 (1951) (equally divided count).

13. Bailey v. Richardson, *supra* note 12.

14. Shelley v. Kraemer, 334 U.S. 1, 13 (1948) (Vinson, Ch. J.).

15. Skinner v. Oklahoma *ex rel.* Williamson, 316 U.S. 535, 536 (1942) (Douglas, J.).

16. Skinner v. Oklahoma *ex rel.* Williamson, *supra* note 15.

17. See *e.g.*, Lamont Bldg. Co. v. Court, 147 Ohio St. 183, 70 N.E.2d 447 (1946).

18. Shelley v. Kraemer, 334 U.S. 1, 20 (1948) (Emphasis added). See also Brown v. Board of Education, 347 U.S. 483 (1954).

19. Dession, *The Technique of Public Order: Evolving Concepts of Criminal Law,* 5 BUFFALO L. REV. 22, 27 (1955).

20. FRANK, LAW AND THE MODERN MIND 37 (1949).

21. N.Y. PEN. LAW §§ 730, 731.

22. N.Y. PEN. LAW § 1030.

23. N.Y. PEN. LAW § 1550.

24. N.Y. PEN. LAW § 2142.

25. 18 U.S.C. § 4 (1958).

26. 18 U.S.C. §§ 1651–1654 (1958).

27. 18 U.S.C. § 953 (1958).

28. See generally SUTHERLAND, WHITE COLLAR CRIME (1949).

29. SHAW, THE CRIME OF IMPRISONMENT 33–34 (1946). For a converse example of a sanction, maintained on the books, though too severe for present needs, see Winer, *An Appraisal of Criminal and Civil Penalties in Federal Tax Evasion Cases,* 33 B.U.L. REV. 387 (1953).

30. CARDOZO, LAW AND LITERATURE 100–101 (1931).

31. Fisher v. United States, 328 U.S. 463, 484 (1946) (dissent).

32. 6 WIGMORE, EVIDENCE § 1845 (3d ed. 1940).

33. *Id.* at 375–376.

34. See generally *id.* §§ 1856–1859.

35. A handful of jurisdictions, notably Minnesota, has pioneered in securing to the criminal defendant by statute such rights of pretrial discovery as the inspection of the reported testimony of witnesses before Grand Juries. See *id.* at § 1855a. An increasing scope of pretrial discovery of chattels and

documents including confessions is secured to the criminal defendant throughout the country, albeit rarely as a *right* and almost exclusively in the courts' discretion, which has been exercised sparingly but with increasing freedom. See Arens & Meadow, *Psycholinguistics and the Confession Dilemma*, 56 COLUM. L. REV. 19 (1956), and cases cited therein.

36. See comparative law materials in DESSION, CRIMINAL LAW, ADMINISTRATION & PUBLIC ORDER 313–14 (1948).

37. See *e.g.*, 64 Stat. 476 (1950), 5 U.S.C. 22-1 (1958); BUREAU OF NATIONAL AFFAIRS, GOVERNMENT SECURITY AND LOYALTY, A MANUAL OF LAWS, REGULATIONS AND PROCEDURES 15:101 (1956).

38. *Id.* 15:108; see *e.g.*, Bailey v. Richardson, *supra* note 12; Peters v. Hobby, 349 U.S. 331 (1955).

39. BARTH, THE LOYALTY OF FREE MEN 109 (1951).

40. Peters v. Hobby, *supra*, note 38, at 350–351.

41. Knauff v. Shaughnessy, 338 U.S. 537, 551 (1950) (Jackson, J., dissenting).

42. I LEA, A HISTORY OF THE INQUISITION 437 (1887).

43. See SOUSA, APHORISMI INQUISITORUM, lib. II, Cap XVII, 168: (Lisbon 1630): "In crimino haeresis cum maiori diligentia examinandi sunt testes: moneri enim debent, ne falsum testimonium dicant, prece, pretio, odio, coniuratione aut alio affectu. Interrogentur de antecendentibus, consequentibus, de occasione et causa, de tempore et loco, de causa scientiae, an viderint vel auderint: interrogentur de personis quae interfuerunt, de pertinacia, de affectu, de furore, ira, de conditione personae, similibus." See also FARINACCI, TRACTATUS DE HAERESI, (Venice 1620), Quaest. CLXXXVIII, § VI: "Ut propterea de inimicitia testium Inquisitores debeant ex officio interrogare tam ipsos testes, quam etiam inquisitum et diligenter inquirere."

44. See ESMEIN, A HISTORY OF CONTINENTAL CRIMINAL PROCEDURE 211–250 (1913).

45. See Ploscow, *The Development of Present-Day Crminal Procedures in Europe and America*, 48 HARV. L. REV. 433, 452 (1935).

46. *Ibid.* 47. *Id.* at 451.

48. RADIN, *The Permanent Problems of the Law*, ABA, JURISPRUDENCE IN ACTION 415, 431 (1953).

49. FRANK, COURTS ON TRIAL 80 (1949). 50. *Id.* at 85.

51. *Id.* at 81. 52. *Id.* at 82.

53. CUTLER, SUCCESSFUL TRIAL TACTICS 229 (1949).

54. Frank, *op. cit. supra* note 49, at 123. See generally MORGAN, SOME PROBLEMS OF PROOF UNDER THE ANGLO-AMERICAN SYSTEM OF LITIGATION (1956).

55. See *e.g.*, Dougherty v. Milliken, 163 N.Y. 527, 533, 57 N.E. 757, 759 (1900).

56. VII WIGMORE, EVIDENCE § 1923 (3d ed. 1940).

57. MCCORMICK, EVIDENCE 23 (1954).

58. In People v. Jones, 42 Cal. 2d 219, 266 P.2d 38 (1954), the court held psychiatric testimony showing absence of sexual deviation in defendant admissible as bearing on the improbability of the commission of a crime involving sexual perversion charged in the indictment. See also Falknor & Steffen, *Evidence of Character*, 102 U. PA. L. REV. 980 (1954), and Curran, *Expert Psychiatric Evidence of Personality Traits*, 103 U. PA. L. REV. 999 (1955).

59. Dession, Freedman, Donnelly & Redlich, *Drug-Induced Revelation and Criminal Investigation,* 62 YALE L.J. 315, 326 (1953).

60. See generally Bratt v. Western Airlines, Inc., 155 F.2d 850 (10th Cir.), *cert. denied,* 329 U.S. 375 (1946).

61. People v. Rice, 159 N.Y. 400, 410, 54 N.E. 48 (1899).

62. See Strauss, *The Qualification of Psychiatrists as Experts in Legal Proceedings,* 2 LAW & CONTEMP. PROB. 461 (1935).

63. *Id.* at 463.

64. See generally KEETON, TRIAL TACTICS AND METHODS 214–15 (1954).

65. See FRANK, COURTS ON TRIAL 141–42 (1949).

66. VIII WIGMORE, EVIDENCE § 2348 (3d ed. 1949).

67. *Id.,* at § 2349, 669–70.

68. *Id.,* at § 2353 and cases cited therein.

69. State v. Fox, 79 Mo. 109, 112 (1883).

70. Johnson v. Hunter, 144 F.2d 565 (10th Cir. 1944); see FRANK, *supra* note 65, at 112–16 for a discussion of the general consequences of such decisions.

71. See BONTECOU, THE FEDERAL LOYALTY-SECURITY PROGRAM 114–45 (1953); YARMOLINSKY, CASE STUDIES IN PERSONAL SECURITY (ed. 1955); EMERSON & HABER, POLITICAL AND CIVIL RIGHTS 564–65 (1st ed. 1952).

72. Sacher v. United States, 343 U.S. 1, 37–38 (1952) (dissent).

73. Public opinion polls on Hauptmann's guilt were thus published by the press in Hauptmann's trial for the kidnapping of the Lindbergh baby in New Jersey. See Ludwig, *Journalism and Justice in Criminal Law,* 28 ST. JOHN'S L. REV. 197, 199 (1954).

74. Ludwig, *supra* note 73 at 198–99 (footnotes omitted); See WERTHAM, THE CIRCLE OF GUILT (1956) for the deleterious effect of journalistic sensationalism in serving to conceal essential facts in something other than the *cause célèbre.*

75. See *e.g.,* Nye v. United States, 313 U.S. 33 (1941); Pennekamp v. Florida, 328 U.S. 331 (1946); Bridges v. California, 314 U.S. 252 (1941).

76. DENNING, THE ROAD TO JUSTICE 67–8 (London 1955).

77. See *e.g.,* Moore v. Dempsey, 261 U.S. 86 (1923).

78. Denial of change of venue for Communists, charged with conspiracy, has thus been sustained on the ground that community feeling in any other area was not likely to have differed from that in which the trial was held. United States v. Messarosh, 223 F.2d (3d Cir.) *rev'd on other grounds,* 352 U.S. 1 (1956). Changes of venue upon application of the defendant moreover are entrusted to the broad discretional powers of the trial court. See Allen v. United States, 4 F.2d 688 (7th Cir. 1925) *Cert. denied,* 267 U.S. 597. See generally Orfield, *Venue of Federal Criminal Cases,* 17 U. PITT. L. REV. 375 (1956).

79. See generally Ludwig, *supra* note 73.

80. Denning, *op. cit. supra* note 76 at 68.

81. The King v. Parke (1903), 2 KB 432, 437. See also R. v. Evening Standard (1924), 40 T.L.R. 833.

82. The King v. Parke *supra* note 81.

83. Frank, *Words and Music,* 47 COLUM. L. REV. 1259, 1276 (1947).

4: SANCTIONING MEASURES AND THE SHARING OF SKILL

1. See generally, ANDERSON, (ed.), CREATIVITY AND ITS CULTIVATION (1959).

2. For scope of occupational licensing throughout the nation see THE COUNCIL OF STATE GOVERNMENTS, OCCUPATIONAL LICENSING LEGISLATION IN THE STATES 78–79 (1952); for limits upon this legislative power see Wormuth, *Legislative Disqualifications as Bills of Attainder,* 4 VAND. L. REV. 603 (1951).

3. GELLHORN, INDIVIDUAL FREEDOM AND GOVERNMENT RESTRAINTS 202 (1956). See generally THE COUNCIL OF STATE GOVERNMENTS, *op. cit. supra* note 2, at 54–56.

4. GELLHORN, *op. cit, supra* note 3, at 125; see also Kotch v. Pilot Commissioners, 330 U.S. 552 (1947).

5. See generally OVERHOLSER, THE PSYCHIATRIST AND THE LAW (1953).

6. Contrast the availability of European facilities as described by Ploscowe, *The Expert Witness in Criminal Cases in France, Germany, and Italy,* 2 LAW & CONTEMP. PROB. 504–06 (1935).

7. Dession, *The Technique of Public Order,* 5 BUFFALO L. REV. 22, 36 (1955).

8. CALLISON, COURTS OF INJUSTICE 97 (1956). 9. *Ibid.*

10. Hampton v. North Carolina Pulp Co., 49 F. Supp. 625 (E.D., N.C. 1943) *rev'd per curiam,* 139 F.2d 840 (4th Cir. 1944).

11. The right of the court to call expert witnesses independently of the litigants (*ex mero motu*), though authoritatively established, 9 WIGMORE, EVIDENCE § 2484 (3d ed. 1940), is altogether too rarely invoked.

12. Thorn v. Worthington Skating Rink Co., L.R. 6 Ch. D. 415, 416 (1876) (Jessel, M. R.).

13. Morgan, *Suggested Remedy for Obstructions to Expert Testimony by Rules of Evidence,* 10 U. CHI. L. REV. 285 292–93 (1943); *cf.* generally CALLISON, *op. cit. supra* note 8, at 103–05, 107.

14. MCCORMICK, EVIDENCE 32 (1954). But compare the elasticity of such case law as State v. Sturtevant, 96 N.H. 99, 70 A.2d 909 (1950).

15. People v. Hawkins 109 N.Y. 408, 410, 17 N.E. 371, 372 (1888); but *cf.* Blunt v. United States, 244 F.2d 355 (D.C. Cir. 1957).

16. MAUDSLEY, RESPONSIBILITY IN MENTAL DISEASE 107 (1892).

17. Contrast this approach with the Continental European setting in which the work of the expert "begins in the preliminary stages" and "the task he must do is set out for him by the investigating magistrate." Ploscowe, *supra* note 6, at 507.

18. Dession, *The New Federal Rules of Criminal Procedure II,* 56 YALE L.J. 197, 219 (1947).

19. Ploscowe, *supra* note 6, at 507.

20. 2 WIGMORE, EVIDENCE § 682 at 807 (3d ed. 1940). For a recent description of an effective nonadversarial use of forensic psychiatry in Europe, see Langfeldt, *Some Outlines of Forensic Psychiatry in Norway,* 110 AM. J. PSYCHIATRY 599 (1954).

21. See 2 WIGMORE, *op. cit. supra,* note 20 at § 686.

22. See *e.g.,* Schuler v. Cudahy Packing Co., 223 Iowa 1323, 275 N.W. 39 (1937); *cf.* Meaney v. United States, 112 F.2d 538 (2d Cir. 1940). See generally Annot. 67 A.L.R. 10 (1930).

23. See generally Ploscowe, *The Expert Witness in Criminal Cases in France, Germany, and Italy*, 2 LAW & CONTEMP. PROB. 504 (1935); Arens & Killian, *Use of Psychiatry in Soviet Criminal Proceedings*, 41 J. CRIM. L. & CRIMINOL. 423 (1950).

24. MORGAN & MAGUIRE, CASES ON EVIDENCE 827 (3d ed. 1951). Compare the contrasting attitudes exemplified by St. Louis Mining & Smelting Co. v. State Industrial Commission, 113 Okla. 179, 241 Pac. 170 (1925), and McAuliffe v. Metropolitan Life Ins. Co., 93 N.J.L. 189, 107 Atl. 258 (1919). See generally MORGAN & MAGUIRE *supra* and cases cited therein.

25. *E.g.*, Arais v. Kalensnikoff, 10 Cal. 2d 428, 74 P.2d 1043 (1937); Berry v. Chaplin, 74 Cal. App. 2d 652, 169 P.2d 442 (Dist. Ct. App. 1946).

26. WEIHOFEN, MENTAL DISORDER AS A CRIMINAL DEFENSE 338 (1954). "It is interesting to note what percentage of the defendants committed for observation [upon criminal charges] are found to be insane by the hospital authorities. In Colorado during the first 22 years that the law [providing for the possibility of hospital commitment for observation] was in effect, 26% were reported insane. In Maine, it was 40% over a 10 year period. In Vermont over a period of 29 years 26.8% were reported to be insane, defective delinquents or psychopathic personalities. In Ohio, over a period of 20 years, 17% were found insane. In South Carolina during the first three years' operation of that state's law, 32% were reported insane." See HURWITZ, CRIMINOLOGY 192–93 (Copenhagen 1952) for evidence of comparable and higher incidence of psychic abnormality among prisoners investigated in Denmark.

27. See generally WEIHOFEN, *op. cit. supra* note 26, at 330–40.

28. MASS. GEN. LAWS ch. 123, § 100 as amended (Supp. 1959).

29. WEIHOFEN, *op. cit. supra* note 26, at 345–46.

30. Rudstedt, Prison Without Bars, The American Swedish Monthly, Nov., 1947, P. 15.

31. Turnbladh, *Substitutes for Imprisonment*, 293 ANNALS 112, 113–14 (1954).

32. Rudstedt *supra* note 30, at 31. See also Schlyter, Les Dispositions Sur La Responsibilité Pénale Dans La Code Pénale Suédois, XII Commission Internationale Pénale et Pénitentiare, Recueil de Documents en Matiere Pénale et Penitentiaire 16–21 (1946).

33. See *e.g.*, United States v. Hiss, 88 F. Supp. 559 (S.D., N.Y. 1950) (psychiatric testimony founded predominantly on courtroom observation); and *compare*. People v. Cowles, 246 Mich. 429, 224 N.W. 387 (1929); *with* State v. Driver, 88 W. Va. 479, 107 S.E. 189 (1921). For the importance of the detection of the litigious paranoid in civil litigation see Lasswell & McDougal, *Legal Education and Public Policy: Professional Training in the Public Interest*, 52 YALE L.J. 203, 283 (1943).

34. FRANK, LAW AND THE MODERN MIND 107 (1930). See generally FRANK, COURTS ON TRIAL 100 (1949); LASSWELL & MCDOUGAL, *supra* note 36, at 283.

35. See *e.g.*, State *ex. rel.* Kelly v. Wolfer, 119 Minn. 368, 138 N.W. 315 (1912).

36. Excerpted from Vold, *Does the Prison Reform?*, 293 ANNALS 42, 44 (1954).

37. BUREAU OF PRISONS, U.S. DEPT. OF JUSTICE, A REPORT OF THE WORK OF THE FEDERAL BUREAU OF PRISONS, 65 (1958). See *e.g.*, *id.*, at 64 for the following table.

RECIDIVISM BY OFFENSE

Repeaters among Prisoners Committed to Federal Institutions under Sentence of More than One Year, Fiscal Year Ended June 30, 1958 (By Percentage)

	Number of Repeaters	*Percent*
All Offenses	10,322	66.6
Selective Service Act	142	12.0
Embezzlement	111	16.2
Income Tax	65	23.1
Military Court-martial Cases	90	40.0
Juvenile Delinquency, Federal	812	40.9
Marihuana	283	48.8
Juvenile Deliquency, D.C.	97	56.7
Other Offenses	1,012	58.4
Robbery	222	65.3
Narcotic Drugs	1,094	65.8
Liquor	1,221	67.0
Larceny, Except Auto	754	72.7
Forgery	1,021	74.7
White Slave Traffic	108	75.9
Transporting Stolen Motor Vehicle	2,785	78.6
Securities, Transporting False or Forged	210	79.5
Immigration	295	81.7

38. *Id.* at 47; See generally ABRAHAMSEN, WHO ARE THE GUILTY? 227–56 (1952).

39. See generally SUTHERLAND, THE PRINCIPLES OF CRIMINOLOGY 460–85 (5th ed. Cressey rev. 1955); our best penal institutions, represented by the federal prison system which, as noted above, registers something in the neighborhood of 60% as the proportion of recidivists among "long termers," have shown a steady increase in inmates, as shown by the following table, excerpted from U.S. Dept. of Justice, Bureau of Prisons, REPORT OF THE WORK OF THE FEDERAL BUREAU OF PRISONS, 65 (1958):

PERCENTAGE OF COMMITMENTS

Selected Year	*Recidivists*	*With one*	*With two*	*With three or more*
1958	6,871	30.4	21.8	47.8
1956	6,452	33.6	22.0	44.4
1954	6,717	33.0	23.4	43.6
1952	5,903	33.4	23.2	43.4
1950	6,004	33.9	22.4	43.7
1948	5,420	34.9	21.6	43.5
1946	5,674	36.9	22.9	40.2
1944	4,728	37.2	21.7	41.0
1943	4,548	36.1	22.4	41.5

40. For the use of psychiatric facilities in a more enlightened setting see Stürup, *How Can Psychiatric Science be Applied in Prisons with Regard Both to the Medical Treatment of Certain Prisoners and to the Classification of Prisoners and Individualization of the Regime?*, Twelfth International Penal Penitentiary Congress, Preparatory Papers, The Hague (1950).

41. Ultimate aims of prison life, proclaimed by the American Prison Association, as quoted in SUTHERLAND, *op. cit. supra* note 39, at 471.

42. *Id.* at 471. 43. See *e.g.*, *id.* at 471–74.

44. See generally *id.* at 463–68, 471.

45. Almost half the States pay no wages; the rest pay wages which appear diminutive. The federal system appears to be the best with "wages ranging from 4 to 40 cents per day" in 1940. *Id.* at 524.

46. The following summary of the State prison-labor situation of a nationwide level is provided by BARNES & TEETERS, NEW HORIZONS IN CRIMINOLOGY 733–34 (2d ed. 1951).

> 1. A certain large percentage of men are completely idle. . . .
>
> 2. A large percentage (greatly exceeding the optimum) is employed in maintenance work. . . .
>
> 3. A certain small percentage is in industrial pursuits, actually producing commodities. But this work rarely involves a full working day—three hours in some prisons, four in some, rarely six, and almost never eight. In some prisons distasteful factory work (jute mill or weaving shop) is reserved for the hard-boiled prisoner and is disciplinary rather than reformatory. . . .
>
> 4. A very small percentage is employed at clerical work. . . .
>
> 5. A number of inmates small in some prisons and larger in others work in trinket shops or cells. . . .

The situation in federal prisons, although better, still seems to leave most prisoners outside the scope of productive employment. *Id.* at 746. See also, BUREAU OF PRISONS, DEPT. OF JUSTICE, REPORT OF THE WORK OF THE FEDERAL BUREAU OF PRISONS 34 (1958): "Our budgetary situation forced us to operate our institutions with an average of 3,856 employees, 41 fewer than . . . (the previous year). Yet our average population soared to an all-time high. . . . Accordingly we were forced to make certain changes in the distribution and placement of the custodial force, which meant that in many instances coverage was spread uncomfortably thin."

47. SUTHERLAND, *op. cit. supra* note 39, at 484–85.

48. *Id.* at 497–504. See generally Floch, *Are Prisons Outdated?*, 47 J. CRIM. L., C. & P.S. 444 (1956).

49. NATIONAL COMM'N ON LAW OBSERVANCE & ENFORCEMENT, REPORT ON PENAL INSTITUTIONS, PROBATION AND PAROLE 170 (1931). "One thing is clear, that what we do now is wrong, perhaps completely wrong. We have failed to reform the criminal. In plain honesty we ought to admit that in what we have been doing we have missed our ends. . . . We have long known that arrest, trial and imprisonment have had little bearing upon turning a criminal into a law-abiding citizen." Tannenbaum, CRIME AND THE COMMUNITY, 474–475 (1938). See generally *id.* 474–78.

50. BARNES & TEETERS, *op. cit. supra* note 46, at 633.

51. *Id.* at 758–86.

52. Turnbladh, *Substitutes for Imprisonment*, 293 ANNALS 112, 114 (1954).

53. The California Institution for Men at Chino, provides one of but few promising examples. See BARNES & TEETERS, *op. cit. supra* note 46 at 565; Fox, *Michigan's Experiment in Minimum Security Penology*, 41 J. CRIM. L., C. & P.S. 150 (1950). See also Scudder, *The Open Institution*, 293 ANNALS 79 (1954). Consider the widespread employment of the genuinely open institution providing genuinely rehabilitative treatment, for close to ⅓ of all criminal convicts in Sweden. See generally GORANSSON, SOME ASPECTS OF THE SWEDISH PRISON SYSTEM (Stockholm 1955). See also Fox, *supra* at 156–57:

"The . . . results show a tendency for the men from the minimum security institution [in Michigan] to be more successful on parole than similar men who served in the maximum security institutions."

54. See *e.g.*, Sington, *Redeeming the Murderer,* The Nation, Feb. 9, 1957, p. 117.

55. See *e.g.*, Sachs, *Zur Behandlung von kriminellen Psychopathen in Danemark,* 38 MONATSCHRIFT FUR KRIMINOLOGIE UND STRAFRECHTSREFORM 69 (Zurich-Vienna, Aug. 1955).

56. See Evans, *Correctional Institution Personnel—Amateurs or Professionals?,* 293 ANNALS 70 (1954). See generally TAPPEN (ed.), CONTEMPORARY CORRECTION (1951); Note, 33 NEB. L. REV. 467, 473–74 (1954).

5: SANCTIONING MEASURES AND THE SHARING OF WELL-BEING

1. Dession, *The Technique of Public Order,* 5 BUFFALO L. REV. 22, 38 (1955). See also BLOCH & FYNN, DELINQUENCY 403 (1956): "The chief Problem is the lack of diversity of resources. In effect, when disposition requires the use of these facilities, the court is forced to use them for a variety of children whose individual needs may not be met by the available programs."

2. Dession, *Psychiatry and the Conditioning of Criminal Justice,* 47 YALE L.J. 319, 328 (1938).

3. See Wash. Post Sept. 23, 1959, p. A3, cols. 6–8.

4. DEUTSCH, THE SHAME OF THE STATES 138 (1948). See generally BACHMAN, HEALTH RESOURCES IN THE UNITED STATES (1952); DEUTSCH, THE MENTALLY ILL IN AMERICA (1949).

5. See *e.g.*, Powell v. Risser, 375 Pa. 60, 70, 99 A.2d 454, 458 (1953), for an example of judicial tolerance in our mental hospitals of "unnecessary or reckless use of violent measures which steal away physical assets from one already robbed of the treasures of a sound mind."

6. See *e.g.*, Farber v. Olkon, 40 Cal. App. 2d 503, 254 P.2d 520 (Sup. Ct. 1953).

7. See *e.g.*, O'Rourke v. Halcyon Rest, 281 App. Div. 838, 118 N.Y.S. 2d 693 (2d Dept. 1953).

8. DRUMMOND, THE SEX PARADOX 82 (1953); see the development of the same ideas in Arens, Book Review, 14 LA. L. REV. 913 (1954).

9. See *e.g.*, Gasperini v. Manginelli, 196 Misc. 547, 92 N.Y.S. 2d 575 (Sup. Ct. 1949); Farber v. Olkon, *supra,* note 6.

10. Chodoff, *Loyalty Programs and Mental Health in the Washington Area,* 16 PSYCHIATRY 399 (1953) (emphasis added).

11. *Id.* at 400 (emphasis added). 12. *Id.* at 399.

13. *Id.* at 400. 14. See *e.g.*, FROMM, THE SANE SOCIETY (1955).

15. Chodoff, *supra* note 10, at 400. For the effects of another form of loyalty and security measure in the form of loyalty oath screening device in academic employment, see Sanford, *Individual and Social Change in a Community Under Pressure,* 9 J. OF SOCIAL ISSUES 25 (1953); see generally BONTECOU, THE FEDERAL LOYALTY-SECURITY PROGRAM 101–56 (1953); Jahoda & Cook, *Security Measures and Freedom of Thought,* 61 YALE L.J. 295 (1952).

16. See *e.g.*, Adler v. Board of Educ., 342 U.S. 485 (1952); Garner v. Board of Pub. Works, 341 U.S. 716 (1951).

17. See generally GILLIN, CRIMINOLOGY AND PENOLOGY 530–43 (1927); GRUNHUT, PENAL REFORM 169 (1948); GLUECK, CRIME AND JUSTICE 55–59 (1936).

18. SUTHERLAND, PRINCIPLES OF CRIMINOLOGY 472 (5th ed. Cressey rev. 1955).

19. ABRAHAMSEN, WHO ARE THE GUILTY? 232 (1952); see also ALEXANDER & HEALY, ROOTS OF CRIME 304 (1935). But see the record of such psychiatrically directed foreign institutions as Herstedvester, discussed in Sachs, *Zur Behandlung von kriminellen Psychopathen in Danemark,* 38 MONTASSCHRIFT FUR KRIMINOLOGIE UND STRAFRECHTSREFORM 69 (Zurich-Vienna, Aug. 1955). One may note in passing that the scientific study of interviewing prison inmates for nontherapeutic purposes still seems to be in its infancy in this country. See *e.g.,* Sorensen, *Interviewing Prison Inmates,* 42 J. CRIM. L. & CRIMINOL. 180 (1950).

20. See generally DEUTSCH, THE SHAME OF THE STATES (1948); Miller v. Overholser, 206 F.2d 415 (D.C. Cir. 1953). It can be assumed that reduction in brutality in the treatment of the mentally ill in public institutions since the forties is ascribable solely to the fact that the more seriously disturbed have been rendered more tractable by the "tranquilizers."

21. Deutsch, *supra* note 20, at 139; see also Wertham, *A Psychiatrist Looks at Psychiatry and the Law,* 3 BUFFALO L. REV. 41, 48 (1953). *But cf.* world survey of the treatment of mental patients, carried out by WORLD HEALTH ORGANIZATION (WHO), *Hospitalization of Mental Patients,* A SURVEY OF EXISTING LEGISLATION 77 (Geneva 1955): "In addition to seeing that patients are not unjustifiably detained, . . . [an] inspectorate is . . . concerned [in many countries] with ensuring that patients are properly treated. To this end inspectors . . . are allowed access to hospitals at any time and patients and their relatives are permitted to approach them with complaints. Details of the treatment provided are also recorded and the inspectors have access to such records. A number of countries have provisions limiting the use of mechanical restraint. . . ."

22. See *e.g.,* BUREAU OF PRISONS U.S. DEPT. OF JUSTICE, REPORT OF THE FEDERAL BUREAU OF PRISONS, 18 (1958). See following table, *ibid.,*

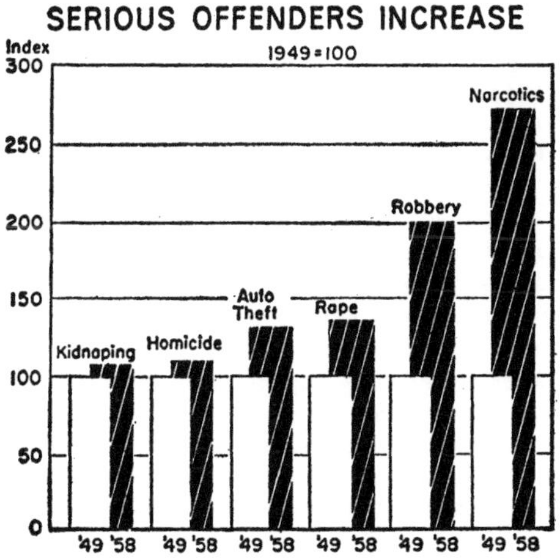

23. Dession, *supra* note 1, at 40; See CANTOR, CRIME, CRIMINALS AND CRIMINAL JUSTICE 152 (1932).

24. See *e.g.*, MOLEY, POLITICS AND CRIMINAL PROSECUTION (1929).

25. MacCormick, *The Prison's Role in Crime Prevention*, 41 J. CRIM. L. & CRIMINOL. 36, 42 (1950). See also CALLISON, COURTS OF INJUSTICE 502–3 (1956); KEFAUVER, CRIME IN AMERICA (1951); WOOD & WAITE, CRIME AND ITS TREATMENT (1941).

26. See Special Comm. to Investigate Organized Crime in Interstate Commerce, 1st S. REP. No. 307, 82d. Cong. 1st Sess. (1951). *Third Interim Report.*

27. For the classic insistence on certainty in the infliction of negative sanctions for criminal transgressions as an indispensable element of social protection see generally BECCARIA, AN ESSAY ON CRIMES AND PUNISHMENT (1st ed. 1767). For a more modern view see MANNHEIM, CRIMINAL JUSTICE AND SOCIAL RECONSTRUCTION 203–18 (1946). An apt summary of contemporary realities has been provided by MOLEY, OUR CRIMINAL COURTS xi (1930): "In spite of the revered phrase of Aristotle, the administration of criminal justice is a government of men, not laws."

28. Caldwell, *Why is the Death Penalty Retained?*, 284 ANNALS 45, 50 (1952).

29. Dession, *The Technique of Public Order*, 5 BUFFALO L. REV. 22, 37 (1955).

30. Rudstedt, Prisons Without Bars, The American Swedish Monthly, Nov. 1947, p. 14.

31. Pearson, *The Right to Kill in Making Arrests*, 28 MICH. L. REV. 957, 966 (1930), and cases cited therein. See generally Perkins, *The Law of Arrest*, 25 IOWA L. REV. 201, 272–73 (1940).

32. Pearson, *id.* at 968–69, and cases cited therein; Perkins, *id.* at 276–78. See generally 1 ALEXANDER, THE LAW OF ARREST IN CRIMINAL AND OTHER PROCEEDINGS, §§ 94–95 (1949); ORFIELD, CRIMINAL PROCEDURE FROM ARREST TO APPEAL 26–27 (1947).

33. See *e.g.*, ANNUAL REPORTS OF THE DEP'T OF POLICE OF THE CITY OF BUFFALO, N.Y., for the years 1946–1955 as a representative example of operations in a contemporary metropolitan center. Almost 4% of all homicides reported in Buffalo during that period were the direct result of police activity.

34. See *e.g.*, REITH, THE BLIND EYE OF HISTORY 172 (1952); for a survey of English police operations see MORIARTY, POLICE PROCEDURE AND ADMINISTRATION (4th ed. 1944).

35. See NATIONAL COMM'N ON LAW OBSERVANCE AND ENFORCEMENT, REPORT ON LAWLESSNESS IN LAW ENFORCEMENT 153 (1931); PRESIDENT'S COMMITTEE ON CIVIL RIGHTS, TO SECURE THESE RIGHTS 25 (1947); see also *In re* Fried, 161 F.2d 453, 459 (2d Cir. 1947) (Frank, J.): "The 'third degree' and cognate devices alarmingly persist in this country."

36. See *e.g.*, Watts v. Indiana, 338 U.S. 49 (1949); Haley v. Ohio, 332 U.S. 596 (1948); McCormick, *Some Problems and Developments in the Admissibility of Confessions*, 24 TEXAS L. REV. 239 (1946).

37. See *e.g.*, Bader, *Coerced Confessions & The Due Process Clause*, 15 BROOKLYN L. REV. 51, 70 (1948).

38. See *e.g.*, McNabb v. United States, 318 U.S. 332 (1943).

39. THE INDIAN EVIDENCE ACT (Act No. 1 of 1872 as amended) § 25.

40. THE INDIAN EVIDENCE ACT (Act No. 1 of 1872 as amended) § 26; the

entire principle would appear to involve no more than the logical extension of the doctrine of McNabb v. United States, *supra* note 38.

41. See *e.g.*, Kauper, *Judicial Examination of the Accused—A Remedy for the Third Degree*, 30 MICH. L. REV. 1224 (1932); Keedy, *The Preliminary Investigation of Crime in France*, 88 U. PA. L. REV. 692 (1940).

42. See *e.g.*, Colyer v. Skeffington, 265 Fed. 17 (D. MASS. 1920); REPORT OF THE PRESIDENT'S COMMITTEE ON CIVIL RIGHTS, *op. cit. supra* note 35 at 25–29; Plumb, *Illegal Enforcement of the Law*, 24 CORNELL L. Q. 337 (1939).

43. *Compare* Trupiano v. United States, 334 U.S. 699 (1948), *with* United States v. Rabinowitz, 339 U.S. 56 (1950). See generally CLARK, THE RISE OF FEDERALISM 41–44 (1938); Beisel, *Control Over Illegal Enforcement of the Criminal Law*, 34 B.U.L. REV. 413 (1954).

44. For an example, drawn from another culture see YOUNG, IMPERIAL JAPAN 238–49 (1938); for a projection of contemporary possibilities in East and West see Lasswell, *The Interrelations of World Organization and Society*, 55 YALE L.J. 889 (1946); as to existing realities at home concerning the "investigation of beliefs" see LOWENTHAL, THE FEDERAL BUREAU OF INVESTIGATION 444–65 (1950); MEIKLEJOHN, FREE SPEECH AND ITS RELATION TO SELF-GOVERNMENT, X (1948); for an example of explicit statutory authorization of such practices, specifically, the investigation of the "loyalty" of "Fulbright Scholars," among others, see 62 Stat. 13 (1948), 22 U.S.C. § 1434 (1958).

45. See *e.g.*, Chodoff, *Loyalty Programs and Mental Health in the Washington Area*, 16 PSYCHIATRY 399 (1953).

46. See *e.g.*, 62 Stat. 13 (1948), 22 U.S.C. § 1434 (1958).

47. Smith, *Municipal Police Administration*, 146 ANNALS 1 (1929).

48. See *e.g.*, Donnelly, *Judicial Control of Informants, Spies, Stool Pigeons, and Agents Provocateurs*, 60 YALE L.J. 1091 (1951).

49. Olmstead v. United States, 277 U.S. 438, 478 (1928).

50. MCNABB v. United States, 318 U.S. 332, 343 (1943) (Frankfurter, J.).

51. 2 MAY, CONSTITUTIONAL HISTORY OF ENGLAND 275 (1874).

52. ELLIOTT, CONFLICTING PENAL THEORIES IN STATUTORY CRIMINAL LAW 134–35 (1931).

53. Turnbladh, *Substitutes for Imprisonment*, 293 ANNALS 112, 114 (1954). See also Note, 33 NEB. L. REV. 467 473 (1954).

54. See generally Smith, *Police Systems in the United States* (2d ed. rev. 1960).

55. See *e.g.*, 58 Stat. 697 (1944), 42 U.S.C. § 250 (1958). For a discussion of expanded and "more effective methods of prevention, diagnosis and treatment of psychiatric disorders" throughout the nation under federal auspices see BACHMAN, *op. cit. supra* note 4, at 142–49. "There is [in our mental hospitals today] a direct correlation between . . . [rising] personnel ratios and the increased discharge rates." Rusk, *Gains Over Mental Ills*, N.Y. Times, April 28, 1957, 1, p. 82, col. 4. See also 69 Stat. 42 U.S.C. 382 (1955), § 242 (b) (1958) (Mental Health Study Grants).

56. Dession, *Psychiatry and the Conditioning of Criminal Justice*, 47 YALE L.J. 319, 339 (1938) (Emphasis added).

57. *Ibid.* 58. *Id.* at 340.

6: SANCTIONING MEASURES AND THE SHARING OF AFFECTION

1. NELSON, DIVORCE AND ANNULMENT § 2.05, at 25 (2d ed. 1945).

2. *Id.* at 26.

3. *Id.* at 49–50. See recommendations for change in dealing with divorce problems reproduced in HARPER, PROBLEMS OF THE FAMILY 771–73 (1952). A few jurisdictions, such as New Mexico, have in fact provided for divorce on the basis of incompatibility as if to prove the exception. See *e.g.*, N.M. Stat. Ann. §§ 22-7-1 (1953).

4. See Peele, *Social and Psychological Effects of Alimony,* 6 LAW & CONTEMP. PROB. 283 (1939).

5. See *e.g.*, Bunim v. Bunim, 298 N.Y. 391, 83 N.E.2d 848 (1949).

6. GELLHORN, CHILDREN AND FAMILIES IN THE COURTS OF NEW YORK CITY 310 (1954).

7. *Ibid.*

8. See *e.g.*, Lamont Bldg. Co. v. Court, 147 Ohio St. 183, 70 N.E.2d 447 (1946).

9. N.Y. CIV. PRAC. ACT. §§ 826–827.

10. N.Y. CIV. PRAC. ACT. §§ 902–903.

11. CLARK, CODE PLEADING 154 (1947).

12. N.Y. CIV. PRAC. ACT. §§ 643, 650, 651.

13. APPLETON, NEW YORK PRACTICE 276 (5th ed. 1957). For underlying statutory authorization see N.Y. CIV. PRAC. ACT. § 764.

14. See *e.g.*, N.Y. INS. LAW § 166.

15. See *e.g.*, GORANSSON, SOME ASPECTS OF THE SWEDISH PRISON SYSTEM 8 (Stockholm 1955); SELLIN, RECENT PENAL LEGISLATION IN SWEDEN (Stockholm 1947); Goransson, *The Treatment of Offenders in Sweden,* HOWARD LEAGUE PAMPHLET (London 1949); Rudstedt, Prisons Without Bars, The American Swedish Monthly, Nov. 1947, p. 14. For a description of Mexico's institutionalization of "conjugal visits" in the prison system of that country see TEETERS, WORLD PENAL SYSTEMS 172 (1944).

16. See generally KINSEY, SEXUAL BEHAVIOR IN THE HUMAN MALE 224–25 (1948); ELLIOTT, CRIME IN MODERN SOCIETY 718 (1952).

17. BARNES & TEETERS, NEW HORIZONS IN CRIMINOLOGY 448 (2d ed. 1951).

18. KINSEY, *op. cit. supra* note 16, at 664.

19. *Ibid.* See generally LINDNER, STONE WALLS AND MEN 454–69 (1946); Karpman, *Sex Life in Prison,* 38 J. CRIM. L. & CRIMINOL. 475 (1948). The obviation of such consequences of incarceration under Swedish law can be seen in GORANSSON, SOME ASPECTS OF THE SWEDISH PRISON SYSTEM, *op. cit. supra* note 15, at 7–8.

20. N.Y. INS. LAW § 166.

21. See *e.g.*, N.Y. PEN. LAW § 2041 (1921), § 2042 (1946).

22. See generally I ABBOTT, THE CHILD AND THE STATE (1947).

7: SANCTIONING MEASURES AND THE SHARING OF RECTITUDE

1. United States v. Dotterweich, 320 U.S. 277, 286 (1943) (Murphy, J. dissenting); see also Schneiderman v. United States, 320 U.S. 118 (1943).

2. See *e.g.*, American Tobacco Co. v. United States, 328 U.S. 781 (1946); United States v. Dotterweich, *supra* note 1; United States v. Patten, 226 U.S. 525 (1913); People v. Wagner, 245 N.Y. 143, 156 N.E. 644 (1927); see also Pinkerton v. United States, 328 U.S. 640 (1946).

3. See Dunn, *Conscious Parallelism Reexamined,* 35 B.U.L. Rev. 225 (1955).

4. See *e.g.*, Note, 17 U. Chi. L. Rev. 148 (1949); *see also;* remarks of Vyshinski in the role of public prosecutor, in *People's Commissariat of Justice Report of Court Proceedings in the Case of the Anti-Soviet "Block of Rights & Trotskyites,"* 694–95 (Moscow 1939), reproduced in part in Dession, Criminal Law, Administration & Public Order 525, p. 98 (1948).

5. See generally Hall, Principles of Criminal Law 279–322 (1947).

6. See *e.g.*, Note, 62 Harv. L. Rev. 276 (1948); Note, 17 U. Chi. L. Rev. 148 (1947). *Compare* Interstate Circuit Inc. v. United States, 306 U.S. 208 (1939), *with* Dennis v. United States, 341 U.S. 494 (1951).

7. N.Y. Pen. Law § 1932; *cf.* similarly mild criminal penalization by way of fine under the Sherman Act, 26 Stat. 209 (1890), 15 U.S.C. §§ 1–2 (1958).

8. See also Shaw, The Crime of Imprisonment 34 (1946): "Commercial civilization presents an appalling spectacle of pillage and parasitism, of corruption in the press and in the pulpit, of lying advertisements which make people buy rank poisons in the belief that they are health restorers, of traps to catch the provision made for the widow and the fatherless and divert it to the pockets of company promoting rogues, of villainous oppression of the poor and cruelty to the defenceless; and it is arguable that most of this could, like burglary and forgery, be kept within bearable bounds if its perpetrators were dealt with as burglars and forgers are dealt with today." Arnold, The Folklore of Capitalism (1937); Berle, The Twentieth Century Capitalist Revolution 112 (1954); Rusche & Kircheimer, Punishment and Social Structure 198–201 (1939).

9. Herbert, Holy Deadlock 28 (1934).

10. Miller, Criminal Law, 438 (1934), and cases cited therein.

11. Kinsey, Sexual Behavior in The Human Male 392 (1949).

12. Drummond, The Sex Paradox 29 (1953).

13. The crime of "sodomy," for example, can involve heterosexual as well as homosexual practices. See Miller, *op. cit supra* note 10, at 437, and cases cited therein.

14. See respective tables of variations in the severity of penalization in the various states for "sodomy" and "lewd acts with children" in Drummond, The Sex Paradox 350–52, 354–55 (1953).

15. Bentham, Principles of Morals and Legislation, ch. XVII, § XIX.

16. Elliott, Conflicting Penal Theories in Statutory Criminal Law 209 (1931).

17. See *e.g.*, Royal Commission on Capital Punishment, Memoranda and Replies to a Questionnaire Received from Foreign & Commonwealth Countries 681–868 (London 1949). See generally Scott, The History of Capital Punishment (London 1950).

18. 70 Stat. 571 (1956), 21 U.S.C. § 176b (1958).

19. See Comment, *Capital Punishment, People's Defense or Judicial Murder,* 1 Archives of Crim. Psychodynamics 941 (1955). See generally Alexander & Staub, The Criminal, The Judge, and The Public (Rev. ed. 1956).

20. See Solesbee v. Balkcom, 339 U.S. 9, 14 (1950) (Frankfurter, J. dissenting).

21. 1 WHARTON, CRIMINAL LAW § 77 (1932).

22. At least in the context of capital crime, official morality seems reflective of the spirit of Carlyle's justification of the death penalty as consistent with Nature's dictate of "natural wrath," "planted . . . against [the criminal] in every God-created human heart. . . . 'Caitiff, we hate thee; . . . Not with a diabolic but with a divine hatred. . . . As a palpable deserter from the ranks where all men, at their eternal peril are bound to be: . . . we solemnly expel thee from our community; and will, in the name of God, not with joy and exultation, but with sorrow stern as thy own, hang thee on Wednesday next. . . .'" (XX CARLYLE, WORKS [*Latter Day Pamphlets*] 75–77 [London 1907]); see also Comment, *Capital Punishment, People's Defense or Judicial Murder*, 1 *Archives of Crim. Psychodynamics* 941 (1955).

23. See excerpts from Judge Bazelon's Brandeis Memorial Lecture, Wash. Post, March 24, 1960, p. A20, col. 6.

24. Elliott, *op. cit. supra* note 16, at 220. "Three motives, deterrence, vengence, and social utility seem to be embodied in the habitual criminal laws. Such laws are apparently enacted in the belief that the initiate in crime, recognizing that a second or subsequent offense brings a severer penalty, will take care lest he fall again (and that) the state . . . has greater abhorrence for the individual who refused to reform and who . . . commits his second, third or fourth felony. Social utility enters in demanding permanent incarceration of those who are insusceptible to reformatory treatment. Which motive is uppermost is not easy to determine. . . ." *Id.* at 187.

25. Dession, *The New Federal Rules of Criminal Procedure II*, 56 YALE L.J. 197, 256 (1947).

26. See *e.g.*, KANT, THE PHILOSOPHY OF LAW 195–96 (Edinburgh, 1887): "The Penal Law is a Categorical Imperative; and woe to him who creeps through the serpent-windings of Utilitarianism to discover some advantage that may discharge him from the Justice of Punishment, or even from the due measure of it. . . . For if Justice and Righteousness perish, human life would no longer have any value in the world."

27. STEPHEN, GENERAL VIEW OF THE CRIMINAL LAW OF ENGLAND 99 (1863). See also the discussion of this view in HOLMES, THE COMMON LAW 41–42 (1881). But cf., the policy conception expressed by Target, one of the five Napoleonic codifiers, early in the 19th century: "It is certain that vengeance must not be the principle of punishment. . . . It is . . . the necessity of punishment which renders it legitimate. The infliction of suffering upon the guilty is not the end-all of the law. . . . If after the commission of the most heinous offense one could be sure that the offense would never be repeated, the punishment of the last malefactor would constitute a fruitless barbarism and . . . exceed the power of the law." FOIGNET & DUPONT, DROIT CRIMINEL 23 (Paris, 1944), (translation supplied).

28. See *e.g.*, BOGART & KEMMERER, ECONOMIC HISTORY OF THE AMERICAN PEOPLE 488–506 (1947); BURNS, THE DECLINE OF COMPETITION (1936); STOCKING & WATKINS, CARTELS IN ACTION (1946); FEDERAL TRADE COMMISSION, MERGER MOVEMENTS (1948).

29. ARNOLD, FOLKLORE OF CAPITALISM 208 (1937).

30. MACIVER, THE WEB OF GOVERNMENT 346–47 (1947).

31. Arnold, *op. cit. supra* note 29, at 227.

32. SUTHERLAND, WHITE COLLAR CRIME 38 (1949); the underlying statute is found in IND. ANN. STAT. § 10–2103 (1956).

33. SUTHERLAND, *op. cit. supra* note 32, at 46–47.

34. See *e.g.*, ADAMS, THE STRUCTURE OF AMERICAN INDUSTRY (rev. ed. 1954); CLARK, SOCIAL CONTROL OF BUSINESS 125–27 (1939); DIRLAM & KAHN, FAIR COMPETITION (1954); See generally SCHUMPETER, CAPITALISM, SOCIALISM AND DEMOCRACY 81–87 (1950).

35. GELLHORN, CHILDREN AND FAMILIES IN THE COURTS OF NEW YORK CITY 286 (1954).

36. Kinsey, *op. cit. supra* note 11, at 665.

37. MANNHEIM, CRIMINAL JUSTICE AND SOCIAL RECONSTRUCTION 3 (1946).

38. "Criminal syndicates in this country make tremendous profits and are due primarily to the ability of such groups . . . to secure monopolies in . . . illegal operations. . . ." Special comm. to Investigate Organized Crime in Interstate Commerce, *Third Interim Report*, S. REP. No. 307, 82d Cong., 1st Sess. 1 (1951). The committee found in some cities that law enforcement officials aided and protected gangsters and racketeers to maintain their monopolistic position in particular rackets.

39. Brooks, *Corruption in American Politics and Life* 187 (1910).

40. See SPECIAL COMM. REPORT, *supra* note 38; see also Graham, *Morality in American Politics* (1952).

41. See SPECIAL COMM. REPORT, *supra* note 38.

42. SHAKESPEARE, MEASURE FOR MEASURE, Act V, Scene I, Lines 320–21.

43. See BUREAU OF PRISONS, U.S. DEPT. OF JUSTICE REPORT OF THE WORK OF THE FEDERAL BUREAU OF PRISONS, (1958).

44. *Id.*, at 6.

45. See DEPT. OF JUSTICE, BUREAU OF PRISONS REPORTS for Years 1950–1955.

46. See BUREAU OF PRISONS *op. cit. supra* note 43, at 64.

47. For a discussion of English development, see I RADZINOWICZ, A HISTORY OF ENGLISH CRIMINAL LAW; TURNER & WINFIELD, PENAL REFORM IN ENGLAND 30 (London 1940).

48. See *e.g.*, N.J. REV. STAT. § 2A: 164 *et seq.* (1953).

49. Bentham, *op. cit.*, *supra* note 12, Ch. XIII, § 1.

50. SHAKESPEARE, KING LEAR, Act IV, Scene 6, Lines 151–55.

8: SANCTIONING MEASURES AND THE SHARING OF WEALTH

1. Baldwin v. G.A.F. Seelig, Inc., 294 U.S. 511, 527 (1935) (Cardozo, J.).

2. See generally Paulsen, *The Persistence of Substantive Due Process in the States*, 34 MINN. L. REV. 91 (1950).

3. Language applied by the Court to state and federal regulations alike appears in United States v. Carolene Prod. Co., 304 U.S. 144, 153 (1938), dealing with the validity of federal legislation.

4. Yick Wo v. Hopkins, 118 U.S. 356, 373–74 (1886).

5. Stern, *The Problems of Yesteryear—Commerce and Due Process*, 4 VAND. L. REV. 446, 459 (1951).

6. See generally Dean Milk Co. v. Madison, 340 U.S. 349 (1951); Goesaert v. Cleary, 335 U.S. 464 (1948); Southern Pac. Co. v. Arizona, 325 U.S. 761

(1945); Baldwin v. G.A.F. Seelig, Inc., 294 U.S. 511 (1935); Yick Wo v. Hopkins, 118 U.S. 356 (1886).

7. See *e.g.*, Southern Pac. Co. v. Arizona, 325 U.S. 761, 767 (1945) (Stone, Ch. J.): "When the regulation of matters of local concern is local in character and effect and its impact on the national commerce does not seriously interfere with its operation, and the consequent incentive to deal with them nationally is slight, such regulation has been generally held to be within state authority."

8. RUTLEDGE, A DECLARATION OF LEGAL FAITH 68 (1947).

9. See 26 STAT. 209 (1890), 15 U.S.C. §§ 1–2 (1958).

10. Appalachian Coals Inc. v. United States, 288 U.S. 344, 359 (1933) (Hughes, Ch. J.).

11. United States v. Aluminum Co. of America, 148 F.2d 416, 428 (2d Cir. 1945) (L. Hand, J.).

12. Appalachian Coals Inc. v. United States, *supra* note 10, at 360.

13. See *e.g.*, Nash v. United States, 229 U.S. 373 (1913).

14. HUGHES, THE SUPREME COURT OF THE UNITED STATES 231 (1928). Significantly, a somewhat vague common law meaning does attach to these terms. See Nash v. United States, *supra* note 13; United States v. Addyston Pipe and Steel Co., 85 Fed. 271 (1898), *modified by* 175 U.S. 211 (1899).

15. 26 STAT. 209 (1890), 15 U.S.C. §§ 1–2 (1958).

16. Standard Oil Co. v. United States, 221 U.S. 1 (1911).

17. Adams, *The "Rule of Reason," Workable Competition or Workable Monopoly?*, 63 *Yale L.J.* 348, 349 (1954), and cases cited therein.

18. See Oppenheim, *Federal Antitrust Legislation*, 50 *Mich. L. Rev.* 1139, 1150–52 (1952); Handler, *A Study of the Construction and Enforcement of the Anti-Trust Laws* 19 (TNEC Monograph 38, 1941).

19. Adams, *supra* note 17, at 352.

20. United States v. Aluminum Co. of America, 148 F2.d 416, 432 (2nd Cir. 1945). For the early attitude of the Supreme Court see United States v. United States Steel Corp., 251 U.S. 417 (1920).

21. American Tobacco Co. v. United States, 328 U.S. 781 (1946).

22. See Adams, *supra* note 17, at 352–53, and cases cited therein.

23. Searls, *The Antitrust Laws from the Viewpoint of a Private Practitioner*, 1950 INSTITUTE ON ANTITRUST LAWS AND PRICE REGULATIONS 71, 79 (1950).

24. *Id.*, at 84.

25. United States v. Columbia Steel Co., 334 U.S. 45, 527–28 (1948).

26. KRONSTEIN & MILLER, REGULATION OF TRADE 274 (1953).

27. *Supra* note 20.

28. Kahn, *A Legal & Economic Appraisal of the "New" Sherman and Clayton Acts*, 63 YALE L.J. 293, 305 (1954). See also Dunn, *Conscious Parallelism Reexamined*, 35 B.U.L. REV. 225 (1955).

29. 64 STAT. 1125 (1950), 15 U.S.C. § 18 (1958).

30. United States v. E. I. duPont de Nemours & Co., 353 U.S. 586 (1957) (Brennan, J.). See *id.* at 592: "We hold that any acquisition by one corporation of all or any part of the stock of another corporation, competitor or not, is within the reach of the section whenever the reasonable likelihood appears that the acquisition will result in a restraint of commerce or in the creation of a monopoly of any line of commerce."

31. Weston, *Restatement of Antitrust Law: Salient Features of the Attorney General's Committee Report,* 24 GEO. WASH. L. REV. 1, 10 (1955).

32. See *e.g.,* MACIVER, THE WEB OF GOVERNMENT 348 (1947): "If such [antitrust] measures are capable at all of dealing with the problem it is necessary that simpler criteria of monopolistic tendencies be agreed upon and that they be maintained without deviation or exception." See also Adams, *Supra* note 17, at 352–53, and cases cited therein. See BAIN, BARRIERS TO NEW COMPETITION 220 (1956): "The probability is that legislative supplementation of existing [antitrust] law would be required on a number of points in order to support an effective policy regarding the limitation on barriers to entry, and the precise character of desirable supplements could be specified only after detailed further study."

33. Nash v. United States, 229 U.S. 373, 377 (1913); see also United States v. Sullivan, 332 U.S. 689 (1948).

34. *Compare,* United States v. Cohen Grocery Co., 255 U.S. 81 (1921), *with* Levy Leasing Co. v. Siegel, 258 U.S. 242 (1922), and A. B. Small Co. v. American Sugar Refining Co., 267 U.S. 233 (1925).

35. Laski, *The Basis of Vicarious Liability,* 26 YALE L.J. 105, 130 (1916).

36. See *e.g.,* Shushan v. United States, 117 F.2d 110 (5th Cir.), *cert. denied,* 313 U.S. 574 (1941). People v. Marcus, 261 N.Y. 268, 185 N.E. 97 (1933). See generally Annot., 133 A.L.R. 1055 (1941).

37. People v. Ferguson, 134 Cal. App. 41, 52, 24 P.2d 965, 970 (1933).

38. State v. Foster, 22 R.I. 163, 168, 46 Atl. 833, 835 (1900); the language is quoted with approval from Hoover v. State, 59 Ala. 57, 60 (1877).

39. See DAVIS, ADMINISTRATIVE LAW 168–69 (1951), and cases cited therein.

40. Barlowe, *Water Rights for Irrigation in Michigan,* 36 MICH. AGRIC. EXPER. STATION A BULL. 30 (1953).

41. See generally THE COUNCIL OF STATE GOVERNMENTS, OCCUPATIONAL LICENSING LEGISLATION IN THE STATES (1952).

42. GELLHORN, INDIVIDUAL FREEDOM AND GOVERNMENTAL RESTRAINTS 126–27 (1956).

43. See *e.g.,* INT. REV. CODE OF 1954, § 11 as amended.

44. BUTTERS & LINTNER, EFFECT OF FEDERAL TAXES ON GROWING ENTERPRISES 15–16 (1945).

45. High corporate taxes would appear to be particularly inhibitive of the development of the small enterprise, dependent on retained earnings for expansion and it may be pointed out in this connection that it is possible "to relieve the tax burden on most small, growing companies without greatly diminishing Federal revenues." *Id.* at 4.

46. See Platt & Tanner, *Paying Dividends,* in THE ENCYCLOPEDIA OF TAX PROCEDURES 899 (Lasser ed. 1956). The combination of personal and corporate profit taxes, as described, would seem to maximize the over-all repressive effects on private investment and productivity. Significantly, however, this will sometimes not turn out to be the case in actual practice since such repressive effects as become perceptible are dependent not on the fact of the "second and substantial bite out of the earnings already subjected to the corporate tax" but on the precise size or aggregation of the two "bites" in each individual instance. See BUTTERS & LINTNER, *op. cit. supra* note 44, at 28.

47. See *e.g.*, Dean Milk Co. v. Madison, 340 U.S. 349 (1951) (5-to-3 decision).

48. See OPPENHEIM, *The Nature and Extent of State Trade Barrier Legislation*, COUNCIL OF STATE GOVERNMENTS, (Proceedings, National Conference on Interstate Trade Barriers, 1939) 23, and analysis furnished. *Id.* at 37–38.

49. COUNCIL OF STATE GOVERNMENTS, *id.* at 37–38.

50. *Ibid.;* see also Lockhart, *State Tax Barriers to Interstate Trade*, 53 HARV. L. REV. 1253 (1940).

51. 330 U.S. 552 (1947). 52. *Id.* at 555.

53. *Id.* at 562. 54. *Id.* at 564.

55. *Id.* at 565; comparable eccentricity in comparable judge-made law, sustaining state licensing regulation against constitutional challenge, is presented by Goesart v. Cleary, 335 U.S. 464 (1948).

56. 9 MCQUILLIN, MUNICIPAL CORPORATIONS (3d ed.) § 26.60.

57. *Ibid.; Cf.* State v. Thompson, 135 Me. 114, 190 Atl. 255 (1937).

58. MACIVER, *op. cit. supra* note 32, at 348.

59. DIMOCK, FREE ENTERPRISE AND THE ADMINISTRATIVE STATE 43 (1951). See generally FEDERAL TRADE COMMISSION, THE MERGER MOVEMENT (1948); NUTTER, THE EXTENT OF ENTERPRISE MONOPOLY IN THE UNITED STATES, 1899–1939 (1951); see also MUND, MONOPOLY (1933).

60. ARNOLD, THE FOLKLORE OF CAPITALISM 207 (1937).

61. *Ibid.* See generally Sharp, *Monopolies and Monopolistic Practices*, 2 U. CHI. L. REV. 301 (1935).

62. See *e.g.*, BOWMAN & BACH, ECONOMIC ANALYSIS AND PUBLIC POLICY 588 (2d ed. 1949): "The inadequacy of staff and resources available for antitrust enforcement has been a glaring defect of public policy." See also SWISHER, AMERICAN CONSTITUTIONAL DEVELOPMENT 420–35 (1954).

63. MACIVER, *op. cit. supra* note 32, at 345; *cf.* generally OSBORN, OUR PLUNDERED PLANET (1948).

64. Railroad Comm'n v. Romas & Nichols Oil Co., 311 U.S. 570, 575 (1941).

65. See *e.g.*, Ellis, *Some Current, and Proposed Water-Rights Legislation in the Eastern States*, 41 IOWA L. REV. 237 (1956).

66. See *e.g.*, THE COUNCIL OF STATE GOVERNMENTS, STATE EXPENDITURES FOR JUDICIAL AND LAW ENFORCEMENT PURPOSES (1954); 261 ANNALS 46–126 (1954).

67. The range of estimates varies. See *e.g.*, BIGGS, THE GUILTY MIND 225, n. 36 (1955): "It is a fact that 30 per cent of police are killed or injured in line of duty. Since the crime bill in this country is certainly in excess of ten billion dollars a year, our critical attitude and stinginess toward our law enforcement officers are ludicrous." A recent estimate is that "the annual cost of crime today would exceed twenty billions of dollars." CALLISON, COURTS OF INJUSTICE 305 (1956).

68. Dession, *The Technique of Public Order*, 5 BUFFALO L. REV. 22, 38–39 (1955).

69. Alexander, *Do Our Prisoners Cost Too Much?*, 293 ANNALS 35, 36 (1954).

70. *Id.* at 39. 71. *Id.* at 40.

72. GORANSSON, SOME ASPECTS OF THE SWEDISH PRISON SYSTEM 5 (Stockholm 1955).

73. See generally Rudstedt, Prisons Without Bars, The American Swedish Monthly, Nov., 1947, p. 14.

9: THE IMPACT OF SANCTIONING UPON POWER

1. Schneiderman v. United States, 320 U.S. 118, 167 (1943) (Rutledge, J. concurring). See also Luria v. United States, 231 U.S. 9, 22 (1913): "Under our Constitution, a naturalized citizen stands on an equal footing with the native citizen in all respects save that of eligibility to the Presidency."

2. Schneiderman v. United States, *supra* note 1, at 131 (Murphy, J.).

3. See *e.g.*, Knauer v. United States, 328 U.S. 654 (1946); Baumgartner v. United States, 322 U.S. 665 (1944).

4. Schneiderman v. United States, *Supra* note 1, at 135.

5. United States v. Schlotfeldt, 136 F.2d 935 (7th Cir. 1943) *Cert. denied,* Krause v. United States, 327 U.S. 781 (1946).

6. See Meyer v. United States 141 F.2d 825 (5th Cir. 1944) (Hutcheson, J.).

7. *Id.* at 826; significantly the court reversed a judgment of denaturalization for fraud, resting on the expression of political views subsequent to naturalization.

8. 66 Stat. 260 (1952) 8 U.S.C. § 1451(a) (1958). See also United States v. Fisher, 137 F. Supp. 519 (N.D. Ill. 1955).

9. 66 Stat. 260 (1952), 8 U.S.C. § 1451(c) (1958).

10. 66 Stat. 269, 8 U.S.C. § 1484(a).

11. *Ibid.*

12. Lapides v. Clark, 176 F.2d 619, 620 (D.C. Cir.), *cert. denied,* 338 U.S. 860 (1949).

13. 328 U.S. 654, 678 (1946).

14. EMERSON & HABER, POLITICAL AND CIVIL RIGHTS 250 (1st ed. 1952).

15. Comment, *Disenfranchisement by Means of the Poll Tax,* 53 HARV. L. REV. 645 (1940); see also Snider, AMERICAN STATE AND LOCAL GOVERNMENT 105 (1950); EMERSON & HABER, *op. cit. supra* note 14, at 280.

16. Breedlove v. Suttles, 302 U.S. 277 (1937) (Butler, J.).

17. *Id.* at 283.

18. SNIDER, *op. cit. supra* note 15, at 103.

19. EMERSON & HABER, *op. cit. supra* note 14, at 306–9; see also SNIDER, *op. cit. supra* note 15, at 108–9.

20. Guinn v. United States, 238 U.S. 347 (1915).

21. Davis v. Schnell, 81 F. Supp. 872, *aff'd,* 336 U.S. 933 (1949); but *cf.* Franklin v. Harper, 205 Ga. 779, 55 S.E.2d 221 (1949), *appeal dismissed for want of a substantial federal question,* 339 U.S. 946 (1950). See also Note, *Validity of Electoral Qualifications Under 14th and 15th Amendments,* 49 COLUM. L. REV. 1144 (1949).

22. See generally MEIKLEJOHN, FREE SPEECH AND ITS RELATION TO SELF-GOVERNMENT (1948).

23. See *e.g.*, O'BRIAN, NATIONAL SECURITY AND INDIVIDUAL FREEDOM (1955).

24. CAL. PEN. CODE ANN. § 11401 (West 1956). For discussion of comparable legislation in other countries see 2 U.S. Code Cong. Serv. 81st Cong., 2d Sess., 3887, 1950.

25. Whitney v. California, 274 U.S. 357 (1927).

26. *Id.* at 372.

27. *Id.*, 372–373. 28. *Id.*, 373. 29. 18 U.S.C. § 2385 (1958).

30. *Ibid.* The constitutionality of the enactment has not yet been adjudicated by the Supreme Court. See *e.g.*, Scales v. United States, 260 F.2d 21 (4th Cir.), *cert. granted*, 358 U.S. 917 (1958), *ordered for reargument*, 360 U.S. 924 (1959).

31. Dennis v. United States, 341 U.S. 494 (1951).

32. Yates v. United States, 354 U.S. 298, 318 (1957).

33. Yates v. United States, *supra* note 32, at 340 (Black, J., concurring in part and dissenting in part).

34. Yates v. United States, *supra* note 32, at 339 (Black, J.). 35. *Ibid.*

36. Mr. Justice Jackson, concurring, in Dennis v. United States, 341 U.S. 494, 578 (1951): "I add that I have little faith in the long-range effectiveness of this conviction to stop the rise of the Communist movement. Communism will not go to jail with these Communists."

37. See LASSWELL, NATIONAL SECURITY AND INDIVIDUAL FREEDOM (1950).

38. See *e.g.*, POPPER, THE OPEN SOCIETY AND ITS ENEMIES (1956).

39. 18 U.S.C. § 2385 (1958). 40. *Ibid.*

41. CHAFEE, FREE SPEECH IN THE UNITED STATES 470 (1941).

42. *Ibid.* Less significantly, it may nonetheless be observed that the "membership clause" may pose a serious problem in "double jeopardy" in that it seems to duplicate some of the penalties of the earlier clauses for what may well turn out to be substantially identical conduct. See *e.g.*, Morgan v. Devine, 237 U.S. 632, 639 (1915).

43. Krulewitch v. United States, 336 U.S. 440, 446 (1949), (Jackson, J., concurring). *Compare* Interstate Circuit Inc. v. United States, 306 U.S. 208 (1939), *with* Dennis v. United States, 341 U.S. 494 (1951). See generally Sayre, *Criminal Conspiracy*, 35 HARV. L. REV. 393 (1922); Note, 62 HARV. L. REV. 276 (1948).

44. See Dennis v. United States, 341 U.S. 494, 579 (1951) (Black, J., dissenting): "At the outset I want to emphasize what the crime involved in this case is, and what it is not. These petitioners were not charged with an attempt to overthrow the government. They were not charged with overt acts of any kind designed to overthrow the government. The charge was that they *agreed to assemble and to talk and publish certain ideas at a later date:* The indictment is that *they conspired to organize the Communist Party and to use speech or newspapers and other publications in the future* to teach and advocate the forcible overthrow of the government." (Emphasis added).

45. Grunewald v. United States, 353 U.S. 391, 404 (1957) (Harlan, J.): *cf.* Krulewitch v. United States 336 U.S. 440 (1949), Delli Paoli v. United States, 352 U.S. 232 (1956). For a more restrictive legal view of the onus for collective criminality see Wagner, *Conspiracy in Civil Law Countries*, 42 J. CRIM. L. & CRIMINOL. 171 (1951).

46. 61 Stat. 136, 146, (1947) 29 U.S.C. § 141, § 159(h) (1958).

47. American Communications Ass'n v. Douds, 339 U.S. 382 (1950). See generally Wormuth, *Legislative Disqualifications as Bills of Attainder*, 4 VAND. L. REV. 603, 614–17 (1951).

48. 64 Stat. 987 (1950) 50 U.S.C. §§ 781–826 (1958).

49. 68 Stat. 775 (1954) 50 U.S.C. §§ 841–844 (1958).

50. 64 Stat. 992 (1950) as amended, 50 U.S.C. § 784 (1958).

51. 64 Stat. 977 (1950) 50 U.S.C. §§ 791–793 (1958).

52. 64 Stat. 1001 (1950) 50 U.S.C. § 793 (1958).

53. The Communist Control Act, for example, in part repetitive and in part extensive, of the provisions of the Internal Security Act, is bound to furnish a fertile source of confusion and bewilderment to busy administrators. See *e.g.*, Comment, 64 YALE L.J. 712 (1955); the incompatibility of dominant strands of such legislation with democratic doctrine has been lucidly demonstrated by the late Professor Chafee. See Chafee, *The Registration of "Communist Front" Organizations in the Mundt-Nixon Bill,* 63 HARV. L. REV. 1382 (1950).

54. See Arens, *Conspiracy Revisited,* 3 BUFFALO L. REV. 242 (1954).

55. See *e.g.*, Communist Party v. Subversive Activities Control Bd., 277 F.2d 78 (D.C. Cir., 1959), *cert. granted,* 361 U.S. 951 (1960).

56. For an example of state programs, see Adler v. Board of Educ. 342 U.S. 485 (1952), and the declaration by Mr. Justice Minton, for the Court (*id.* at 493): "One's associates, past and present, as well as one's conduct, may properly be considered in determining fitness and loyalty." See also Garner v. Board of Pub. Works, 341 U.S. 716 (1951).

57. See *e.g.*, Warren, *Blessings of Liberty* 1955 WASH. U.L.Q. 105, 106–7; Jahoda, *Morale in the Federal Civil Service,* 300 ANNALS 110 (1955).

58. See O'BRIAN, *op. cit. supra* note 23.

59. Dession, *The Technique of Public Order: Evolving Concepts of Criminal Law,* 5 BUFFALO L. REV. 22, 39 (1955).

60. For citations to such state laws see McDougall v. Green, 335 U.S. 281 (1948) (per curiam).

61. McDougall v. Green, *supra* note 60, at 283.

62. *Ibid.* See also Note, 16 U. CHI. L. REV. 499 (1949).

63. McDougall v. Green, *supra* note 60, at 288 (Douglas, J., dissenting).

64. Colegrove v. Green, 328 U.S. 549, 552 (1946) (Frankfurter, J.).

65. Colegrove v. Green, *supra* note 64, at 556.

66. Friedmann, *Corporate Power, Government by Private Groups and the Law,* 57 COLUM. L. REV. 155, 165 (1957).

67. See GROSS, THE LEGISLATIVE STRUGGLE, 17–36 (1953). See generally BROOKS, POLITICAL PARTIES OR ELECTORAL REFORMS (1923); SAIT, AMERICAN PARTIES AND ELECTIONS, 413–470 (1942).

68. "In the *laissez-faire* of contemporary politics there are immense inequalities among interests. Some, like business and industry may be represented by a multitude of associations seemingly organized to speak for every conceivable sub-interest; whereas other interests like consumers, are either not organized at all or are inadequately or incompletely organized." MCKEAN, PARTY AND PRESSURE POLITICS, 629 (1949). See also generally, SWISHER, THE THEORY AND PRACTICE OF AMERICAN NATIONAL GOVERNMENT, 205–218 (1951).

69. FRIEDMANN, AN INTRODUCTION TO WORLD POLITICS, 71 (3d ed. 1956).

11: THE SANCTIONING PROCESS

1. The type of scientific information available is indicated in *Somatic Radiation Dose for the General Population; The Ad Hoc Committee of the National Committee on Radiation Protection and Measurements, 6 May, 1959,* 131 SCIENCE 482 (1960).

2. Crimes that are rarely reported are consensual sex acts, petty thefts, frauds, blackmail, traffic or motor vehicle violations, gambling, prostitution, black market and other white collar violations. Sellin, *The Significance of Records of Crime,* 67 L.Q. REV. 489, 494–99 (1951); SUTHERLAND, PRINCIPLES OF CRIMINOLOGY 25 (5th ed. Cressey rev. 1955).

Sellin reports that the number of cases of shoplifting known to three Philadelphia department stores was greater than the total number of thefts of all kinds in the entire city which were known to the police. SELLIN, RESEARCH MEMORANDUM ON CRIME IN THE DEPRESSION 69 (1937).

From November 1, 1947, to April 30, 1948, 1,576 persons were apprehended by store detectives for thievery from four stores in the Loop area of Chicago, but in only 137 cases was a report made to the police department either as to the offense or the person caught in the offense. Letter from Virgil W. Peterson, cited in TAFT, CRIMINOLOGY 21 (1950).

In New York State, the only ground for divorce is adultery. Every time a divorce is granted, therefore, a judge certifies to his belief that adultery was committed by the defendant husband or wife. But the left hand of the law does not know what the right hand is doing. In the year 1948, for example, approximately 6,000 divorces were granted in New York City alone, yet the Annual Report of the Police Department for the same year does not disclose a single arrest for adultery. PLOSCOWE, SEX AND THE LAW 156 (1951).

And a recent study of the "bad-check problem" in the State of Nebraska concluded that: "On the average, only about two per cent of the bad checks returned by the bankers get to the officials; and instead of prosecuting as required by law, the officials are chiefly engaged in collecting the checks under threat of criminal prosecution." BEUTEL, EXPERIMENTAL JURISPRUDENCE 406 (1957).

3. Concerning both the bar and social scientists consult Riesman, *Toward an Anthropological Science of Law and Law Enforcement,* 57 AM. J. SOC. 121 (1951); Llewellyn, *Law and the Social Sciences,* 62 HARV. L. REV. 1286 (1949).

4. In recent history the Caryl Chessman case provides a dramatic picture of the alternatives that our system provides under some circumstances to the adjudged guilty party.

5. The University of Chicago Law School studies of jury response have reported pertinent findings; *e.g.,* Strodtbeck, *Sex-Role Differentiation in Jury Deliberation,* 20 SOCIOMETRY 300 (1956).

6. Anthropologists and sociologists sometimes arrive at distinctions roughly equivalent to those made here. See PROPOSIL, KAPAUKU PAPUANS AND THEIR LAW, Yale University Publications in Anthropology, No. 54 (1958), especially Part 4; HOEBEL, THE LAW OF PRIMITIVE MAN (1954); MALINOWSKI, INTRODUCTION TO HOGBIN, LAW AND ORDER IN POLYNESIA (1934); RADCLIFFE-BROWN, STRUCTURE AND FUNCTION IN PRIMITIVE SOCIETY (1952). Also, Schwartz, *Social Factors in the Development of Legal Control: A Case Study of Two Israeli Settlements,* 63 YALE L.J. 471 (1954).

7. The late WALTER B. CANNON phrased the conception of homeostasis in a manner intelligible to scholars in fields other than physiology in WISDOM OF THE BODY (1932), greatly contributing to the understanding of systemic as distinct from "single factor" analysis. Among American social scientists TAL-

COTT PARSONS has been especially suggestive. See, for example, THE SOCIAL SYSTEM (1951). Further LASSWELL, ANALYSIS OF POLITICAL BEHAVIOUR; AN EMPIRICAL APPROACH (1948), especially Part II. A. Ch. 2. Also MERTON, SOCIAL THEORY AND SOCIAL STRUCTURE (1945).

8. See Sutherland, *The Diffusion of Sexual Psychopath Laws*, 56 AM. J. SOC. 142 (1950).

9. Greenberg, *Social Scientists Take the Stand; A Review and Appraisal of Their Testimony*, 54 MICH. L. REV. 953 (1956); Rose, *The Social Scientist as Expert Witness*, 40 MINN. L. REV. 205 (1956); *Content Analysis—A New Evidentiary Technique*, 15 U. CHI. REV. 910 (1948); *Public Opinion Surveys as Evidence: The Polsters Go To Court*, 66 HARV. L. REV. 498 (1953); Blum & Kalvin, *The Art of Opinion Research: A Lawyer's Appraisal of an Emerging Science*, 24 U. CHI. L. REV. 1 (1956); Arens & Meadow, *Psycholinguistics and the Confession Dilemma*, 56 COLUM. L. REV. 19 (1956).

10. For background see BRINTON, A HISTORY OF WESTERN MORALS (1959); NICHOLSON, GOOD BEHAVIOR; BEING A STUDY OF CERTAIN TYPES OF CIVILITY (1955). The most influential theories of criminology originated in Europe.

11. See *e.g.*, The Library of Congress, *Manual of the Legislative Reference Service* (1950); Council of State Governments, *Manual for the Interstate Exchange of Legislative Service Agency Publications* (1957).

12. On this and many points connected with the bar hints can be obtained in BLAUSTEIN, PORTER & DUNCAN, THE AMERICAN LAWYER: A SUMMARY OF THE SURVEY OF THE LEGAL PROFESSION (1954).

13. See Davis, *Crime in Colorado Newspapers*, 57 AM. J. SOC. 325 (1952), confirming the hypothesis that the amount of crime news in the press, and state crime rates do not vary consistently.

14. *E.g.*, on the "correctional cycle," see CARR, DELINQUENCY CONTROL 223 (1950). A preliminary sketch of the adjustment of business to regulation: LANE, THE REGULATION OF BUSINESS MEN (1954); see Aubert, *White Collar Crime and Social Structure*, 58 AM. J. SOC. 263 (1952).

15. Hints of this appear in connection with the study of internal security policy in the United States. See BROWN, LOYALTY AND SECURITY; EMPLOYMENT TESTS IN THE UNITED STATES (1958); GELLHORN ed. THE STATES AND SUBVERSION (1952); CARR, THE HOUSE COMMITTEE ON UN-AMERICAN ACTIVITIES (1952); BONTECOU, THE FEDERAL LOYALTY-SECURITY PROGRAM (1953); YARMOLINSKY ed. CASE STUDIES IN PERSONAL SECURITY (1955).

16. Recent developments are outlined in NELSON, MERGER MOVEMENTS IN AMERICAN INDUSTRY 1895–1956 (1959); see Bain, *Industrial Concentration and Anti-Trust Policy, in* GROWTH OF THE AMERICAN ECONOMY, Ch. 32, 46 (Williamson ed. 1951).

17. For a rudimentary model of the "reform cycle" in city politics see LASSWELL & KAPLAN, POWER AND SOCIETY 247 (1950). Further, see KORNHAUSER, THE POLITICS OF MASS SOCIETY (1959).

18. RUSCHE & KIRCHHEIMER, PUNISHMENT AND SOCIAL STRUCTURE (1939). Concerning "capitalistic" institutions as a whole consult: MAX WEBER ON LAW IN ECONOMY AND SOCIETY (RHEINSTEIN ed. tr. 1954); RENNER, THE INSTITUTIONS OF PRIVATE LAW AND THEIR SOCIAL FUNCTIONS (Kahn-Freund ed. tr. 1949); ROSTOW, PLANNING FOR FREEDOM; THE PUBLIC LAW OF AMERICAN CAPITALISM (1959); BONGER, CRIMINALITY AND ECONOMIC CONDITIONS (tr.

1916) and critique by THOMAS, SOCIAL ASPECTS OF THE BUSINESS CYCLE (1927). Corresponding syntheses of theory and data are not yet possible for "socialist" or "communist" institutions. See, however, Karev, *The Forthcoming Reform in U.S.S.R. Criminal Law,* with comment by Berman, HARV. L. RECORD p. 1, col. 2 (May 1, 1958); Berman, *Soviet Law Reform—Dateline Moscow 1957,* 66 YALE L.J. 1191 (1957); Lipson, *The New Face of 'Soviet Legality,' Problems of Communism* 22 July–Aug. 1958; Kirchheimer, *The Administration of Justice and the Concept of Legality in East Germany,* 68 YALE L.J. 705 (1959).

19. See Millspaugh, *Trial By Mass Media?* 13 PUB. OP. Q. 328 (1949), a study of Baltimore newspapers in a murder case; Klapper & Glock, *Trial By Newspaper,* 180 SC. AM. 16 (1949); on *Hearings by House Un-American Activities Committee on E. U. Condon;* also, BERELSON, CONTENT ANALYSIS 1, 488 HANDBOOK OF SOCIAL PSYCHOLOGY (LINDZEY ed. 1954); LASSWELL & LEITES, LANGUAGE OF POLITICS; STUDIES IN QUANTITATIVE SEMANTICS (1949); TRENDS IN CONTENT ANALYSIS (Pool ed. 1959); GEORGE, PROPAGANDA ANALYSIS (1959); DOVRING, ROAD OF PROPAGANDA (1959). On legal language in general see Probert, *Law and Persuasion: The Language-Behavior of Lawyers,* 108 PA. L. REV. 35 (1959).

12: THE STRATEGY OF SANCTIONING

1. For background in connection with all objectives see HALL, STUDIES IN JURISPRUDENCE AND CRIMINAL THEORY (1958); GENERAL PRINCIPLES OF CRIMINAL LAW (1947); McDougal, *Perspectives for an International Law of Human Dignity,* PROC. AM. SOC. INT. L. 107 (1959). In contrast with the policy oriented approach see Wechsler, *Toward Neutral Principles of Constitutional Law,* 73 HARV. L. REV. 1, 34 (1959). See the critiques by Pollak, 108 U. PA. L. REV. 1, 31 (1959), and Black, 69 YALE L.J. 421 (1959).

2. Consult McDougal and Feliciano, *International Coercion and World Public Order; The General Principles of the Law of War,* 67 YALE L.J. 771 (1958); McDougal and Feliciano, *Legal Regulation of Resort to International Coercion: Aggression and Self-Defense in Policy Perspective,* 68 YALE L.J. 1057 (1952); Wechsler, *The American Law Institute: Some Observations on Its Model Penal Code,* 42 A.B.A.J. 321 (1956); Wechsler, *The Challenge of a Model Penal Code,* 65 HARV. L. REV. 1097 (1959). Comparative animal studies of aggression deal with "external events," not with perspectives about events. Hence despite their lucidity animal researches are marginally pertinent. An excellent summary of this work is SCOTT, AGGRESSION (1958).

3. Recognition that predispositions of the kind mentioned—involving orientations connected with culture, class, interest, personality, and level of crisis—affect the judge and other decision makers was a principal result of American legal realists. In general see Llewellyn, *Some Realism about Realism—Responding to Dean Pound,* 44 HAR. L. REV. 1222 (1931); FRANK, LAW AND THE MODERN MIND (1930). Further, the selections from Cardozo, Haines, Hutcheson, Llewellyn, Frank and F. S. Cohen in COHEN & COHEN, READINGS IN JURISPRUDENCE AND LEGAL PHILOSOPHY, ch. 6 (1951). Some empirical researches: Gaudet, *The Differences Between Judges in the Granting of Sentences of Probation,* 19 TEMPLE L.Q. 471 (1946); LAZAR, *The Human Sciences and Legal Institutional Development: Role and Reference Group Concepts*

Related to the Development of the National Railroad Readjustment Act, 31 NOTRE DAME LAW. 414 (1946).

4. For example, the Poisson distribution. See JAMES & JAMES, MATHEMATICS DICTIONARY 296 (1959).

5. "Communication" and "coordination" occur in every "interaction," the distinction depending upon the relative prominence of subjective and non-subjective events. All subjective events may be called "symbols" and all non-subjective events "resources." "Signs" thus are resources specialized to communication. See LASSWELL & KAPLAN, POWER AND SOCIETY, chs. 2, 6 (1950); MORRIS, SIGNS, LANGUAGE AND BEHAVIOR (1946); MEAD, MIND, SELF AND SOCIETY (1934).

6. See Lasswell & Donnelly, *The Continuing Debate over Responsibility: An Introduction to Isolating the Condemnation Sanction,* 68 YALE L.J. 869 (1959). By permission this article has been freely drawn upon.

7. The maximization postulate has been employed in the classical models designed to explain economic choices. The urge to use "operational indexes" has sometimes been allowed to obscure the point that "concepts" are not exhausted by the indexes selected by scientific observers to connect the most comprehensive theoretical models with empirical contexts. See HEMPEL, FUNDAMENTALS OF CONCEPT FORMATION IN EMPIRICAL SCIENCE (1952). Economists employ "indifference analysis" to discover the alternative which the chooser expects will leave him in the most advantageous position. No other alternative is perceived as worth the cost of adoption. Problems arise in moving from the perspective of particular participants to the aggregate of participants. See ARROW, SOCIAL CHOICE AND INDIVIDUAL VALUES (1951); BAUMOL, WELFARE ECONOMICS AND THE THEORY OF THE STATE (1952); Schelling, *An Essay on Bargaining,* AM. ECON. REV. 281 (1956). Economists have been slow to adopt the concept of the self with its subsystems having demand and expectation systems more or less distinctive from the demand-expectation pattern of "the whole man."

8. See Part II, ch. 11, note 2.

9. This is particularly true of youthful offenders. See RUBIN, CRIME AND JUVENILE DELINQUENCY 95 (1958).

10. Andenaes, *General Prevention—Illusion or Reality?,* 43 J. CRIM. L., C. & P.S. 176 (1952).

11. BORCHARD, CONVICTING THE INNOCENT (1932); FRANK & FRANK, NOT GUILTY (1957); KOESTLER, REFLECTIONS ON HANGING (1957); Donnelly, *Unconvicting the Innocent,* 6 VAND. L. REV. 20 (1952).

12. In United States v. Kaplan, Judge Weinfeld was persuaded "that the prosecutor's view that an innocent man has been convicted is correct and that a grave miscarriage of justice has taken place." 101 F. Supp. 7, 11 (S.D.N.Y. 1951). He reluctantly concluded, however, that no legal procedure existed for freeing Kaplan and that his only source of redress was executive clemency. For some inexplicable reason Kaplan's application for pardon was denied. FRANK & FRANK, NOT GUILTY 111 (1957). See also Donnelly, *Unconvicting the Innocent,* 6 VAND. L. REV. 20 (1952).

13. In 1939, Thomas J. Pendergast, a party leader in Kansas City, Missouri, and Robert E. O'Malley, Superintendent of the Insurance Department of Missouri, entered a guilty plea to the charge of attempting to evade the pay-

ment of income taxes on amounts received by them in connection with the settlement of litigation on fire insurance premium rebates. In a long memorandum, District Judge Otis listed the principles governing his sentences and dealt with certain criticisms of the sentences as too lenient. See United States v. Pendergast, 28 F. Supp. 601, 602, 607, 609 (W.D. Mo. 1939). Perhaps the classic statement of the problems of a judge in imposing sentence is ULMAN, THE TRIAL JUDGE'S DILEMMA: A JUDGE'S VIEW IN PROBATION AND CRIMINAL JUSTICE 109 (Glueck ed. 1933).

14. Consider, for example, the remarks of Judge Kaufman in the *Rosenberg* case. See RECORD, vol. 2, bk. 4, pp. 1613–15, Rosenberg v. United States, 344 U.S. 838 (1952). See also United States v. Hurt, 9 U.S.C.M.A. 735, 27 C.M.R. 3 (1958), affirming the conviction and death sentence of an Army sergeant who was charged with raping and murdering a five-year-old Okinawan girl. Apparently, feeling was so high against Americans that the commanding general found it necessary to consult with "the civilian Chief Executive, the Speaker of the Legislature, the Chief Justice of the Ryuku Islands, the President of the University of the Ryukyus, and the President and Managing Editors of the civilian newspapers." *Id.* at 759.

15. The term "correctional" or "corrective" is used by us without "penal" or "criminal" connotations. We are aware that these connotations are often present, yet alternative categories typically suffer from similar disadvantages. The perspective with which we view the "corrective" problem is outlined in Dession & Lasswell, *Public Order Under Law: The Role of the Advisor-Draftsman in the Formation of Code or Constitution*, 65 YALE L.J. 174 (1955).

16. ERIKSON, CHILDHOOD AND SOCIETY (1950).

17. Erikson, *Growth and Crises of the "Healthy Personality,"* in PERSONALITY IN NATURE, SOCIETY, AND CULTURE 185 (2d ed., Kluckhohn & Murray, 1955).

18. Concerning development see Jean Piaget, particularly his THE LANGUAGE AND THOUGHT OF THE CHILD (Warden transl. 1926); JUDGMENT AND REASONING IN THE CHILD (Warden transl. 1928); THE CHILD'S CONCEPTION OF THE WORLD (Tomlinson transl. 1929); and THE MORAL JUDGMENT OF THE CHILD (Gabain transl. 1932). An exhaustive guide to the *Language Development in Children,* including "good" and "bad" categories of reference, is by Dorothea McCarthy, in CARMICHAEL, MANUAL OF CHILD PSYCHOLOGY 476 (1st ed. 1946). A particularly careful account of the growth of the self as put forward by George Herbert Mead is NATANSON, THE SOCIAL DYNAMICS OF GEORGE H. MEAD (1956). Sigmund Freud's hypotheses about the acquisition of conscience are abundantly considered in *The Psychoanalytic Study of the Child* (annual since 1945). The adolescent phase of development in our civilization is well known for the "moral" problems that young people face. In this connection, see SYMONDS, ADOLESCENT FANTASY; AN INVESTIGATION OF THE PICTURE-STORY METHOD OF PERSONALITY STUDY (1949).

19. See Keedy, *A Remarkable Murder Trial: Rex v. Sinnisiak*, 100 U. PA. L. REV. 48 (1951). See YOUNG, AMERICAN MINORITY PEOPLES 246 (1932): "If our desirable penal objectives may be said to be the protection of society and its members from criminal injury, and not just revenge, why not extend the principle of individualization to minorities, as is already being done in a haphazard, occasional manner and has been done more thoroughly for our Indians and Negroes in slave days?"

20. Functional diseases are those free of organic lesions sufficient to account for the pathology. In this connection, we recognize, there are very troublesome questions of drawing a definitional line.

21. See the interesting case of United States v. Kunak, 5 U.S.C.M.A. 346, 17 C.M.R. 346 (1954), and Dr. Guttmacher's discussion of it in Model Penal Code § 4.01, app. B, at 175 (Tent. Draft No. 4, 1955).

22. See CLECKLEY, THE MASK OF SANITY (3d ed. 1955); GUTTMACHER, *Diagnosis and Etiology of Psychopathic Personalities as Perceived in Our Time*, in CURRENT PROBLEMS IN PSYCHIATRIC DIAGNOSIS 139 (Hoch & Zubin ed. 1953).

23. Particularly those suffering from severe organic brain disease. See ENGLISH & FINCH, INTRODUCTION TO PSYCHIATRY chs. 18–19 (2d ed. 1957); ALEXANDER & STAUB, THE CRIMINAL, THE JUDGE AND THE PUBLIC 93 (rev. ed. 1956); CLECKLEY, THE MASK OF SANITY (3d ed. 1955).

24. See ELLIOTT, CRIME IN MODERN SOCIETY 179–82 (1952); HOOVER, MASTERS OF DECEIT (1958); WEST, THE MEANING OF TREASON (1947).

25. See Elliott, *supra* note 24, at 187–88, 193–94 (1952); 2 EMERSON & HABER, POLITICAL AND CIVIL RIGHTS IN THE UNITED STATES 1176–96 (2d ed. 1958).

26. See LASSWELL, PSYCHOPATHOLOGY AND POLITICS (1930); LASSWELL, POWER AND PERSONALITY (1948); EYSINCK, POLITICAL PERSONALITY (1954); Zink, *A Case Study of a Political Boss*, 1 PSYCHIATRY 527 (1938).

The usual effect of legal action against indoctrinated revolutionaries in the United States is to assist their propaganda technique of exploiting the courtroom situation. In 1919 and 1920 the Communists were under heavy fire from law enforcement officers in Washington, D.C., and elsewhere over the nation. The first tactic of the Communists was to refuse to testify. But Benjamin Gitlow, Charles Ruthenberg, and Isaac Ferguson developed a more durable tactic of condemning the judge and the court. See HOWE & COSER, THE AMERICAN COMMUNIST PARTY, A CRITICAL HISTORY (1919–1957), at 49–60 (1957). See also GATES, THE STORY OF AN AMERICAN COMMUNIST (1958). And Professors Loewenstein and Riesman have ably discussed how the Fascists and Nazis used libel and libel law as a major political weapon, and how defamation of opponents is one of the standard devices of political propaganda. See Loewenstein, *Legislative Control of Political Extremism in European Democracies* (pts. 1–2), 38 COLUM. L. REV. 591, 725 (1938); Riesman, *Democracy and Defamation: Control of Group Libel*, 42 COLUM. L. REV. 727 (1942); Riesman, *Democracy and Defamation: Fair Game and Fair Comment* (pts. 1–2), 42 COLUM. L. REV. 1085, 1282 (1942). If libel suits were brought, the courtroom was used as an arena for further vilification and abuse. For a similar tactic in this country, see Gordon, *Fascist Field Day in Chicago*, 166 THE NATION 98 (1948).

27. Model Penal Code § 3 (Tent. Draft No. 8, 1958). See also Note, *Manslaughter and the Adequacy of Provocation: The Reasonableness of the Reasonable Man*, 106 U. PA. L. REV. 1021 (1958).

28. See CRESSEY, OTHER PEOPLE'S MONEY (1953); PETERSON, THE EMBEZZLER (1947).

29. See *e.g.*, article 62 of the Italian Penal Code, which provides: "The following circumstances, when they are not constitutive elements thereof or special extenuating circumstances, extenuate the offence: (1) Having acted for motives of special moral or social value. (2) Having reacted when in a

state of anger caused by an unjust act of another. (3) Having acted at the suggestion of a tumultuous crowd. . . . (4) Having in crimes against patrimony, or which may in some manner injure patrimony, caused to the victim of the offence patrimonial injury of exceedingly trifling extent. (5) When an act committed with criminal intent by the injured person, in addition to the act or omission of the guilty party, has co-operated in causing the event to occur. (6) Having before the trial fully repaired the injury by means of compensation and, when possible, restitution."

An elaborate analysis of the aggravating and mitigating circumstances recognized by American courts appears in Hall, *Reduction of Criminal Sentences on Appeal* (pts. 1–2), 37 COLUM. L. REV. 521, 762 (1937). See also the criteria for withholding sentence of imprisonment and for placing a defendant on probation in Model Penal Code § 7.01 (Tent. Draft No. 2, 1954).

30. This problem arises frequently in conspiracy cases in which the question is whether or not original agreement contemplated the subsequent "overt acts." See *e.g.*, Kotteakos v. United States, 328 U.S. 750 (1946); Rex v. Meyrick, 21 Crim. App. R. 94, 45 T.L.R. 421 (Ct. Crim. App. 1929). See also Goldstein, *Conspiracy to Defraud the United States*, 68 YALE L.J. 405, 410 (1959).

31. The classic study is HENTIG, THE CRIMINAL AND HIS VICTIM (1948). The entrapment cases are also relevant. See Donnelly, *Judicial Control of Informants, Spies, Stool Pigeons, and Agent Provocateurs*, 60 YALE L.J. 1091, 1098–15 (1951).

32. Judicial measures against defendants who are conscious of their own rectitude frequently lead to a more generalized rejection of the dominant social system. Eugene Victor Debs, for example, was sentenced for contempt of court for violating an injunction against railway strikers in 1895. In prison, Debs spent much of the time reading and shortly announced his conversion to socialism. See 5 DICTIONARY OF AMERICAN BIOGRAPHY 183 (1943).

33. See Hall, *Ignorance and Mistake in Criminal Law*, 33 IND. L.J. 1 (1957).

34. Codes usually use the terms "recklessness" and "negligence" as categories of culpability. Model Penal Code § 2.02 (Tent. Draft No. 4, 1955).

35. See the Little Rock integration opinion, Cooper v. Aaron, 358 U.S. 1 (1958).

36. This seems to have been the view of District Judge Lemley in the Little Rock case. Aaron v. Cooper, 163 F. Supp. 13 (E.D. Ark. 1958).

37. See the segregation cases, Brown v. Board of Educ., 347 U.S. 483 (1954), 349 U.S. 294 (1955).

38. The demand to impose suffering may be widespread throughout all or many social classes in the body politic and it may peculiarly characterize some interest groups and personalities. During periods of crises, too, sadistic demands may be most intense. One must not lose sight of the fact that examination of a specific culture will show that it is characterized by permissive or even adulatory evaluations of cruelty in the name of punishment. But there is no place for cruelty as an end in itself in a value system committed to human dignity. See Ewing, *Punishment as Viewed by the Philosophers*, 21 CAN. B. REV. 102 (1943); ROYAL COMMISSION ON CAPITAL PUNISHMENT, REPORT 17 (1953). Concessions made to the glorification of cruelty in the name of punishment are justified only when the net gains outweigh the costs (as to all values

involved). Since estimates of the kind required cannot be made by means of explicit rules, the prospects for human dignity are best when decision makers are human beings who gain no gratification by imposing cruelty.

39. See HALL, GENERAL PRINCIPLES OF CRIMINAL LAW 19–60 (1947).

40. In classical Greece the initiator of certain policies was liable to suffer exclusion from the body politic. Concerning the demand to punish and the rise of middle class formations see RANULF, THE JEALOUSY OF THE GODS AND CRIMINAL LAW AT ATHENS; A CONTRIBUTION TO THE SOCIOLOGY OF MORAL INDIGNATION (2 v. 1933–34).

41. A recent discussion is Mannheim, *Some Aspects of Judicial Sentencing Policy*, 67 YALE L.J. 961 (1958).

42. See *e.g.*, materials in DESSION, CRIMINAL LAW, ADMINISTRATION & PUBLIC ORDER 207–32 (1948); BUNN, JURISDICTION IN PRACTICE OF THE COURTS OF THE UNITED STATES (4th. ed. 1938).

43. See *e.g.*, GOODRICH, HANDBOOK OF THE CONFLICT OF LAWS 1–45, 166–225 (1949).

44. See generally KELLOR, ARBITRATION IN ACTION (1941).

45. Concerning coalition alignments in decision processes, CHAMBERLAIN, THE PRESIDENT, CONGRESS AND LEGISLATION (1946); more generally, GROSS, THE LEGISLATIVE STRUGGLE: A STUDY IN SOCIAL COMBAT (1953); Cantwell, *Public Opinion and the Legislative Process*, 55 AM. POL. SCI. R. 924 (1946); SHUBIK, STRATEGY AND MARKET STRUCTURE (1959).

46. Sample points are discussed in: Note, *The Nature and Consequences of Forensic Misconduct in the Prosecution of a Criminal Case*, 54 COLUM. L. REV. 946 (1954); Note, *Prosecutor Forensic Misconduct—"Harmless Error"?*, 6 UTAH L. REV. 108 (1958); Note, *Local Prejudice in Criminal Cases*, 54 HARV. L. REV. 679 (1941); Note, *The Right to an Impartial Federal Jury in the Event of Prejudicial Pretrial Publicity*, 53 COLUM. L. REV. 651 (1953); Note, *Controlling Press and Radio Influence on Trials*, 63 HARV. L. REV. 840 (1950); DEVLIN, THE CRIMINAL PROSECUTION IN ENGLAND (1958).

47. See Dession & Lasswell, *Public Order Under Law: The Role of the Advisor-Draftsman in the Formation of Code or Constitution*, 65 YALE L.J. 174 (1955).

48. Dession, *The Technique of Public Order: Evolving Concepts of Criminal Law*, 5 BUFFALO L. REV. 22 (1955).

49. Recent theoretical analyses have been put forward by Morgenthau, Liska, Morton Kaplan, Arthur Lee Burns, and others. See also Schelling, *Bargaining, Communication, and Limited War*, 1 CONFLICT RESOLUTION 19 (1957); STONE, LEGAL CONTROLS OF INTERNATIONAL CONFLICT (1954); DE VISSCHER, THEORY AND REALITY IN PUBLIC INTERNATIONAL LAW (tr. 1957); McDougal, *op. cit. supra*, note 2. For a review of research see Lasswell, *The Scientific Study of International Relations*, 12 YEARBOOK OF WORLD AFFAIRS 1 (1958).

50. HUNTER, REVOLUTION: WHY, HOW, WHEN? (1940); MANNHEIM, IDEOLOGY AND UTOPIA: AN INTRODUCTION TO THE SOCIOLOGY OF KNOWLEDGE (1936); GROSS, THE SEIZURE OF POLITICAL POWER (1958).

51. See Lasswell, *Legislative Policy, Conformity and Psychiatry* in PSYCHIATRY AND THE LAW (Hoch & Zubin ed. 1955).

52. Bibliography of the Charter of the United Nations, UN Headquarters Library, Bibliographical Series No. 3 (1955); WILCOX AND MARCY, PROPOSALS FOR CHANGES IN THE UNITED NATIONS (1955).

53. Concerning the constitutive questions that arise in federal systems consult, MCWHINNEY, JUDICIAL REVIEW IN THE ENGLISH-SPEAKING WORLD (1956).

54. LANE, POLITICAL LIFE, HOW PEOPLE GET INVOLVED IN POLITICS (1959) provides a summary of data concerning representation.

55. Koontz, *Extent of Administrative Regulation in Economic Affairs,* 221 ANNALS 13.

56. *Id.* at 14. See generally HURST, LAW AND THE CONDITIONS OF FREEDOM, ch. 2 (1956); CLARK, THE RISE OF A NEW FEDERALISM 138–145 (1938).

57. PEGRUM, THE REGULATION OF INDUSTRY 308 (1949).

58. Problems of regulating the flow of communications in a democratic society are dealt with by Mayo, *The Limited Forum,* 22 G. WASH. L. REV. 261 (1954); *The Free Forum, ibid.,* 387 (1954).

59. Herring, GROUP REPRESENTATION BEFORE CONGRESS (1929); PUBLIC ADMINISTRATION AND THE PUBLIC INTEREST (1936); FEDERAL COMMISSIONERS (1936). See the papers on *Power Blocs and the Operation of Economic Forces* by Lewis and Hildebrand, with discussion by Hoover and Chamberlin, 49 AM. EC. R. 384 (1959). Commentary upon Berle, Galbraith and others.

60. LATHAM, THE GROUP BASIS OF POLITICS (1952).

61. HOFSTADTER, AGE OF REFORM (1952); BLAISDELL, AMERICAN DEMOCRACY UNDER PRESSURE (1957); GARFINKEL, WHEN NEGROES MARCH: THE MARCH ON WASHINGTON MOVEMENT IN THE ORGANIZATIONAL POLITICS FOR FEPC (1959); VOSE, CAUCASIONS ONLY; THE SUPREME COURT, THE NAACP, AND THE RESTRICTIVE COVENANT CASES (1959).

62. For data see DORFMAN, THE ECONOMIC MIND IN AMERICAN CIVILIZATION (5 v. 1946–1959). On model building, data relations and policy see, for instance, SCHOEFFLER, THE FAILURES OF ECONOMICS; A DIAGNOSTIC STUDY (1955); KNIGHT, FREEDOM AND REFORM; ESSAYS IN ECONOMICS AND SOCIAL PHILOSOPHY (1947).

63. The role of intellectuals and businessmen in United States society is characterized by SHILS, TORMENT OF SECRECY (1956). See SUTTON, HARRIS, KAYSEN, TOBIN, THE AMERICAN BUSINESS CREED (1956); concerning lawyers, Krastin, *The Lawyer in Society—A Value Analysis,* W RESERVE L.R. 409 (1957); HORSKY, THE WASHINGTON LAWYER (1953); Miller, *American Lawyers in Politics and Business,* 60 YALE L.J. 66 (1951); Wardwell & Wood, *Informal Relations in the Practice of Criminal Law,* 62 AM. J. SOC. 48 (1956).

64. Concerning academic standards under modern conditions see Riesman, *Some Observations on the 'Older' and the 'Newer' Social Sciences,* 319 in THE STATE OF THE SOCIAL SCIENCES (White ed. 1956).

65. The situation is succinctly stated in CORSON, EXECUTIVES FOR THE FEDERAL SERVICE (Preface by H. Emmerich), (1952).

66. MCCORMICK, DAMAGES 275 (1935). 67. *Id.* at 280.

68. *Id.* at 276; for a specific illustration of punitive damages in a tort case see Cramer v. Atlantic Coast R. Co., 214 S.C. 71, 51 S.E.2d 174 (1948).

69. Mintz v. Premier Cab Ass'n Inc., 127 F. 2d 744 (D.C. Cir. 1942); for a sampling of damage verdicts in personal injury cases see IV SCHWEITZER, CYCLOPEDIA OF TRIAL PRACTICE 2158–2217 (1954).

70. McCLINTOCK, EQUITY 59–69 (1948).

71. Recent studies of behavior and norm, or of articulated norm: COHEN, ROBSON & BATES, PARENTAL AUTHORITY; THE COMMUNITY AND THE LAW (1958); STOUFFER, COMMUNISM, CONFORMITY, AND CIVIL LIBERTIES (1955); SNYDER, ALCOHOL AND THE JEWS; A CULTURAL STUDY OF DRINKING AND SOBRIETY (1958). See Smigel, *Public Attitudes Toward 'Chiseling' with Reference to Unemployment Compensation,* 18 AM. SOC. R. 59 (1953).

72. See Lasswell, *The Impact of Psychiatry upon Jurisprudence,* OHIO L.J. (1960); *Impact of Psychoanalytic Thinking on the Social Sciences* in THE STATE OF THE SOCIAL SCIENCES (White ed. 1956).

73. The Isaac Ray Award Books of the American Psychiatric Association are of great importance in clarifying the interconnections of law and psychiatry. On a historical point see Reid, *Understanding the New Hampshire Doctrine of Criminal Insanity,* 69 YALE L.J. 367 (1959). The standard work is Guttmacher & Weihofen, PSYCHIATRY AND THE LAW (1952).

74. Psychiatrists and lawyers are both involved in the search for a suitable language. See the enlightened comment by Judge Bazelon in Briscoe v. United States, 248 F. 2d 640, 644 (D.C. Cir. 1957); also that of Judge Prettyman in Carter v. United States, 252 F. 2d 608, 617 (D.C. Cir. 1957).

13: THE STUDY OF THE SANCTIONING SYSTEM

1. The significance of "traumatic" episodes has been stressed in Freud's psychoanalytic theory. William I. Thomas spoke of "significant experiences" in personality growth. Arnold J. Toynbee dealt wtih challenge and response patterns in his Study of History. Equivalent conceptions are to be found in every psychological or sociological field.

2. Systematic elite studies provide important data concerning the environmental factors which have moulded the predispositions with which decision makers enter various situations. The detailed investigation of perspectives (identifications, demands, expectations) is at an early stage. We interpret findings to date as significant for disclosing the multiplicity of relatively dynamic and self-limiting coalitions which operate within our fundamental patterns of public order. For example: MILLS, THE POWER ELITE (1956); HUNTER, COMMUNITY POWER STRUCTURE (1953), and subsequent books; WARNER, YANKEE TOWN SERIES, and related publications; VIDICH & BENSMAN, SMALL TOWN IN MASS SOCIETY (1958); Matthews, *U.S. Senators; A Study of the Recruitment of Political Leaders* (unpub. Ph.D. diss. Princeton, 1953); Schmidthauser, *The Justices of the Supreme Court,* 3 MIDWEST J. OF POL. SCI. 1 (1959); Rossi, *Community Decision,* in APPROACHES TO THE STUDY OF POLITICS 363 (Young ed. 1958); BENDIX, HIGHER CIVIL SERVANTS IN AMERICAN SOCIETY (1949); NEWCOMBER, THE BIG BUSINESS EXECUTIVE; THE FACTORS THAT MADE HIM, 1900–1950 (1955); WARNER AND ABLEGGAN, OCCUPATIONAL MOBILITY IN AMERICAN BUSINESS AND INDUSTRY, 1928–1952 (1955), and the recent studies by Eulau, Marvick, Janowitz, and others.

3. See LEIGHTON, CLAUSEN & WILSON, EXPLORATIONS IN SOCIAL PSYCHIATRY (1957).

4. The importance of providing environmental support for a conflictful personality is often demonstrated in Alcoholics Anonymous. When expected

events fail to occur the faith and loyalty of group members are undermined unless they are in contact with one another. See FESTINGER, RIECKEN & SCHACHTER, WHEN PROPHECY FAILS (1956). Also AMERICAN PRISON ASS'N, A MANUAL OF CORRECTIONAL STANDARDS 379–89 (1954); AMERICAN PRISON ASS'N, *Services to the Discharged Offender,* in CONTEMPORARY CORRECTION 380 (Tappan ed. 1951).

5. Skolnick, *Toward a Developmental Theory of Parole,* AM. SOC. R. 542 (1960).

6. Parole studies include Schuessler, *Parole Prediction: Its History and Status,* 45 J. CRIM. L., C. & P. S. 425 (1954); OHLIN, SELECTION FOR PAROLE: A MANUAL OF PAROLE PREDICTION (1951).

7. Prison studies include: CLEMMER, THE PRISON COMMUNITY (1958); MCCLEERY, POLICY CHANGE IN PRISON MANAGEMENT, Governmental Research Bureau, Mich. State U. (1957); SYKES, THE SOCIETY OF CAPTIVES: A STUDY OF A MAXIMUM SECURITY PRISON (1958).

8. On suicide: HENRY & SHORT, SUICIDE AND HOMICIDE (1954). For culture contrast see AFRICAN HOMICIDES AND SUICIDES (Bohannan ed. 1959).

9. The specific patterns mentioned here do not exhaust the mechanisms at the disposal of an individual for maintaining perspectives that he can tolerate. In general see the ego defense devices by which symbol events at the conscious level are kept relatively free of anxiety: FREUD, THE EGO AND THE MECHANISMS OF DEFENCE (1946); FESTINGER, THEORY OF COGNITIVE DISSONANCE (1957).

10. Returning to Skolnick's analysis.

11. See JANIS, PSYCHOLOGICAL STRESS (1958). GRINKER & SPEIGEL, MEN UNDER STRESS (1945).

12. The multi-valued orientation needs eventually to be applied to every participant in the context of sanctioning. In order to describe the predispositions with which each wave of young people enters the adult phase of the body politic it is important to conduct periodic surveys, and to analyze the configuration of factors that have affected the success or failure of the socialization process. In principle, surveys can be designed to provide an adequate sampling of each time-section from the beginning to the end of life. The larger outlines of a sanctioning system (within a legal and social system) can be described with little attention to the perspectives of participants. But the finer structure of a system can be discerned only when characteristic perspectives (attention-perception systems; identification, demand and expectation systems) are integrated with operational data, thus revealing the total dynamics (inner, outer) of the individual and group participants who are interacting with one another in the myth-technique patterns constituting personality and culture. See, MYERS & ROBERTS, FAMILY AND CLASS DYNAMICS IN MENTAL ILLNESS (1959), which builds on Hollingshead and Redlich's work; HYMAN, POLITICAL SOCIALIZATION (1959); LANE, POLITICAL LIFE; HOW PEOPLE GET INVOLVED IN POLITICS (1959); LIPSET, POLITICAL MAN (1959); BURDICK & BRODBECK, AMERICAN VOTING BEHAVIOR (1959); STRAUSS, MIRRORS AND MASKS; THE SEARCH FOR IDENTITY (1959); FOOTE & COTTRELL, IDENTITY AND INTERPERSONAL COMPETENCE; A NEW DIRECTION IN FAMILY RESEARCH (1955); WHITING & CHILD, CHILD TRAINING AND PERSONALITY; A CROSS CULTURAL STUDY (1953); MEAD & WOLFENSTEIN, CHILDHOOD IN CONTEMPORARY CULTURES (1955); and the classical researches of the Gluecks. Also Lasswell, *Political Constitution and Individual Character,* 46 PSYCHOAN. AND PSYCHOAN. R. 3 (1959–60).

13. Goldhamer & Speier, *Some Observations on Political Gaming,* 12 WORLD POLITICS 71 (1959). The following paragraphs have drawn freely from Lasswell, *Technique of the Decision Seminar,* 4 MIDWEST J. OF POL. SCI. 213 (1960).

14. Goldhamer and Speier mention Northwestern, Columbia, Massachusetts Institute of Technology, and West Point.

15. For a critical review see OSBORN, APPLIED IMAGINATION: PRINCIPLES AND PROCEDURES OF CREATIVE THINKING (rev. ed. 1957).

16. The permissive approach to audience participation in part reflects the guidance approach of Carl Rogers and others. See PSYCHOTHERAPY AND PERSONALITY CHANGE (Rogers & others, eds. 1954). Also SLAVSON, THE PRACTICE OF GROUP THERAPY (1947).

17. For role playing theory see LEWIN, FIELD THEORY IN SOCIAL SCIENCE; SELECTED THEORETICAL PAPERS (Cartwright ed. 1951); MORENO, WHO SHALL SURVIVE? FOUNDATIONS OF SOCIOMETRY, GROUP PSYCHOTHERAPY AND SOCIODRAMA (1953); Guetzkow, *Building Models About Small Groups,* in APPROACHES TO THE STUDY OF POLITICS (Young ed. 1958).

18. See PERRY & KENT, TOOLS FOR MACHINE LITERATURE SEARCHING (1958). Machine programming is intimately connected with recent advances in symbolic logic. Of great interest is MULL, *The Quarterly Newsletter of the Electronic Data Retrieval Committee of the American Bar Association,* edited at Yale Law School by Layman E. Allen and others (1959–). Machines are also adaptable to teaching. See the succinct summary given by the great innovator in this field, B. F. Skinner, *Teaching Machines,* 128 SCIENCE 969 (1958).

19. Professor Allan R. Holmberg was in charge of the Vicos Project. See *The Research and Development Approach to the Study of Change,* 17 HUMAN ORGANIZATION 12 (1958).

20. For example: HAWLEY, THE CHANGING SHAPE OF METROPOLITAN AMERICA; DECENTRALIZATION SINCE 1920 (1956); Vold, *Extent and Trend of Capital Crimes in the U.S.,* 234 ANNALS 1 (1952).

21. Kemp, *Mathematical Treatment by Dorothy Swaine Thomas of Social Data Arranged in Time Series,* in METHODS IN SOCIAL SCIENCE (Rice ed. 1931); HENRY & SHORT, SUICIDE AND HOMICIDE, Appendices 1–5 (1954); GOLDHAMER & MARSHALL, PSYCHOSIS AND CIVILIZATION (1953); ARROW, *Mathematical Models in the Social Sciences,* in POLICY SCIENCES: RECENT DEVELOPMENTS IN SCOPE AND METHOD (Lerner & Lasswell eds. 1951); MATHEMATICAL THINKING IN THE SOCIAL SCIENCES (Lazarsfeld ed. 1954); Glock, *Some Applications of the Panel Method to the Study of Change,* in LANGUAGE OF SOCIAL RESEARCH 242 (Lazarsfeld & Rosenberg eds. 1955); SIMON, MODELS OF MEN (1957).

22. Ohlin & Duncan, *The Efficiency of Prediction in Criminology,* 54 AM. J. SOCIOL. 441 (1948–49); Kaplan, Skogstad & Girschick, *The Prediction of Social and Technological Events,* 14 PUB. OP. Q. 93 (1950); SHORT-TERM ECONOMIC FORECASTING, STUDIES IN INCOME AND WEALTH, v. 17, Nat. Bu. of Econom. Research (1955); LONG-RANGE ECONOMIC PROJECTION; STUDIES IN INCOME AND WEALTH, v. 16, Nat. Bu. of Econom. Research (1954); Eulau, *H. D. Lasswell's Developmental Analysis,* 11 WEST. POL. Q. 229 (1958).

23. See BRECHT, POLITICAL THEORY (1959); Lasswell, *Clarifying Value Judgment: Principles of Content and Procedure,* 1 INQUIRY 87 (1958).

24. DAVIDSON & SUPPES, DECISION MAKING; AN EXPERIMENTAL APPROACH (1957); Edwards, *Theory of Decision Making,* 51 PSYCHOL. BULL. 68 (1954); BROSS, DESIGN FOR DECISION (1953); WILLIAMS, THE COMPLEAT STRATEGYST,

BEING A PRIMER ON THE THEORY OF GAMES STRATEGY (1954); LUCE & RAIFFA, GAMES AND DECISIONS (1957); Lasswell, *Current Studies of the Decision Process: Automation versus Creativity*, 8 W. POL. Q. 381 (1955). See Hilgard, *Creativity and Problem-Solving*, and Lasswell, *The Social Setting of Creativity*, in CREATIVITY AND ITS CULTIVATION (Anderson ed. 1959); KUBIE, NEUROTIC DISTORTION OF THE CREATIVE PROCESS (1958); KRIS, PSYCHOANALYTIC EXPLORATIONS IN ARTS (1952); WERTHEIMER, PRODUCTIVE THINKING (1945).

25. MILLS & LONG, THE STATISTICAL AGENCIES OF THE FEDERAL GOVERNMENT (1949).

26. See PUBLIC ADMINISTRATION AND POLICY DEVELOPMENT; A CASE BOOK (Stein ed. 1952); KAYSEN, U.S. v. UNITED SHOE MACHINERY CORPORATION, AN ECONOMIC ANALYSIS OF AN ANTI-TRUST CASE (1956); TENNENT, THE AMERICAN CIGARETTE INDUSTRY; A STUDY IN ECONOMIC ANALYSIS AND PUBLIC POLICY (1950).

27. Failure to follow systematic categories is a major limitation in the reporting of many cases. But see WESTIN, THE ANATOMY OF A CONSTITUTIONAL LAW CASE: YOUNGSTOWN SHEET AND TUBE CO. v. SAWYER; THE STEEL SEIZURE DECISION (1958).

28. EVIDENCE AND INFERENCE (Lerner ed. 1958).

29. The University of Chicago jury study devised an experimental plan which selected juries from among those summoned to official jury duty, subjecting the experimental panels to "playbacks" of cases. Thus the R (response) of jurors was studied by changing the E (environmental factors) or the P (predispositional factors). Such a design makes it feasible, for example, to discover the impact of the judge's instructions upon juries of diverse composition, or of varied instructions upon juries of the same composition. In principle the factors of personality, interest, class, culture, and crisis level can be assessed. See also Edwards, *Experiments: Their Planning and Execution*, ch. 7 in HANDBOOK OF SOCIAL PSYCHOLOGY (Lindzey ed. 1954). Experiments which are conducted under the controlled conditions of a laboratory can be related to the study of the configurations of the larger social context by devising tests which enable experimental results to be concisely predicted from the predispositions displayed by the subjects. The tests can be used to identify the degree to which the P factors are present in the field situation (or the original experiment can be adapted to the field in order to accomplish the same appraisal). In principle tests or experiments can be employed at strategic points in the world community context for the purpose of discovering the P factors that prevail, hence providing essential information for projection and control.

30. Decision seminar technique can be extended from teaching and research to official advisory bodies and to the procedures employed by specialized organs of final commitment. The fundamental conception can be adapted to the needs of the whole electorate in the form of a "social planetarium." See Lasswell, *The Rational Use of Observation*, in HUMAN MEANING OF THE SOCIAL SCIENCES (Lerner ed. 1958).

INDEX

Bei Fragen zur Produktsicherheit wenden Sie sich bitte an:
If you have any questions regarding product safety,
please contact:

Walter de Gruyter GmbH
Genthiner Straße 13
10785 Berlin
productsafety@degruyterbrill.com